MEXICO'S CRUCIAL CENTURY, 1810–1910

The Mexican Experience

William H. Beezley, series editor

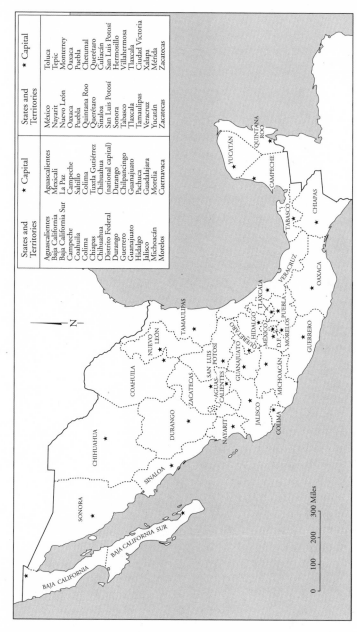

States and Territories	* Capital	States and Territories	* Capital
Aguascalientes	Aguascalientes	México	Toluca
Baja California	Mexicali	Nayarit	Tepic
Baja California Sur	La Paz	Nuevo León	Monterrey
Campeche	Campeche	Oaxaca	Oaxaca
Coahuila	Saltillo	Puebla	Puebla
Colima	Colima	Quintana Roo	Chetumal
Chiapas	Tuxtla Gutiérrez	Querétaro	Querétaro
Chihuahua	Chihuahua	San Luis Potosí	San Luis Potosí
Distrito Federal	(national capital)	Sinaloa	Culiacán
Durango	Durango	Sonora	Hermosillo
Guerrero	Chilpancingo	Tabasco	Villahermosa
Guanajuato	Guanajuato	Tlaxcala	Tlaxcala
Hidalgo	Pachuca	Tamaulipas	Ciudad Victoria
Jalisco	Guadalajara	Veracruz	Xalapa
Michoacán	Morelia	Yucatán	Mérida
Morelos	Cuernavaca	Zacatecas	Zacatecas

Mexico

MEXICO'S CRUCIAL CENTURY, 1810-1910

AN INTRODUCTION

COLIN M. MacLACHLAN
& WILLIAM H. BEEZLEY

UNIVERSITY OF NEBRASKA PRESS • LINCOLN & LONDON

© 2010 by the Board of Regents
of the University of Nebraska
All rights reserved
Manufactured in the
United States of America

⊗

Library of Congress Cataloging-
in-Publication Data
MacLachlan, Colin M.
Mexico's crucial century, 1810–1910 : an
introduction / Colin M. MacLachlan and
William H. Beezley.
p.   cm.—(The Mexican experience)
Includes bibliographical references and index.
ISBN 978-0-8032-2844-3 (pbk. : alk. paper)
1. Mexico—History—19th century. 2. Mexico—
Politics and government—19th century. I. Beezley,
William H. II. Title.
FI232.M2184   2010
972'.03—dc22
2009051621

Set in Adobe Garamond by Bob Reitz.

CONTENTS

ILLUSTRATIONS

MAPS

ACKNOWLEDGMENTS

An intellectual interest does not become a book overnight. Rather, it takes shape slowly over a considerable time, long before it is reduced to words. This book is no exception. Consequently, it is difficult to single out the many intellectual facilitators who have contributed ideas, often in informal settings, that have been internalized and now acted upon. Many of them have published important works and are so acknowledged in the bibliography. It is possible, nonetheless, to thank those who graciously read the manuscript in its various drafts and offered straight-to-the-point evaluations.

It is pleasure to acknowledge friends and colleagues who have helped shape the work in its final stages. Jaime Rodríguez O. read the work several times and made excellent suggestions, all of which have been incorporated. John Hart and Susan Deeds read the work for the University of Nebraska Press and contributed their expertise to the project. Cheryle Champion supplied the cover photograph of an item from her extensive collection of Mexican folk art. Heather Lundine, Bridget Barry, and Joeth Zucco at the University of Nebraska Press provided expert professional guidance through the publication process.

The images reproduced in this volume were originally published in 1900 as the covers of short history books for children written by Heriberto Frías and were drawn by the famous graphic artist, Guadalupe Posada. The series, called "A Mexican Child's

Library," consisted of 110 sixteen-page booklets and was published by the Maucci Brothers in Mexico City. Various libraries in Mexico and the United States have partial collections of
the booklets, but as far as we know, the complete set, in excellent condition, exists only in the Posada Collection of the John
Charlot Archives, the University of Hawaii. We thank the cura-
tor of the collection, Bronwen Solyom, for her assistance with
these images, Ryan S. James for making the digital photographs,
and above all John Charlot for permission to use the images from
the collection.

MEXICO'S CRUCIAL CENTURY, 1810–1910

INTRODUCTION

The National Trauma

In the nineteenth century, the Mexican Republic faced extinction not once but twice. In addition, the federal republic teetered on the verge of fragmenting into microrepublics at least as many times. Mexico lost some 50 percent of its territory to the United States and continued to struggle to find ways of accommodating its northern neighbor while preserving its sovereignty and self-respect. Napoleon III of France came within a hair's breadth of permanently establishing a satellite monarchy on Mexican soil.

In retrospect, that the Mexican Republic survived the crucial first century of independence seems almost miraculous. Mexico spent much of the period attempting to claw its way back to the economic prosperity that had characterized the colonial period before the turn of the nineteenth century.[1]

In the eighteenth century Mexico's resources engendered a level of prosperity that rivaled that of the imperial metropolis. Economic and population growth, the emergence of complex cities, and internal demands changed the relationship between the empire and Spain. Mexican capital and shipping played a significant role in transatlantic commerce. The merchant community in Cádiz included Mexicans as well as other Spanish Americans. Legal and contraband items entered New World ports and markets with little attention to the laws. Spain could not supply goods or absorb sufficient raw materials to serve as

Mexico's only trading partner. Mexico had become part of a global economic system increasingly detached from Spain.[2] In the closing decades of the eighteenth century, the Atlantic world had established a rough commercial equilibrium between the New World's demand for industrial products and Europe's appetite for sugar, cotton, tobacco, cacao, and precious metals; nevertheless, a political rebalancing remained to be worked out.

Meanwhile, North America was undergoing an imperial territorial rearrangement with important implications for Mexico. France and Britain attempted to extend their territorial grasp at the expense of their rivals. The outcome of the French and Indian War (1759–63), part of the worldwide conflict between France and Britain known as the Seven Years' War, eliminated France as an American power and exposed Spanish weakness. In 1803, France's sale of Louisiana to the still fledgling United States destabilized the western frontier of New Spain even before Mexico's independence.

While eighteenth-century reforms imposed on Mexico by Spain led to tension between them, a core foundational culture united them psychologically and culturally. The slow acceptance of the utility of independence can be explained in part by the strength of these shared cultural ties.[3] It took a protracted crisis in Spain to sever the political bonds with the mother country. Even then some Mexican patriots anticipated inviting the Spanish monarch or a Spanish prince to rule an independent Mexico.

Economic and cultural maturity, coupled with the disintegration of imperial order, compelled Mexicans to take responsibility into their own hands. They did so reluctantly, and with good reason. New Spain needed more time to make the transition to an independent nation than history allowed. Tragically, the best hope, the Constitution of 1812, which provided a commonwealth structure, evaporated in the face of events in Spain. The great future predicted by Alexander von Humboldt in the last decade of the eighteenth century ended in civil war, destroying much of 300 years of economic progress. So began the crucial century.

Constructing an independent nation out of the broken parts of colonial New Spain proved harder than anyone imagined. Dramatically opposing views of the nature of an independent nation pitted powerful ideologies against each other. The clash of ideas began almost immediately following the collapse of the Mexican empire (1822–23) of Agustín Iturbide.

The violent political turmoil that racked the Mexican Republic in its first century must be understood as a conflict of ideologies.[4] Liberalism, conservatism, the temporal ideology of the Church, and the emerging agrarian-anarchist ideology in the countryside all collided. Adherents violently challenged the values and activities of those who did not share their ideology. Civil wars, conspiracies, destruction, repression, and executions sullied all the participants.

Nor could the ideological struggle be conducted in isolation from the rest of the world. Emperor Napoleon III visited his dreams of restoring monarchies on a hapless Mexico in 1863. Deploying French troops to install Maximilian on a Mexican throne in the end fatally injured the Conservative agenda. The hard-pressed forces of Benito Juárez eventually triumphed, ending forever the notion of a Mexican monarchy. In the early decades of the crucial century the focus had to be on political survival.

Only after the defeat of the French intervention could Mexicans consolidate their hard-earned gains.

With Porfirio Díaz's seizure of the presidency in 1876, liberalism reached maturity. Conservatism had ceased to be a viable ideology. Díaz chose to informally accommodate the Church but rejected the agrarians, and thus sowed the seeds of the Mexican Revolution of 1910. Under Díaz, political stability obscured the country's unaddressed social vulnerabilities. Nevertheless, the Porfirian peace made possible long-delayed economic development and laid the foundation of a modern Mexico, but one that favored an oligarchy at the expense of most Mexicans.

Throughout this crucial century, a weakened Mexico faced U.S. American territorial ambitions and economic pressure. The United States had to be considered at every turn. The U.S.-Mexican War (1846–48) threatened Mexico's survival as a viable independent nation. The war constituted a defining event for Mexico as well as for the United States, and brought both into close contact. The creation of the Republic of Texas in 1836 was soon followed by war with the United States, and the 1848 Treaty of Guadalupe Hidalgo that ended the conflict left Mexico territorially diminished and demoralized.

As an unanticipated consequence of war and American annexation of Texas, a process of demographic, cultural, and economic convergence began. Along both sides of the new border between the two republics a binational region emerged with roots in both cultures and, increasingly, a shared history.[5] Railways carried the elements of cultural convergence into the heartlands of both republics. Much of the history of the two republics became entwined for better or for worse, but not on the basis of respected equals.

Inequality continues to complicate relations into the present.

The bicentennial celebration of independence (1810–2010) and the centennial of the Mexican Revolution (1910–2010) marked the beginning and the end of the crucial century, but the influence of this century's events lingers on as the twenty-first century unfolds.

Mexico went through a prolonged process of disentangling its destiny from that of the mother country, Spain, a process that was complicated as well as accelerated by Napoleon Bonaparte's desire to subordinate the Spanish monarchy. The crisis, rooted in Spain's economic weakness, ended in state collapse. Unable to confront revolutionary France after 1789, Spain made an unequal peace. A once proud monarchy became a Napoleonic toy subject to financial blackmail and forced alliances. Draining money from the empire to pay off the French bought time, but not a solution. In Mexico, the enforcement of the Law of Consolidation (1804), which ordered the conversion of clerical assets into bonds and remission of the proceeds to Spain, caused an economic crisis. In Mexico, most Church assets took the form of loans on land that now had to be sold to pay the debt. Forced disposal of real estate devastated property owners, crippled economic activity, and damaged the rudimentary financial structure of New Spain.

Following the Battle of Trafalgar in 1805, in which the British Navy destroyed the combined French and Spanish fleet, Napoleon sealed the European continent to deny Britain access to European markets. Napoleon's objective, to place his brother Joseph on the Spanish throne, required the abdication of Carlos IV and the elevation of his son, Fernando VII, to the throne. Invited to meet with Napoleon, Fernando unwisely traveled to France and into the hands of Napoleon, who promptly imprisoned him.

Napoleon then forced the transfer of the Spanish crown to his brother Joseph, subsequently proclaimed José I of Spain. The French invasion and occupation of the Iberian Peninsula followed with startling rapidity. The news stunned Spain's American empire, totally unprepared for such a calamity.

Napoleon's Bayonne Constitution of 1808 sought to impose a French constitutional structure on Spain. Many of its liberal articles could be accepted in principle, but not the fact that they had been imposed. Napoleon reorganized the structure of the Spanish government to make it uniform and more efficient; such changes appealed to the *afrancesado* (Francophile) intelligentsia and to an aristocracy anxious to hold on to its privileges. For a majority of Spaniards, however, Napoleon's imposed reforms violated Spain's deeply held political traditions.

An aroused and angry population refused to accept French rule and turned against the aristocracy, which it suspected of being a willing tool of Napoleon. The inevitable revolt began in Madrid on May 2, 1808, and soon engulfed the rest of the nation. By summer, Napoleonic troops were close to being defeated. An alarmed Napoleon took to the field with a force of 300,000 men and reoccupied Madrid in December 1808.

The effort to save Spain from Napoleon went badly. The Junta Central, created by those who had rejected French rule to govern in the absence of the imprisoned Fernando VII, retreated to Cádiz, then to the Island of León, the last morsel of Spain denied Napoleon by the heavy guns of the combined British and Spanish fleet. On January 29, 1810, the newly formed Regency Council, which replaced the Junta Central, took charge of governing the remnants of a once proud nation. Many Spaniards believed the time had come to salvage whatever could be pulled from the ruins.

In Mexico and other parts of the Spanish empire in America, royal officials contemplated their future prospects, and some appeared ready to accept the reality of French control and to serve at the pleasure of the Duque de Berg, France's regent in occupied Spain. Those willing to concede the subordination of Spain and its empire to France underestimated the extent to which Napoleon had offended the Spanish people and frightened those in the empire.

In Spain, resistance to the French occupiers fell to the common people, mainly but not exclusively peasants, who formed small irregular bands that carried on guerrilla warfare. French forces slowly lost control of the countryside, small hamlets, villages, and towns. Intimidation, firing squads, destruction, and rape could not break the insurgency. The French held the major cities but found themselves surrounded by hostile peasantry. Loosely organized guerrilla units cut down French patrols that ventured beyond fortified perimeters. The French had to provide extensive protection for their supply wagon trains as food, fuel, and fodder became difficult to purchase locally or to seize.

Napoleon aroused the ancient, deeply ingrained notion of popular sovereignty that vested the people collectively with the right to rule in the absence of a legitimate king. With collapse of the state, the mantle of authority returned to its original source. Popular sovereignty took the form of unbeatable guerrilla bands. Napoleon made a fatal mistake by removing Fernando VII and his government in Madrid. He eliminated a legitimate if badly discredited government that possibly could have signed a peace treaty and continued to govern subordinate to Paris. The redeployment of French forces to other parts of Europe in 1812 in effect conceded the mistake, and foreshadowed the final French defeat in 1814.

Napoleon's Uncertain Shadow over Mexico

Napoleon's successes in Europe alarmed the Mexican population, fearful that the French would incorporate New Spain, perhaps as part of a peace treaty conceded by a prostrate mother country. To head off any unwanted transfer of territory, many favored political autonomy, but not necessarily independence. European residents in New Spain believed that the creoles secretly wanted independence and that agitation for political autonomy obscured their true motives. Adding to the political uncertainty, New Spain grappled with a difficult transition to a new agricultural production and distribution structure. Urbanization had arrived at the point that local and regional markets surrounding major cities produced food for ever-larger urban concentrations. Competition over foodstuffs and the land to grow what the cities wanted caused rural prices for traditional food items to increase. A severe drought in 1808–9 added to the misery in the countryside. In some areas starvation and famine loomed.

Heightening the degree of suffering, textile manufacturing suffered from competition from cheap imports. In addition, mining experienced rising costs, resulting in mine closures and declining wages. Those able to respond to urban needs profited, while others lost ground. In many parts of the country people remained prosperous. A checkerboard pattern of well-being and impoverishment supplied plenty of recruits for insurrection, and an equal number anxious to hold on to relative prosperity—a perfect recipe for social conflict and civil war.

Meanwhile, events in Europe preoccupied many. Mexicans in the capital and provincial cities and towns, colonial functionaries, military officers, and parish priests struggled to comprehend what it meant for them. Most preferred to wait for clarity, although many feared the worst. Napoleon's actions forced people to make choices that few relished, but to remain in a state of paralysis invited becoming part of the spoils to be divided up around a peace table as the grim terms of defeat unfolded.

In Spain, liberal pragmatists intent on moving beyond simple restoration of a discredited monarchy proposed the creation of a constitutional monarchy. They envisioned a commonwealth encompassing all the kingdoms in Spain and the empire on the basis of political equality. In early 1809, the Junta Central requested that the empire send delegates to represent them in Spain. New Spain responded by appointing an American-born representative, Lardizabal y Uribe, who was already in Spain.

In Mexico, conspiracies abounded, fueled by rumors of an imminent transfer of New Spain to the French. New Spain relied on reasonably well-trained and well-officered colonial militias for security. Only a small number of Spanish soldiers served in Mexico. While New Spain could mount a creditable defense against a French invasion, the most important issue came down to the legitimate authority to govern. The viceroy drew his authority from the Spanish monarchy, but with Fernando VII in French captivity and various juntas claiming popular sovereignty, just who had legitimate authority remained uncertain. Royal officials in New Spain declared themselves to be loyalists, employing putative loyalty to the imprisoned monarch as their claim to governing legitimacy. Distrust ran rampant. Would royal officials side with the French, as many had in Spain? It appeared to be a possibility. The level of uncertainty and distrust spawned a number of conspiracies, most of which could be dismissed.

Two conspiracies, however, drew attention—a group in Valladolid composed of individuals from wealthy families, and another group initiated by Ignacio Allende, Juan de Aldama, and subsequently Father Miguel Hidalgo that mobilized the lower classes. In the fall of 1809, the Valladolid conspiracy took shape. The principal leaders, all natives of New Spain, attracted another thirty conspirators, mostly wealthy native-born individuals but including several prominent Europeans also. The conspirators favored creating a national junta, following the example of Spain, recruiting a military force of 20,000 paid troops, and preparing to repulse a French invasion. Arrest of the Valladolid conspirators ended in their dispersal throughout the country rather than harsh punishment. The authorities took into consideration the high status of most of the conspirators, their reluctance to actually engage in violence, and their support for the monarchy. The viceroy understood that little would be gained and much lost by an overreaction.

Meanwhile the viceroy and his advisers, worried about political instability, clung to the traditional hierarchy of authority, ignoring the reality that the hostage king, Fernando VII, no longer ruled. In the whirlwind of gossip and allegations, the authorities remained indecisive. The arrival of a new viceroy, Francisco Javier Venegas, changed the situation. Faced with a list of the Querétaro conspirators, he ordered their arrest, but his servants passed the information to the wife of the regional administer. The official's wife, the "*Corregidora*" Joséfa Ortiz de Domínguez, sent messengers galloping to warn the conspirators. Aldama brought the news of the plot's discovery to Hidalgo just after midnight. By happenstance, Allende had been visiting Hidalgo at the time. The three conspirators, believing that their countrymen would rise up in support, took action on September 16, 1810.

Hidalgo ordered the ringing of the church bell at eight in the morning, calling together his parishioners, many from outlying areas, who were attending the Sunday market day. The priest exhorted them, with words now lost, asking them to defend the kingdom against those who sought to deliver it into the hands of the French and consequently destroy New Spain's religious culture.[1] He also declared the end of the tribute paid by Indians.[2]

Just how many joined the Hidalgo movement as it made its way through the countryside is impossible to determine, perhaps between 15,000 and 50,000. Given logistical problems, 20,000 would seem a reasonable guess. His troops consisted of creoles, mestizos, Indians, blacks, and various racial mixtures. Those trained in provincial militias offered professional military advice. The sack of Guanajuato, the first major city to fall to Hidalgo's army, shocked New Spain, as did the murder of Spaniards that accompanied the plundering of the city. Hidalgo could not control the burning and looting that occurred as he moved on to the capital. His assumption of the title of captain general of America did not awe his followers, nor did his newly effected uniform of purple trousers, green turban, and gleaming scimitar strengthen his command. In the city of Valladolid, uncontrolled looting continued for two days before it could be stopped. Hidalgo abolished slavery shortly thereafter in an attempt to strengthen popular support. Many feared that New Spain might be consumed by a race war, on the scale of the Haitian slave revolt. Small landholders, including Indians, saw the poor and landless as an economic and social threat. After advancing to within striking distance of Mexico City and suffering heavy casualties, Hidalgo's army retreated.

Hidalgo moved to Guadalajara, where he established his government from November 26, 1810, to January 14, 1811. He ordered the execution of Spaniards rumored to be planning a counterrevolt. Ignacio Allende initially fled to Guanajuato, later joining Hidalgo in Guadalajara. Allende, appalled at the executions ordered by Hidalgo, briefly plotted to poison him in order to end the violence and executions. As the loyalists advanced on Guadalajara, Hidalgo unwisely decided to take the offensive; a six-hour battle destroyed his army. Royalist forces chased the insurgent remnants northward in a ruthless campaign commanded by General Felix Calleja, who had established an enduring reputation for both exceptional competence and cruelty. Hidalgo fell into viceregal hands in March 1811. The execution of Hidalgo and other top leaders ended the threat, or so it seemed. At the time, few could have predicted the chronic insurgency that followed Hidalgo's execution. Suppression of the Hidalgo Revolt provided only a pause in what became ten years of sporadic fighting marked by indiscriminate violence, draconian executions, feverish looting, and the settling of old scores against neighbors, neighboring villages, or arrogant regional officials.

José María Morelos, a mestizo priest and former student of Hidalgo, continued the insurgent cause in the south. Morelos proved a capable commander and developed an effective guerrilla campaign. His army, made up of many African Mexicans and mulattoes from the hot Pacific coastal areas, as well as indigenous and mestizo followers, soon controlled parts of central Mexico, but not the important cities of Veracruz, Puebla, and Mexico. Unfortunately, the success of the insurgency in the south led to internal divisions just as they appeared on the verge of seizing control.

Dissension among the top leadership, particularly between Ignacio Rayón, Hidalgo's former private secretary and lawyer turned insurgent commander, and Morelos, at times played out on the battlefield as they failed to come to each other's assistance. The ambitious Rayón called himself the president of the Suprema Junta and Minister Universal of the Nation, a title that implied political superiority. The search for a solution to the dysfunctional Suprema Junta resulted in the convening of a Sovereign National Congress with deputies elected in the province of Tecpan, created in 1813 by the insurgents, and in clandestine fashion in some areas under viceregal control. On September 14, 1813, Morelos called the national congress into session as a constituent body charged with writing a constitution. In his inaugural speech, written by Carlos María de Bustamante, Morelos evoked the images of pre-conquest Mexico to provide legitimacy for the claims of those of mixed and Indian ancestry, but did not brush aside those of the New World's European descendants.[3] A document, the *Sentimentos de la Nación*, laid out guiding principles for the congress as the deputies began work on the constitution. Article One took the final step of declaring total independence from Spain. Up to that moment all sides, with varying degrees of sincerity, had declared their allegiance to Fernando VII of Spain. Morelos set September 16 as the anniversary of independence, thereby honoring Hidalgo, his former teacher, Ignacio Allende, and Juan de Aldama. Congress proclaimed Morelos supreme generalissimo, but soon stripped him of that title after he lost several battles.

As loyalist forces closed in, the congress fled, writing a constitution as they moved one step ahead of their pursuers. Once completed, the document, in the absence of a printing press, could not be published until October 22, 1814. The Constitution of Apatzingán, named for the last refuge of the insurgent congress, came too late to have an impact. Morelos's insurgency failed to close the ring around Mexico City and suffered repeated defeats that reduced his army to a ragged band of refugees. Eventually, at the battle of Temalaca, Morelos fell into loyalist hands and suffered the same fate as Hidalgo; he was executed on December 22, 1815. Meanwhile, small bands of insurgents avoided extermination and continued to plague loyalist forces, but did not threaten their control.

The internal political struggles of the Morelos insurgency contributed to its ultimate military defeat. Nevertheless, some important achievements must be noted. The abolition of all racial distinctions and the recognition of the contributions of all races, including those of African and European ancestry, reassured those who feared a race war. Moreover, Morelos pulled the classes together, avoiding class warfare. Consequently, his movement attracted a significant number of members of the upper classes, including Doña Leona Vicario, a rich orphan ward of a loyalist, who supplied money and smuggled arms to the insurgents.

Subsequently imprisoned, she escaped, joined the army of Morelos, and administered the army's finances as well as organized medical care. After independence in 1821, a grateful Congress awarded her a hacienda and three houses in Mexico City. Her funeral in 1842 was a national event.

The Constitution of 1812, Imperial Reaction, and Independence

While the Hidalgo and Morelos revolts ground on from 1810 to 1815, Liberals in Spain worked out a new, promising framework of empire. Viceroy Venegas in Mexico received instructions from the Regency Council, representing the imprisoned monarch in Spain, to call elections for representatives to the constituent Spanish Cortes to write a collective constitution for the Spanish world, including Spanish America. The Regency Council also officially abolished the Indian tribute and ordered that land and water rights be examined and redistributed to villages as equitably as possible, with the obligation of villagers to put the land into cultivation immediately. The Regency Council ordered that its instructions be published in New Spain's indigenous languages, not just Spanish. Political participation, intended to be as wide as possible, included local and regional levels and moved down the social structure from creoles and mestizos to include Indians, but not *castas* (racial mixtures), as participants in indirect elections. The viceroy, with a better understanding of the nature of the population than Liberals in Spain, invoked his authority to allow *castas* to vote. Viceroy Venegas disseminated the Regency Council's instructions throughout New Spain on October 9, 1810, three weeks and one day after the outbreak of the Hidalgo Revolt.[4]

Electors selected deputies to represent New Spain in the Cortes. Some dissatisfaction over the number of New World deputies relative to those from various parts of Spain posed a potential problem. They demanded that the same formula used in Spain, which allotted one representative for each population unit of 50,000, be applied in America. They further demanded that all free subjects be counted. Equal representation would shift the balance in favor of America by a three-to-two ratio, an outcome unacceptable to peninsula Spaniards and, if accepted, would have radically reversed the traditional relationship between Spain and its empire.

The introduction of the new constitutional system in the midst of the spreading insurgency in New Spain and the continued French occupation of large parts of Spain underscored the sense of urgency. The Regency Council then resigned, passing sovereign legitimacy to the Cortes. The Cortes remained superior to all institutions, including the king or his representatives, who functioned as the executive subject to the legislation of the Cortes.

The American deputies, including the twenty-two deputies from New Spain who made up the majority of American deputies in the Cortes, again raised the issue of equal representation. A compromise was worked out that counted Indians, creoles, and the mixed offspring of both groups, but not all *castas*, for the purpose of determining representation. The compromise resulted in a more or less evenly balanced representation between the empire and Spain.

Each article of the constitution occasioned spirited debate until its promulgation on March 19, 1812. The issue of slavery and the slave trade, which some hoped to abolish, was dropped because of the opposition of representatives from slaveholding regions in Spanish America. A reorganization of the colonial governing structure abolished viceroyalties and the viceregal office. A new office of the *jefe político superior* had military powers as a captain general, as well as political authority. Colonial high courts, the *audiencias*, remained courts, but stripped of their former political and administrative functions.

Miguel Ramos Arizpe, representing Mexico's northern provinces in the Cortes, proposed a new regional administrative structure, the Diputaciones Provinciales, as an intermediate level of authority.[5] Despite some resistance from those who believed it might lead to fragmentation and federalism, the Cortes approved. Seven elected individuals, chaired by an appointed *jefe político*, had provincial responsibilities. Deputies also voted to establish constitutional municipal councils (*ayuntamientos*). Formerly, only the principal cities in New Spain had recognized and sanctioned municipal councils. The new regulations allowed urban centers of at least 1,000 inhabitants to form municipal councils. At least 160 new municipal councils, most of them in Indian towns, came into existence. The Cortes envisioned both the Diputaciones Provinciales and the constitutional *ayuntamientos* as administrative bodies. Provincial deputations theoretically reported directly to the government in Spain, while the municipal councils reported to the provincial government. In reality, both acted politically and represented their constituents.

Such wide-ranging structural changes, together with elections, dramatically changed behavior and attitudes. A flood of short-lived newspapers and pamphlets, stimulated by the freedom of the press provisions of the 1812 Constitution, dealt with such issues as political representation, politics, and trade. Newspapers not only reported events, they also sought to mold public opinion. Newspaper competition to influence public opinion encouraged a sense of civic empowerment among readers. The Constitution of 1812 politicized the population from top to bottom and partially overturned patriarchic obstacles to civic participation.

Derailing the Constitution of 1812

Events in Europe stalled the movement toward an empire-wide representative commonwealth. In 1813, allied troops commanded by British general Arthur Wellington defeated the French at Vitoria, ending the peninsula war. A relieved British Crown promoted him to field marshal and subsequently made him the first Duke of Wellington, in 1814. In kaleidoscopic fashion, everything suddenly changed. With Spain liberated from French occupation, Fernando VII returned to the throne. Most believed he would accept a modified form of a constitutional monarchy; he did not. On May 4, the king abolished the Constitution of 1812, arrested prominent Liberals, and disregarded the contribution of those who had carried on the guerrilla war against the French. Scattered revolts broke out, only to be crushed. Royal displeasure reached across the Atlantic to punish colonial supporters of the constitution. A number of individuals, including the former Indian governor and subsequent councilman in the constitutional *ayuntamiento* of Mexico under the Constitution of 1812, received sentences of six years in exile in the Pacific Ocean colony of the Marianas Islands.

Not only did the king suppress the constitution, he annulled all the laws enacted after his imprisonment. In reality, the Liberal genie had escaped from the bottle and could not be squeezed back into it. Silver shipment to Spain had long since stopped, as the civil war had disrupted the Mexican economy. Both the Mexican and Spanish economies faced collapse. King Fernando, however, refused to endorse free trade and ignored sensible economic suggestions as he concentrated on reestablishing the colonial regime.

In Mexico, the royalist army, reinvigorated by the arrival of some 10,000 troops from Spain and a determined administration animated by the king's restoration, made an all-out effort to crush the insurrection. Between 1813 and 1815, additional Spanish troops arrived, adding to the violence and destruction, as the insurrection fragmented into innumerable small groups. Previous romantic sentiments that favored a hostage king restored turned to disappointment as order and security evaporated.

Spanish civil and military officials controlled the ports, the capital, and the cities along the highway between them. Everywhere else, patches of loyalty and insurgency existed. Banditry in the name of patriotism and patriotism as a guise for banditry ravaged the country. Revenge, retribution, and ambition pushed aside traditional deference to the king, his officers, and administrators. Loyalty to family, community, and local leaders, who provided a degree of personal security and protection from sporadic looting, replaced reliance on the ineffectual authority in Mexico City. Local leaders negotiated with others in the murky politics of self-interest to become regional warlords. The systemic breakdown of order could not be stopped.

A brief spasm of hope occurred with the 1820 revolt in Spain that restored the Constitution of 1812: one more slim opportunity remained to construct a representative transatlantic common-wealth. New Spain dutifully held an election for new deputies to the restored Cortes. Nevertheless, many concentrated on ensuring that some sort of a functioning system would be in place, in case the king abolished the constitution again. The issue of equal representation again emerged but would be laid aside. A more worrisome structural issue involved the preservation of Mexico as one territorial entity. The 1812 charter required each province to report to Madrid directly, theoretically fragmenting Mexico's territorial unity. In the event that the restored constitution did not survive and gave way to independence, various parts might declare their independence as separate nations. Equally troubling, the royalist army and the clergy remained ambivalent, even hostile, to the 1820 revival of Spanish constitutionalism.

In response to such fears, New Spain's deputies to the Cortes boldly proposed the establishment of three separate regencies in America, each to be governed by a Spanish prince, but under the Constitution of 1812. The regencies would be loosely connected with Spain on the basis of political equality, assume a share of the Spanish debt, continue the special trade ties, and cooperate on defense. The proponents of New World regencies cited the example of Canada, which could have joined the United States but instead chose its existing form of monarchist government. An alternative plan called for autonomy without a resident prince but with some form of integrated legislature. The Cortes rejected the proposals, thereby deciding the issue in favor of independence.

In Mexico, militia colonel Agustín de Iturbide began to seek support for a plan somewhat along the lines of that suggested by New Spain's deputies to the Cortes. He concluded that only a political solution could end the ongoing insurgency. Moreover, counterinsurgency tactics that had worked previously could not be implemented under the restrictions imposed by the Constitution of 1812. Colonel Iturbide's brutal reputation as a counterinsurgency commander gave him some political credibility among disheartened royalists as he sought to develop a consensus for a Mexican solution to the impasse.

Once a reasonable consensus had been forged, Iturbide issued the Plan of Iguala, calling for a constitutional monarchy. The plan offered protection to the Church and declared equality for all Mexicans, while guaranteeing the rights of Spaniards—and declared Mexico's independence from Spain. Fernando VII or a Spanish prince would be invited to come to Mexico to serve as the head of state. While few believed that the Spanish monarch would accept, the idea of a prince seemed possible, until the king refused to allow the several princes available to consider the offer. The plan did not provide a role for Iturbide, although it stated that in the event a Spanish prince could not be enticed, Mexicans could select their own monarch.

The Plan of Iguala pulled together a coalition of *jefes*, *caudillos*, clerics, and others. These men favored redemption from political uncertainty with an independent nation. The plan exaggerated Iturbide's commitment to replace nothing but the king's representatives. His offer to leave the warlords alone, with the hint of improved opportunities, became an appeal for fraternity and equality. He rallied the people and reassured the clerics with the promise to protect the Roman Catholic Church, threatened by an enlightened liberalism that many associated with the detested French. The Plan of Iguala offered "Three Guarantees:

Independence, Religion, and Equality," symbolized in the tricolor flag. The guarantees facilitated the building of temporary coalitions, most notably with Vicente Guerrero, who governed a region in the south. The royalist army generally accepted the Plan of Iguala, although the Army of the Three Guarantees numbered only some 1,500 men and could not have prevailed on the battlefield. Only a few garrisons, such as the one in Mexico City, held out.

In July 1821, Juan O'Donojú, appointed political chief and captain-general by the Spanish Cortes, arrived in Mexico, where he found most of the country under the control of Iturbide's forces and his allies. Faced with this reality, he met with Iturbide in the city of Córdoba, where he signed a treaty conceding Mexican independence. Since the Plan of Iguala appeared to be the same as the proposal for New World monarchies, which O'Donojú incorrectly believed had been approved by the Cortes, the new political chief ordered the withdrawal of royal troops from Mexico City. A triumphant Iturbide entered the city on September 27, 1821. The two men appointed a Sovereign Governing Junta, which formally declared independence on September 28.[6] The Sovereign Governing Junta named a regency council that included O'Donojú and Iturbide among its five members. Unfortunately, O'Donojú died shortly thereafter, leaving Iturbide as the most important member of the regency council. Meanwhile, royalist forces in the impenetrable fortress of San Juan de Ulúa in Veracruz harbor refused to accept Mexico's independence; they remained there, more prisoners than a garrison, for several years.

Out of this struggle, an independent people obtained two heroes and the challenges of creating a workable government and a united people. Padre Hidalgo became an enduring symbol, challenging his countrymen to take risks for the future they wanted, to face death for ideals they valued, and to demand more out of life than subsistence. He became the first Liberal hero. Agustín de Iturbide became an enduring symbol that incited his countrymen to live in reality by accepting society as they had been born into it, to practice pragmatic politics based on coalitions of strongmen, and to rely on local military or landholding elites to maintain order. He became the first Conservative hero of independence.

Of the three guarantees, only one required action. Independence carried with it Iturbide's commitment to monarchism. Most inhabitants, having known no other form of government, assumed that a monarchy was the most stable political structure. In contrast, the idea of a republic appeared radical and risky. Iturbide and an assembly of like-minded men attempted for some months to find a new king willing to govern Mexico. When they failed, Iturbide, with the backing of popular groups and the army, assumed the crown. The Mexican empire included the captaincy-general of Guatemala, not previously part of New Spain. From the outset, Iturbide insisted on being a strong executive, while the legislature, following the tradition of the Spanish Cortes, insisted on its dominance. The difficulty of creating a king out of a militia colonel did not trouble Iturbide.

The Mexican Empire
Emperor Agustín shook off his personality as Iturbide, the ambitious pragmatist and political broker. In a rash moment, he came to believe in the veracity of his own magic show and abandoned

the manipulation that had enabled him to proclaim independence and grab the crown. The right to rule appeared to be a matter of form. His coronation, modeled on Napoleon's imperial extravaganza, complete with borrowed and fake jewels and the elevation of close relatives to the nobility, bordered on farce.

The commanders and local bosses, who in order to survive had endured ten years of violence during which patriotic idealism had given way to betrayal, revenge, brutality, murder, and suspicion, had little patience with the emperor's new-found pretensions. The regal Iturbide jailed opponents, dismissed Congress, and replaced it with a Junta Nacional Instituyente, a privy-council subordinate to him. The desire for regional autonomy, a consequence of decades of disorder as well as the decentralization of the Constitution of 1812, conflicted with the emperor's centralism. Nor did his former supporters appreciate the emperor's tendency to rely on military officers and force rather than persuasion. Nevertheless, all agreed on the need for a national government, but resisted the taxes necessary to support it. Virtually every region had suffered economically and understandably wanted to keep resources within their province. The Mexico City elite failed to grasp that the constitutional municipalities and the provincial deputations created under the Constitution of 1812 meant the dissolution of the political supremacy of Mexico City.

Disgruntled Masons, including Miguel Ramos Arizpe and Mariano Michelena, recognized the widespread disillusionment with the empire and joined other opponents under the banner of the Plan of Casa Mata that demanded the election of a new congress. Significantly, it did not propose the establishment of a republic or the removal of Iturbide. Instead, it followed the lead of Spanish liberalism by asserting the superiority of congress and the restoration of provincial autonomy. Almost immediately, the provincial deputations supported the Plan of Casa Mata. Ominously, military men organized a "Liberation Army," anticipating the use of force. The emperor's refusal to compromise made his forceful removal a question of timing. A stubborn but in the end realistic Emperor Iturbide reconvened the old congress and abdicated the throne on March 19, 1823, leaving the nation without an executive and with demands for a new congress unaddressed.

The former captaincy-general of Guatemala separated amicably from the Mexican empire with Iturbide's abdication. In Central America, only Chiapas elected to remain part of Mexico. Meanwhile, politicians in Mexico City struggled to ensure the political unity of what remained. The failure of Iturbide's empire left only the option of a republic. Whether it would be a federal or centralized one remained to be determined. The remote northern marches (today the southwestern United States) demanded autonomy to meet indigenous threats and political flexibility to compensate for their isolation.

Few, however, anticipated the fundamental problems that independence brought out of the colonial shadows. Many understood that viceregal politics reflected the monarchist structure and values of a viceroyalty. Some, but not all, also understood that a patriarchal monarchy and its hierarchical social ladder, which had defined society for more than 300 years, had become archaic. Nevertheless, envisioning its effective replacement required an imaginative leap, and subsequently bitter experience. Not all Mexicans accepted reality, nor could the political culture be purged rapidly of ingrained notions and tendencies. The association of monarchies with arbitrary power made a weak national executive attractive and influenced the structure of the first republican constitution, but with unintended consequences.

The Early Republic's Sociopolitical Context

As Spanish power in New Spain collapsed, conspiratorial politics moved out of the viceroy's palace and into civil society in the form of secret societies such as the Guadalupes. Without actual power, secret societies and their influence varied greatly, depending on plots, schemes, and the manipulation of prominent individuals. Secret agendas by small, closed, conniving groups precluded frank and open debate and encouraged self-serving attempts to mold public opinion. For many traditionalists, Agustín's brief empire did not end their desire for a Mexican monarchy. Tradition, the Church, a social hierarchy set within a patriarchal society—in effect, a monarchy—suggested orderly political continuity to most Conservatives. In contrast, Liberals' seeming preference for abrupt change with little room for compromise and a tendency to make sweeping pronouncements in the name of progress created political and social confusion.

The fundamental split between Conservatives and Liberals meshed with the debate over federalism and centralism. States anxious to control their economic resources favored federalism, while Mexico City supported federalism but with enhanced powers at the national level, suggesting a drift toward centralism. One could be a Conservative and a federalist or a Liberal and a centralist, depending on one's geographic location within the nation. In general, state elites believed themselves the heirs of Spanish liberalism's decentralization and regional autonomy. Although most provincial elites agreed on the importance of a center of the union, they placed their state's survival above national well-being.

In the capital, a rudimentary party system emerged in the form of Masonic lodges. The Masonic order had roots in the eighteenth-century Enlightenment as an organizational home for intellectuals anxious to confront archaic values. Conveniently divided into two branches, the Masonic lodges provided a home for Liberals (York Rite) and Conservatives (Scots Rite), although the division between them blurred over the issue of the structure of the republic. The Scots Rite's membership included both Liberals and Conservatives until 1825. With the establishment of the York Rite lodge, the Masonic Mexican movement split into two groups. That the American representative in Mexico, Joel Ponsett, had openly supported the founding of the York Rite lodge caused lasting resentment among Conservatives. Liberal Masonic opposition to the Scots Rite lodge transformed the two movements into partisan organizations. Attempts to bridge the widening division within the Masonic political elite led to elaboration of a Mexican Masonic Rite. The Rito Nacional Mexicano Supreme Council emerged in the early 1830, borrowing ritual and structure from the Scots Rite movement, but it had little success.

The Masonic movement functioned as a poor substitute for an inclusive party system able to formulate broad sociopolitical objectives. As a consequence, negotiated political accommodations between different social groups could not be made, and the fabric of national unity could easily be torn. In addition, the absence of sufficient patronage, coupled with elite distrust of the masses, checked the impulse to create broad national parties. At the state level a party system did not evolve because of the effectiveness of family camarilla politics, which had developed a reasonably effective consensus, if an elite one, in each state.

Masonic lodges reinforced the notion that the political and social order depended on the wisdom of a small number of individuals. Whereas both Liberals and Conservatives distrusted the masses, they did so for different reasons. On the question of what group represented the essence of nationality, both Conservatives and Liberals agreed that it lay with the creole population, defined not necessarily on racial factors but on an individual's identification with European civilization. Nevertheless, despite basic agreement on national identity, deep philosophical divisions existed between Conservatives and Liberals. The reluctance of many Conservatives to relinquish a monarchist political structure stemmed from doubts that the population could dispense with patriarchal institutions of such long standing. Both groups agreed that the lower classes needed to be directed, but the Conservatives rejected the idea they could or should be molded into modern Mexicans, stripped of superstitions, culture, and attachment to the Church. In contrast, Liberals viewed the Indian population as caught in a state of static dependency. Colonial paternalism, in their view, had degraded the Indian population. Secular schooling and an end to priestly control became Liberal objectives tied to the urgent need to develop a modern economy. In the Liberal view, the Church fostered superstition and backwardness, prolonged dependency, and saddled Indians with religious expenses that drained their pitiful resources. Another option, European immigration and intermarriage, appeared attractive to many as a means of revitalizing the Mexican people and filling an under-populated northern Mexico. Above all, action had to be taken to modernize Mexico and its population.

The extent to which Liberals understood themselves to be revolutionaries remains unclear. That they believed they had a mission to overcome the past and plunge boldly into the future cannot be doubted. All levels of consciousness came under pressure. Everyday activities conducted in private or in public appeared to require aggressive action by Liberal reformers.

The Difficult Transition to a Republic

Much to the anger of provincial politicians, the Plan of Casa Mata's call for new elections would not be honored by the reconvened congress. In reaction, Oaxaca established a provincial governing junta, while Yucatán created its provincial administrative junta; in effect, both became quasi-independent states. Guadalajara caused the most concern. Guadalajara's long-standing opposition to Mexico City as the seat of national authority had roots deep in the colonial period. Its provincial deputation declared that it accepted the reconvened national congress, but only for the purpose of calling an election for a constituent congress to write a federal constitution. Other provinces insisted they existed as sovereign entities, while the capital, Mexico City, declared that only the nation could be sovereign. The constitutional municipalities also demanded a role, declaring that regional issues could only be understood and addressed by those in that region and not by distant governments in Mexico City or elsewhere.

Those intent on establishing a strong central government in Mexico City refused to back down. Finally, General Santa Anna, attempting to gain national attention, on his own authority announced the formation of a military organization, the Protector of Liberty Army, to fight if necessary for a federal republic. Rejecting intimidation, the government in Mexico City sent its own army to confront Santa Anna. After negotiations failed, the two armies made ready for battle. Fortunately, last-minute talks resolved the situation, and the immediate threat of civil war subsided.

Another standoff between Guadalajara and the reconvened congress occurred over the dispatching to that province of an official with the military title of captain-general, an indication that Mexico City intended to take harsh measures. Not surprisingly, Guadalajara refused to receive the new appointee and sent troops to stop him from entering the province. To make their point even blunter, the provincial political authorities transformed their province into the "Free State of Jalisco." As a sovereign state it elected a constituent legislature, issued its own constitution, and declared that it would be governed by the laws of the Constitution of 1812. If a federal union were created, however, Jalisco would join. Zacatecas followed the example of Jalisco. An angry national congress issued secret orders to General Nicolás Bravo to attack the two would-be states, cloaking its intended aggression as a desire to ensure tranquility. Both states mobilized their militias and deployed them on the border. Prudently, General Bravo halted at the last minute, and both sides agreed to talk.

The confrontation between the national regime and the two states aroused the entire nation. Sovereignty became the central issue, with the states insisting that the center of the union had sovereignty only on those issues that pertained to the entire nation, while the states had internal sovereignty. Meanwhile, armies under the command of the national government took up positions on the borders of four provinces. A civil war seemed inevitable. Fortunately, the national congress backed down and voted in favor of a settlement.

The second constituent congress convened on November 7, 1823, with instruction to elaborate a federal structure acceptable to the provinces. The new constitution drew on the 1812 Spanish Constitution as well as the 1787 Constitution of the United States. The Mexican constitution recognized joint sovereignty but separate functions. The constitution provided for a federal president, Senate, and Chamber of Deputies elected in a manner decided by each state. State legislators voted for the president and vice president, with the candidate with the most votes becoming president. The national congress tallied the votes and announced the results. Election by the states and confirmation by the national congress mirrored the same procedure initially followed by the United States. It made the national congress the political arbitrator of who became president and vice president in the event of ties and put potentially contentious rivals at the highest level of the national government.

Divided tax authority strengthened the municipalities and the states but reduced the office of president to that of an impoverished national administrator. The administration depended on the states to contribute funds to augment inadequate revenues from import and export taxes. The national congress dominated the other branches of the federal government but had a subordinate relationship to state legislatures. Each state decided the extent of legislative freedom enjoyed by its representatives. Consequently, actual power lay with state politicians drawn from recognized families. Federal senators and deputies represented the interests of their particular state, and secondarily those of the nation as a whole. The provinces won. The unity of the nation had been preserved temporarily, but the issue of a strong central government did not disappear.

Politically, both state and national legislatures rested on a municipal foundation that extended into rural Mexico. Municipalities had administrative and police authority over subordinate towns and villages within their jurisdiction. Officials collected taxes and dispensed them within the municipality as well as passed revenues on to the state level. A network at the district level tied municipalities together as an informal political force. State legislatures had political influence at the national level but little ability to control municipalities or create strong institutions within their state. Militias, theoretically controlled at the state level, relied on municipalities to supply militiamen. A deeply flawed constitution invited extralegal manipulations to make things work. Out of necessity, a national political elite emerged in the capital, eventually unbalancing the 1824 arrangement as the national elite drifted toward centralism.

Guadalupe Victoria (1786–1843), the first president under the Constitution of 1824, had sufficient prestige to hold the 1824 arrangement together. Schooled at the seminary in Durango and inspired by Hidalgo, he fought with Morelos, achieving the rank of general. With independence, he favored placing an insurgent in the presidency within a republican structure. His opposition to Emperor Iturbide, who as a royalist officer had fought against insurgents, resulted in his imprisonment. After escaping, Guadalupe Victoria fled to Veracruz to join other disgruntled opponents of Iturbide rallying around the Plan of Casa Mata. Guadalupe Victoria served on the three-man Supreme Executive Power that governed (1823–24) after the abdication of Iturbide until the Constitution of 1824 went into force. Guadalupe Victoria became president and Nicolás Bravo became vice president.

Creating a National Identity

The need to create a separate national identity became a problem with independence. Detaching from Spain after 300 years of a Hispanic legitimacy required a painful rejection. A search for Spanish vices to provide an excuse to denounce what they had previously embraced settled on imagined stereotypes mixed with bits of objective reality. Mexicans' exaggerated the extent of the wealth of Spanish merchants and their political influence. Together with Spain's apparent unwillingness to recognize Mexican independence, anti-Spanish stereotypes unleashed a wave of emotions that roiled the new republic. Inexperienced politicians, driven by the masses, could not deal with the threats to social stability and the economy and the challenge to their ability to direct civil society. Massive displays of anti-Spanish hostility forced both the national and state governments to propose punitive measures.

The state of Jalisco dismissed Spaniards from the militia and disarmed them. In the state of México, several prominent military men advocated the removal of Spaniards from the government, maintaining that Mexicans had a right to fill such positions. The most serious disorder occurred in the capital, where a military mutiny broke out in 1824 in favor of expulsion. General José María Lobato, at the head of the movement, demanded that all Spaniards be purged from the bureaucracy. In the end, General

Lobato bowed to government pressure, but other commanders had to be put down by force.

Armed bands roamed the countryside, killing Spaniards and looting estates. A rumored reinvasion by royalists added to the hysteria. Guadalupe Victoria prudently floated loans in London to equip the army and purchase warships to isolate the Spanish garrison in the fort of San Juan de Ulúa. The subsequent 1826 bankruptcy of the firm responsible for floating the loan made access to the full proceeds impossible, causing a financial crisis. The public blamed the Spaniards for the situation. The surrender of the Spanish garrison of San Juan de Ulúa on September 15, 1825, provided some relief from public pressure, but not entirely.

Liberals saw the anti-Spanish issue as politically too opportune to be relinquished, while Conservatives cautiously attempted to curb expulsion demands. The public correctly believed the Scots Rite Masons to be pro-Spanish. Proto-party politics as practiced by the *Yorkinos* fed on the anti-Spanish mood in the streets and directed it against the Conservatives. They seized on a doubtful conspiracy, but one sufficient to kept tensions high. Father Joaquín Arenas allegedly plotted to restore Spanish power as the only way to save religion, but once discovered, he refused to implicate others. It is not clear whether a plot existed or whether he was expressing personal outrage. Father Arenas had a reputation as a crackpot, and certainly as an inept conspirator. Eventually, four other Spaniards would be swept up in the presumed plot, including General Gregorio Arana, the major author of the anti-Iturbide Plan of Casa Mata. A military court dominated by Yorkist (Yorkinos) Masons sentenced Father Arenas and General Arana to be shot in the back as traitors.

Fueled by rumors of conspiracies real or imagined, public pressure forced congress to take up the issue of Spanish residents and their removal from the country. The president and others understood that expulsion would be an economic blow, but they could not resist the public's demand for action. An expulsion law passed on December 20, 1827, represented a victory for the Liberals, although the many exemptions meant that not all Spaniards fell under the law. Some left Mexico voluntarily rather than risk vigilante attacks on their shops or estates. An accurate count of those expelled is not possible, but official statistics indicate that 770 fell under the provisions. Of more significance, 1,977 enjoyed exemptions, 523 under Article Seven, which exempted those who had rendered notable service to Mexico during the independence period, and skilled professionals, broadly defined. The states exempted 1,154.[7] It became obvious that the national congress and state legislatures could be driven by public hysteria orchestrated in part by the Yorkinos. Many lawmakers privately resented their inability to deliberate calmly and rationally. The number of exemptions granted made the point. Public anger reached new levels as it became evident that the law of 1827 had removed very few Spaniards from the country. Predictably, Liberals implied that the pro-Spanish Conservatives lacked patriotism. Conservatives, fearful that they would not be able to defend their interests in the face of an outrage public or in congress, resorted to rebellion. The rebellion, initially led by Manuel Montaño, a hacienda manager with military experiences but politically not very influential, would soon be taken over by prominent Scots Rite Masons, including Vice President Nicolás Bravo, the Grand Master of the Scots Rite Masons. Bravo's small force could not counter the 2,000-men army commanded by General Guerrero. Vice President Bravo, captured and sentenced to exile, sailed for Colombia, along with other supporters of the brief, two-week Montaño revolt. The failed revolt damaged the Scots Rite lodge, effectively ending its influence.[8]

In an effort to calm public agitation over the failure of the 1827 expulsion law, new legislation in March 1829 attempted to remedy the situation. It failed because many of its supporters wanted a political excuse to be outraged but had little interest in deporting their relatives, friends, or personal acquaintances. Outrage and private ambivalence cut across class lines. A determined group of forty lower-class women herded their children into the Chamber of Deputies and presented a petition in favor of exemptions. Nevertheless, a number of former Spanish soldiers too poor to afford to return to Europe would be sent to New Orleans at government expense.

Unaddressed tensions in the early republic burst through with the presidential election of 1829.[9] State legislatures voted for a number of logical candidates, as well as favorite sons with little chance of attracting votes in other states. The tally resulted in the election of a moderate Conservative, Manuel Gómez Pedraza, with eleven votes for president, followed by the Liberal favorite Vicente Guerrero, with nine votes, and Anastaso Bustamante, a Conservative, with six ballots. Ten votes divided among a number of other individuals completed the count. A flawed process failed to definitively indicate the preference of the states, inviting the disappointed to contest the results.

The Liberals who favored Guerrero chose to revolt. With Santa Anna in the lead, they announced the Plan of Perote, which called for the installation of Guerrero as president. Liberal revolts broke out across Mexico, threatening a return to pre-independence violence. A hapless Gómez Pedraza fled the country. The national congress installed Guerrero in the presidency and Bustamante as vice president, and nullified Gómez Pedraza's eleven votes. The attempt to preserve scraps of constitutional procedure and placate Conservatives by allowing Bustamante to be vice president did not undo the damage.

President Vicente Guerrero's reputation rested on his military contribution in the independence struggle in southern Mexico, led by Father Morelos. His heroic status, however, could not override his perceived social deficiencies. His racially mixed parentage and informal education made him unacceptable to many individuals in the government. As president, he relied heavily on Lorenzo Zavala, a radical Liberal who would subsequently become the vice president of the breakaway Texas Republic in 1836.

The difficult and problematic struggle to achieve political stability encouraged pro-colonial-restoration proponents in the Veracruz merchant community and exiled Spaniards to plot to reestablish Spanish rule. A Spanish invasion followed by the reintroduction of modified colonial institutions under the legitimate rule of Fernando VII of Spain seemed feasible. Private funds financed an invasion force under a Spanish general. Rumors of the plan circulated, as did various possible landing sites. Not all believed that it constituted a threat until a force of 4,000 men commanded by General Isidro Barradas landed north of Tampico on July 27, 1829. General Santa Anna immediately assumed most of the responsibility for repelling the invaders. A weak, poorly trained, and underequipped Mexican army directed by

Santa Anna confronted an unwanted occupation force. Those who had financed the invasion erroneously expected that many Spanish residents would join them. The Mexican population refused to supply food or assistance, and guerrillas complicated enemy troop movements, but the climate proved to be the most effective defense. In the end, yellow fever and other tropical diseases decimated the Spanish force. Forty-seven days later they surrendered.

Victory over the invaders did little to help President Guerrero. His legitimacy had been undermined by those who considered him unfit for the presidential office. A spate of rebellions broke out demanding the end of federalism and the establishment of a strong central government. Vice President Bustamante issued the Plan of Jalapa, calling for the removal of Guerrero, and the army deserted the president, who fled the capital. Guerrero's fruitless attempts to regain control ended with his ignominious capture and execution in 1831.

The republic had survived its first tumultuous years, but not well. Both Victoria and Guerrero contended with vice-presidential revolts, constitutional procedures had been blatantly violated, and public opinion had been manipulated to secure political advantage. To further their agenda, the Yorkinos legitimized divisive politics and seriously damaged the government. The Conservatives adopted the same techniques, as both groups came to believe that moderation meant defeat and principles ruled out compromise. Only General Santa Anna emerged from the bitter confusion of the first decades of independence with enhanced prestige. Santa Anna's adherence to a series of successful plans, from Casa Mata to the Plan of Jalapa, and his prominent role in the defeat of the

Spanish invasion made him a national figure. That he would eventually become president seemed foreordained.

The defeat of the Spanish invasion force constituted the one positive episode during the chaotic early years. The decisive rejection of a return to Spanish sovereignty marked the psychological end of the colonial era.

Political and Cultural Obstacles

Liberalism did not underestimate the task at hand. While some reforms could be readily accepted in principle by much of the population and accomplished theoretically with the stroke of a pen, others could not. Decrees such as those abolishing racial distinctions (1822), extinguishing noble titles (1826), and eliminating African slavery (1829) occasioned little resistance. Contested issues such as the social and economic role of the Church could not be disposed of so readily, however. For many Liberals, the Church embodied all the fundamental obstacles to change—a position diametrically rejected by Conservatives.

The power of the Church rivaled that of the government, and the Church remained a competitive force into the twentieth century. Politicians might dominate the republic, but the Church controlled the people and much of the country's wealth. Clerics displayed their prowess in religious parades through city streets, as well as in villages nationwide. Time marked by church bells and a yearly calendar that proceeded from one religious holiday and its obligations to the next kept the Church at the center of community life. Individual and village saints' days celebrations, marriages, baptisms, confirmations, and burials placed religion at everybody's side virtually twenty-four hours a day from birth to death. Politicians of all stripes—Liberals and Conservatives, federalists, centralists, monarchists, and republicans—responded reluctantly or willingly, but always within the religious context of daily life. The extent of the hold of traditional religious beliefs is encapsulated in a common prayer recited by women before intercourse:

> *It is not out of vice*
> *Nor is it out of fornication*
> *But to make a child*
> *In your holy service*[10]

The clergy understood that Liberals sought to subordinate the Church to the government, transform the people into citizens first, and make religion a question of personal choice rather than a defining attribute of Mexican nationality. Thus, when Jalisco's state constitution of 1824 required the clergy to swear allegiance to the new government, they refused. Legislators in Durango and Zacatecas urged the national government to control the Mexican Church rather than wait for an agreement with Rome. Nevertheless, a weak government could not win a direct confrontation with a powerful Church.

The Church retained many responsibilities that had evolved over the colonial centuries. After independence, the clergy found it difficult to adapt, as the emerging state began to encroach on what they believed to be their rightful role. Clerics believed themselves to be under siege and consistently overreacted. Priests urged the people to resist "godless" officials and tended to see every move by the government as an effort to diminish the Church. Nor could the faithful debate with the "heretical philosophies," because the

Church forbade discussion with heretics. When Vicente Roca-fuerte published his *Essay on Religious Toleration* in 1831, calling for the separation of church and state, he ran afoul of the Press Board, which monitored publications to ensure conformity to the Constitution of 1824. The board charged him with violation of the constitution and arrested him. The public trial of Rocafuerte discredited an excessively sensitive, overreaching Church. To the clergy, religious toleration meant first and foremost loss of their authority and remained a divisive issue even after the Liberals succeeded in declaring religious toleration in 1860. A series of reforms challenged clerical influence over women, altered relations between the sexes, and transferred traditional clerical functions to the state. A civil registry law in 1857 led to required civil marriages two years later. A marriage became legal and children legitimate only as result of a civil ceremony. Thereafter the Church's role in this critical social contract became ceremonial and voluntary.

In contrast to Liberal reformers, Conservatives believed that the Church had an important role in maintaining social links that bound society together and provided guidance and control of the indigenous population. They agreed with the Liberals on the inferior nature of the Indian population but rejected the notion that it resulted from colonial paternalism. Both Conservatives and Liberals supported the idea of European immigration to genetically and culturally uplift the indigenous population, but Conservatives insisted that the immigrants be Catholics. With or without immigration, Conservatives insisted that an evolution-ary process would eventually elevate the Indian to an acceptable level of civilization. Meanwhile, Conservatives saw no need to incite trouble by forcing the pace of change. Liberals understood the Conservatives' argument but believed that constructing a viable, independent Mexico could not wait. Slow adaptation to a changing world by a backward people—indeed, the great majority of the nation's population—might well be fatal to Mexico's independent survival.

While both Liberals and Conservatives agreed on the nature of the Indians, they had little faith in the lower classes in general and accepted the notion that an elite must govern the country. Consequently, both ideological camps at different times manipulated the people, an attitude reflected in the 1830 restructuring of the municipal electoral system in the capital. Instead of voting by parishes in Mexico City, the law created 245 wards under the supervision of commissioners appointed by the municipal councils. Each ward held its own primaries, theoretically avoiding manipulation of voters. In fact, commissioners responsible for determining eligible voters saw to it that results went as intended by the political elite. The intent of the 1830 law to restrict the possibility of mob rule evolved into the actual and psychological disenfranchisement of the lower classes that characterized the nineteenth century.

Education as a Panacea

Liberals believed that education could rescue the nation as well as detach the lower classes, Indians, and women from clerical influence. The eighteenth-century view that enlightened women in their maternal role of mothers could play an important part in the development of the citizens lay behind this belief. Moreover, the exclusion of women from certain economic tasks that did not require physical strength made little sense, and their lack of schooling retarded development. Such notions did not convince everyone, but the articulation of the need to rethink women's role had an impact, evident in the 1842 law that theoretically made education mandatory for boys and girls from age seven to fifteen years. The government required all urban concentrations of more than 500 inhabitants to establish a school for each gender. Basic skills, including reading, writing, arithmetic, geometry, languages, and civics, formed the core curriculum. In 1843 the republic had 1,310 primary schools, adding an average of eight more each year until 1857. Private schools run by respectable matrons called *amigas* charged modest weekly fees to teach young girls and small boys the basic elements. Those who attended school seldom proceeded beyond the elementary level, however, and in reality, few children had access to schooling. Rural schooling hardly existed, although literate individuals, such as a priest, might offer tutoring.

A low level of education, even illiteracy, did not preclude a successful career during the colonial era. That changed abruptly in nineteenth century as the industrial revolution spread world-wide. The growing focus on international trade and markets, as well as the need to understand more than the simple mechanics of local commerce, made literacy and the access to knowledge it provided mandatory.

After independence, Liberals, reflecting their Enlightenment origins, felt an urgent need to catch up with the modern world and placed a high economic, social, and political value on educa-tion. With a devastated economy barely able to stay afloat with exploitive loans and with few resources to build schools and train teacher, a sense of frustration characterized most Liberal reformers. Nevertheless, they clung to the belief that education offered the key to the transformation of the people and the modernization of Mexico.

Liberal emphasis on knowledge without the resources to undertake a national educational program widened the gap between urban and rural Mexico and between the classes, and this gap persisted into the twentieth century. The spread of basic literacy in cities owed much to the popularity of the Lancaster method. Developed in England for elementary level instruction, it consisted of one person teaching reading, writing, and simple numbers to individuals, who in turn acted as teaching assistants directed by the head teacher. Essentially a form of organized rote learning, the method seemed to be a cost-effective way to provide mass education. Strictly regimented Lancaster schools could teach several hundred students at a time. A Lancaster Company in Mexico City organized schools employing this method, and in 1842 the company assumed control of elementary education in the capital. Mexico City had four such schools for boys, five for girls, one for both genders, and an adult night school. The method gradually lost favor and was officially replaced in 1890. For all the success of the Lancaster method, the majority of Mexicans lived a rural life and remained illiterate, toiling without the benefit of enlightened ideas or the technological advances available in the cities.

Secondary education employed individual instructors schooled in a particular subject. The course of instruction could be arduous and long. Seminaries provided instruction for men entering the priesthood. Girls generally did not attend school after age twelve, although those with the means and the desire to pursue private instruction could do so, with admirable results. Many accepted the prevailing notion at the time that too much education for women destroyed their marriage prospects, diverted attention from their roles of wife and mother, and disrupted patriarchal relations within the family. Lower-class children of either gender had scant access to secondary education.

Wealthy women had the advantages of money, time, and private tutors. A number of ladies' magazines published beginning in the 1840s mirrored as well as accelerated their progress. The content of such magazines demonstrated that many privileged women had an impressive level of educational sophistication far beyond basic literacy. Letters to the editors, submission of poems, and articles translated from other languages by readers made it obvious what these women demanded from the magazines they supported. Such publications acted as an association of like-minded women, a social network that did not depend on actual acquaintance or physical proximity. They broadened perceptions, shared concerns, and often suggested necessary advances. In 1856, a sympathetic President Ignacio Comonfort received a petition from a women's group to establish a secondary school for less privileged females. Political turmoil delayed its establishment until 1869.

The Economics of Chronic Disorder

The destruction that resulted from the independence struggle threw Mexico into a chronic economic crisis. The prolonged insurgency resulted in the collapse of the mining industry, the economic engine of the former viceroyalty of New Spain. Flooded mines, deserted farmlands, abandoned road networks, and a population loss of an estimated 20 percent led to widespread misery. The economic disruption caused by the insurgency depleted financial resources, degraded the infrastructure, hindered recovery, and limited tax revenues. Observers noted the charred remains of haciendas and modest houses and other signs of past prosperity long after the violence had subsided. Guerrilla violence, nutritional deprivation, and rampant disease took their human and economic toll on an exhausted people. The economic prosperity of the colonial era that had so impressed Alexander von Humboldt in 1799 no longer existed.

Recovery required a half century or more, and began with agonizing slowness in the late 1820s. The government borrowed much of the depleted amount of domestic capital at extremely high interest rates, barely leaving the crumbs for private borrowing. Even then the government had to turn to foreign loans floated in London to prop up a bankrupt state. Draining flooded mines, prospecting for new ones, and repairing the road network to facilitate the transportation of ores required vast amounts of capital. Nevertheless, the reputation of the region's mines, often exaggerated by promoters, attracted European speculators and investors blissfully unaware of the risks. The desire of many uninformed investors to believe in a Mexican cornucopia made selling mining investments possible and disappointment inevitable.

William Bullock, one of the nineteenth century's great showmen, certainly in a class with P. T. Barnum, captured popular attention with such displays as Cromwell's head and Napoleon's battle coach. He recognized the curiosity about Mexico, visited for six months, and returned to England with some 1,000 objects to mount a two-pronged exhibit in the Egyptian Hall in London. The exhibit featured the first European display of Aztec antiquities, which excited great admiration, and another room of contemporary items that fueled investment fever. Bullock's travelogue, *Six Months' Residence and Travels in Mexico* (1824), further heightened "Mexico fever" among a broad segment of the British public, including William Wordsworth and Benjamin Disraeli. Bulloch's promotional activities encouraged imprudent investing. When the speculative Mexican fever ended in 1826, it forced several large British banking houses, including Barclay, Goldschmidt and Company and Herring, into bankruptcy. Herring closed it doors with more than 1.5 million pesos of Mexican government funds on deposit. As a result, Mexico defaulted on its loans in 1827.

Wonder and excitement traveled in both directions. Europe's fantastic new technology seemed to offer the tools to restore the damaged Mexican economy and expand it. Inventions such as steam engines and pumps appeared to be magical solutions to national needs. Heightening the fascination with technology, showmen introduced the general public to other inventions that had yet to have practical applications. In early 1835, French showman Eugene Robertson, in a bullring packed with spectators, stepped into a wicker gondola, ordered the lines of his hot air balloon cast off, and to the amazement of the audience disappeared into the clouds. He came down sixty miles away in a tree in Chalma. A two-balloon repeat performance in honor of Santa Anna's victory at Tampico involved a small balloon carrying a large fanciful portrait of the president into the heavens. In an even larger balloon, Robertson ascended again while waving a Mexican flag. His amazing tour ended with a spectacular show as he and a young, beautiful, adventuresome Mexican woman rose rapidly in a gondola decorated with both the French and Mexican flags.

A less flamboyant demonstration in 1843 featured a diorama with lights behind it that gave the illusion of various times of the day. Mexicans admired the wonders of mechanical invention and embraced technology as the beginning of a new era. They would be correct, but it would not be easy.

Modest economic recovery became evident in the 1840s, although the government remained impoverished and dependent on customs revenues and foreign loans. Agricultural rents slowly improved between 1835 and 1840, and real estate prices slowly began to climb. The textile industry picked up in the 1840s. While mining activity attracted British capital, foreign entrepreneurs, and skilled engineers, the task of draining deep mines frequently bankrupted even the most experienced operators. Nevertheless, mining gradually recovered, encouraged by new discoveries. Guanajuato, devastated by the flooding of the Valencia mine, sprang back with a rich silver strike at La Luz. Nevertheless, limited recovery did not build sufficient momentum to dramatically expand the economy until decades later.

Transportation constituted a major obstacle. In the 1800s the nine major highways, the former *caminos reales*, the royal state roads, provided the basic transportation grid that converged on Mexico City. Routes conformed to the rugged terrain and available mountain passes, making time, not actual distance, the determining factor in travel. The most important roads served the mining regions in the north and the ports on each coast. Primitive feeder roads, little more than mule trails, connected northern mines with the Zacatecas and Pachuca highways. Highways to Acapulco on the Pacific coast and to Veracruz on the Caribbean linked Mexico to Asia and Europe.

The Veracruz to Mexico City highway handled the largest volume of commercial traffic and served as the major entry and exit route for merchants and travelers. Heavy cargo hauled by oxen and mules in trains of several hundred animals, with at times fifty large wheeled wagons, fueled economic activity. Individual mounted riders, the occasional coach, porters carrying litters, and *arrieros* (mule skinners) with strings of fifteen to twenty pack animals, along with herds of cattle, goats, and sheep that moved in both directions, made the route the most important national artery. Off the main highways regional and local roads, sometime trails and paths, provided an unmapped maze known only to local guides. Here burros and porters carried products to market towns. Transportation to the outer rural fringes remained difficult, time-consuming, and costly, leaving large sections of the country isolated. In the extreme northern territories wagon trains required six months to reach Santa Fe, New Mexico, and even longer to reach the remote settlements in Alta California.

The republic required considerable experimentation to find an acceptable balance between the powers of the national government and those of the states. In the states, politicians shared a preference for federalism. The early republican presidents professed to be Liberals, but the extent of their federalism varied. Santa Anna, elected president in 1833 as a Liberal, turned the office over to Valentín Gómez Farías, his vice president, and retreated to his hacienda in Jalapa.

General Santa Anna, as a transitional figure, appealed to those who wanted a peaceful interlude to recover and lick self-inflicted wounds. Santa Anna's ordinary tastes, talents, and wants matched those of his countrymen. His close attention to these shared desires rather than to utopian ideals accounted for his charisma. He learned about himself and his countrymen by living with them in the barracks and campaigning with them across the country. His vice president, Gómez Farías, saw what Mexicans could become, while Santa Anna recognized what both he and they represented already. His emphasis on a common identity expressed not demagoguery but a basic social and political unity not appreciated by the Liberal elite.

Gómez Farías, considered one of the most radical Liberals, represented the first president with a strong ideological agenda. President Gómez Farías reduced the size of the army and ended its special privileges, in accordance with the Liberal idea that a militia composed of citizens could best defend the republic and avoid the tyranny of the sword. He closed the University of Mexico to end clerical influence over advanced learning, reduced clerical demand on scarce capital, and fiscally weakened the Church by declaring the tithe optional rather than mandatory.[1] The president nationalized the Franciscan mission system in California, a preliminary step that the Church feared endangered its more important holdings in the nation's center. In a direct attack on clerical discipline, Gómez Farías promulgated regulations that allowed priests and nuns to renounce their vows and return to civil life. Many young girls entered convents pressured by parents or guardians, well before they realized what a secular life offered. Convent life absorbed resources with little economic utility, and in an underpopulated country prevented marriageable women from forming families. How many nuns and priests took advantage of the law is unknown, but the option of doing so changed their relationship with clerical authorities.

Gómez Farías's reforms proceeded too rapidly. He failed to prepare the shocked public for such radical changes. Apprehensive Conservatives appealed to General Santa Anna to stop his vice president. In addition to pressure from Conservatives, the Church, and the army, large towns and cities felt threatened by the political power that federalism allowed small towns to wield. Such apparently widespread opposition to federalism convinced the general to remove Gómez Farías and reexert his presidential authority over the federal government. He did so dramatically in a coup d'état, technically against his own government. Santa Anna wavered between federalism and centralism before deciding that the republic needed the firm direction that only a centralized government could impose.

Santa Anna ignored the importance of federalism and decreed a centralized government, although he did not reverse many of the reforms imposed by Gómez Farías, including the optional tithe. The army continued to receive the assets of the California missions, and even the renunciation of clerical vows remained law until 1854. Santa Anna ordered states to reduce the size of their militias in order to reduce competing military forces. Zacatecas refused to do so, prompting the general to lead 4,000 troops into the state to teach a harsh lesson.

Santa Anna, calling his regime the government of *Las Siete Leyes* (the Seven Laws), suggested a new departure to deal with political and financial difficulties. The Seven Laws restructured institutions and attempted to reorient the nation away from its attachment to federalism and return control to a national political elite. In addition to spelling out the responsibilities of the various branches of government and the political blueprint of the republic, the laws provided for a national supervisory body. The Supreme Conservative Power had the task of balancing institutional elements in accordance with guidelines that determined the proper direction of the country.

The new Constitution of 1836 converted states into departments under the direction of political bosses appointed by the president. Brushing aside federalism, perhaps the one thing Santa Anna should have left alone, set the stage for political disintegration. Santa Anna failed to recognize that the frontier north had interests that differed from those of central Mexico. He also failed to appreciate the extent of the external threat. Thomas Jefferson's purchase of the Louisiana Territory in 1803 exerted pressure on the provinces of Texas and New Mexico. In addition to the American threat, British, French, and Russian adventurers and seamen probed the coast of California. President Santa Anna's mishandling of the Californios, Nuevo Mexicanos, and Tejanos weakened their attachment to the republic at a vulnerable time.

Revolt in Texas

Defending Mexico's far northern territories appeared to require the establishment of a population buffer against an expanding United States and hostile Indians. Immigration appeared to be the solution, but just what type of immigrant became an issue. Disagreement centered on religion, with the Conservatives favoring Catholics, assuming they would integrate smoothly into Mexico's Catholic culture, while Protestants allegedly threatened that cultural fabric. Emperor Iturbide in an 1823 law established a Catholic religious requirement, following the precedent of the 1821 enactment of the Spanish Cortes. Nevertheless, many Liberals believed that religious toleration and material progress went together. Vicente Rocafuerte, the Mexican representative in London during Guadalupe Victoria's administration, argued for freedom of religion in order to attract northern Europeans, whom he believed to be superior workers. Nevertheless, the Catholic religious requirement theoretically remained in place. Government agents contracted with organizations to recruit and transport immigrants. The few that arrived under colonization contracts swore to become Mexicans, declared their support of the government in Mexico City, and promised to learn Spanish and convert to Catholicism, if necessary.

Despite such efforts, organized immigration to Mexico failed, while informal immigrants from the United States swarmed across the Louisiana border into Texas with little knowledge of legal stipulations, although they likely would have ignored them anyway. The frontier population, whether the migrants came north with Mexican military garrisons, or on their own to obtain land, or from American Louisiana, enjoyed de facto autonomy. They organized their own defenses against Indian raiders and continued to bring duty-free goods from the United States. American settlers, who owned slaves in violation of Mexican law, and others concerned they might be driven out feared an intrusive central government. A combination of interests came together in opposition to Santa Anna's centralized regime. Texas withdrew from the Mexican union, although technically it no longer existed under the new constitution. Other former states reacted in a similar fashion for a variety of reasons.

Between 1836 and 1841, revolts in favor of federalism swept the entire republic. Jalisco mounted seven, the newly designated department of México eight, while Puebla experienced five revolts. Yucatán withdrew from the union and remained independent for some time. A lesser number of revolts occurred throughout the republic. Revolt in Texas, on the nation's northern periphery, caused the most trouble. Mexico, beset by Mayan uprisings in Yucatán (the Caste Wars), and with talk of independence in the silver zones (the Republic of the Sierra Madre), seemed to be coming apart. European bankers, alarmed that the republic verged on disintegration, made incessant demands for repayment of loans. Santa Anna needed to demonstrate quickly and decisively that he could control the country. He recruited an army to end the Texas secession and punish the rebellious Texans and restore confidence.

The revolt in Texas united American settlers and a significant number of Tejanos hoping to force restoration of the federal Constitution of 1824. Austin had talked of Texas independence and possible annexation by the United States earlier, but used the 1824 Constitution to rally the Tejanos against Santa Anna's government. A combined Tejano and Anglo-Texan force fought the Mexican garrison in San Antonio de Béxar in fierce battle, at times house by house, forcing it to surrender and agree to withdraw southward.[2] Responding to news of Santa Anna's advance into Texas, the rebels organized their defense in the largest town in the territory, San Antonio.

Colonel Ben Travis commanded only 173 men, augmented by Davy Crockett, who decided to interrupt his hunting trip to the Rocky Mountains to join the fighting. They unwisely chose to make a stand in the old Franciscan mission called the Alamo. Santa Anna soon placed the Alamo under siege and demanded its unconditional surrender. The Texans decided to fight—a decision that cost all of them their lives, either in the battle or in the execution of prisoners that followed. Santa Anna then made a forced march to Goliad, to confront some 200 rebels. This group, remembering the Alamo, surrendered on Santa Anna's terms. General-President Santa Anna then ordered their execution as bandits and rebels. Only a band of insurgents led by Sam Houston remained.

Houston understood that the survival of his army and the Republic of Texas depended on avoiding battle. For several days he led his men away from Santa Anna, who continued in pursuit, until he reached San Jacinto, part of the modern-day city of Houston. There the exhausted Texans bivouacked. Santa Anna's army came within sight of the Texas picket line and camped as well, the men expecting to attack as soon as they had rested. In a mix-up resulting from overconfidence or miscommunication, the Mexicans failed to post guards. When Houston received word of the unguarded Mexican camp, he ordered an immediate attack. The Texans needed only thirty minutes to overwhelm the sleeping Mexican army in the rather grandly named Battle of San Jacinto.

The Texans recognized the poorly disguised Santa Anna among their prisoners and wanted to execute him along with the rest of their captives. Houston had a different plan: to trade the prisoners, including Santa Anna, for independence. In return for the release of the prisoners and his own life, Santa Anna agreed that his defeated army would retreat south of the Rio Grande, and promised to obtain government recognition of the independence of Texas. President Andrew Jackson, then vacationing in Memphis, Tennessee, received the defeated Mexican general and arranged for the U.S. Navy to transport Santa Anna to Havana, where he could take a ship home to Mexico. Once on Mexican soil, Santa Anna renounced his promise as one made under duress. Rival politicians rejected the general, whom they viewed as a traitor for having traded Texas independence for his release, and laid plans to retake Texas. Plans to attack the Tejanos abruptly became secondary to an immediate threat posed by the French.

French bankers demanded payment of the Mexican debt, including claims for property damage. Louis Napoleon, eager for some international success, sent warships to the port of Veracruz to force payment. Among the many plausible damaged property claims, a petty one stood out. A French baker who had resided

"The Invasion of the North Americans: First Battles" The U.S. invasion in 1846 led to fighting south of Texas, but soon resulted in U.S. victories in California and ultimately in the center of Mexico, with Mexico City occupied by U.S. forces for ten months. Jean Charlot Collection, University of Hawaii at Manoa.

in Mexico City asserted that soldiers had occupied his shop during a political disturbance and eaten all of his pastries, valued at 100 pesos. The Mexican government made the hapless baker's lamented loss symbolic of France's heavy-handed debt collection. Annoyed, the French increased their demands by 200,000 pesos to pay for collection costs. After the Mexicans agreed, the French admiral nevertheless ordered the bombardment of Veracruz. Santa Anna and his men galloped toward the city as the cannons began shelling it. One errant shot struck his right leg, just below the knee. Santa Anna survived, subsequently claiming that his late leg proved the intensity of his patriotism. The Mexican people recorded the episode as the Pastry War.

War with the United States

The U.S. presidential elections in 1844 placed a little-known compromise candidate in office. James K. Polk, a determined expansionist, hoped to oversee the creation of a transcontinental nation. His plan involved forcing the resolution of territorial conflicts with Great Britain, incorporating the Republic of Texas, and building an unstoppable coalition for continental expansionism. In short order, the U.S. Congress annexed Texas, and Polk dispatched diplomats to London and Mexico City with orders to fulfill his campaign pledges. Polk's combination of objectives required making good on his slogan of "54 40 or Fight," to resolve the issue of the Oregon Territory with the British in Canada and purchase Mexican ports on the Pacific coast in order to gain the support of New England merchants interested in the Asian trade. Britain and the United States agreed to a treaty that divided Oregon at the present U.S.-Canadian border, but the

Mexican government ordered the American representatives to leave, making it clear it did not accept the loss of Texas or intend to sell Pacific ports.

After some weeks considering what might justify an invasion of Mexico, Polk confided in his diary that he would request Congress to declare war based on the hostile treatment of his emissary, their bellicose statements in regard to Texas, and their general disrespect for American territorial claims. He worried that congressmen would see his statement as a request to declare war because of rude behavior. Events in the Rio Grande Valley, a region claimed by both Texas and the Mexican border state of Tamaulipas, saved him from this indignity. Reports of an exchange of gunfire between American soldiers and Mexican troops that had crossed the Rio Grande offered a pretext for war. Polk demanded a declaration of war to retaliate for the loss of American blood on American soil.

Congress declared war on Mexico in April 1846 in a close vote, with strong opposition coming from the Whig Party. Opponents, including Abraham Lincoln, denied that the skirmish had occurred on American territory. Free State supporters and abolitionists in western New York state and Ohio demonstrated against the war, concerned that new territorial acquisitions would add to the number of slave states. They opposed conscription and fought military appropriation bills in Congress throughout the war. Southerners generally supported a Mexican war, with most of the opposition coming from the North, although militias from Illinois and other Midwestern states as well as the Northeast served in Mexico.

A substantial number of troops had to be raised and organized as volunteer militias. Recruitment often required coercion of newly arrived immigrants, but unemployment drove many into the ranks. In addition, judges dispatched those accused of crimes, by posing the choice of jail or military service. The regular army relied on immigrants for some 40 percent of its men, but in volunteer regiments such as the First New York Regiment, immigrants far outnumbered the native-born. While the regular army functioned at a higher professional level, the competence of state and volunteer militias varied widely. Consequently, desertions in the war with Mexican reached the highest level of any conflict to date, as did the number of deaths from combat wounds and disease.[3]

Military equipment did not favor one side over the other. Mexicans carried the flintlock barrel-loading muskets of the Napoleonic wars, as did most of the U.S. troops. A few units of the regular army carried a new percussion musket that simplified the process and made reloading faster, although it still required pouring powder down the barrel and a ramrod to pack the balls before firing.[4] Professionalism provided the crucial advantage for the U.S. forces. Major General Winfield Scott used military engineers, and a quartermaster corps to provide support for the army in the field.[5] Nevertheless, many senior officers, including General Zachary Taylor, had little experience other than that gained in the Indian wars.

More than offsetting weaknesses on the North American side, the Mexican government had few financial resources and faced serious internal opposition. The war exposed the deep social and ethnic fissures that lurked just below the surface. In 1844, as it became evident that war loomed, the peasantry of Río Grande, the

Xichú in Guanajuato, revolted against taxes imposed to prepare for war as well as the military draft (*leva*). Unrest in the Sierra Gorda would spread, becoming a wide-scale rebellion in 1847 that lasted until 1850. The American army in Tampico encouraged the extensive arms trade that supported the rebellion, which encompassed parts of four states: Querétaro, Guanajuato, San Luis Potosí, and a small area in the state of Hidalgo.

The states of Puebla, Querétaro, and México passed laws to seize communal land and sell it to raise money for the war, sparking protests and leading to an informal army that withdrew recognition of the federal government. In northern Veracruz state, the Huasteca Veracruzana, Indian groups also protested war measures that appeared to fall heavily on the indigenous population. In the confusion, various large landholders declared in favor of the U.S. invaders, while others supported the government; self-interest rather the patriotism or disloyalty often determined the choice.[6] Desertions of entire militia units composed of reluctant soldiers also hampered the resistance. A severe shortage of competent junior officers and experienced noncommissioned officers hampered effectiveness. Nevertheless, from a senior leadership standpoint, Santa Anna had military skills and organizational talents that surpassed those of General Zackary Taylor. Santa Anna fought General Taylor, who conducted American military operations in northern Mexico, to a draw at Buena Vista. Then Santa Anna moved his forces to the south to protect the capital and confront General Scott, a much more talented officer.

The war also had a psychological aspect, as each side attempted to subvert the other. Mexican government and military officials, keenly aware of anti-Catholicism in the United States, called on

Map 1. The U.S.-Mexican War

their co-religionists in the American army to join them in repulsing "Protestant" expansionism. The San Patricios (Saint Patricks), a battalion composed mainly of deserters from the American forces, suggested that Mexico could count on their Catholic brethren to join them in confronting the United States. While more of a morale booster than a decisive addition to Mexican forces, the San Patricios had a propaganda value and provided a potential magnet for American deserters. The Saint Patrick designation, suggested by John Reilly, the commander of the unit, resulted in the notion that it consisted entirely of Irish immigrants, although only 40 percent fell into that category. In a somewhat different fashion, the American army recruited Mexican irregulars to establish control in outlying areas, suppress guerrilla bands, and serve as scouts. The 200-man Domínguez Raiders, commanded by Manuel Domínguez, served the U.S. Army throughout the war, although subsequently their contributions would be ignored. Ulysses S. Grant, at the time a junior officer, relied on the Raiders to scout out supply routes.

A Precarious American Victory

General Scott concentrated troops at the Mexican port of Tampico on the Gulf of Mexico, then moved down the coast, making an amphibious landing and laying siege to the city of Veracruz in March 1847. A high percentage of untested volunteers made up his army; nevertheless, the landing went smoothly: in five hours 10,000 soldiers landed without encountering enemy resistance. The city of Veracruz had to be taken as fast as possible, before the yellow fever season began, which ran from April to September.[7] Veracruz became an artillery battle with devastating results for the civilian population caught in the smoking ruins. Eventually the defenders surrendered.

The next step involved moving most of his forces to the higher elevations of Jalapa to avoid the impending arrival of yellow fever on the coast. General Santa Anna intended to block them, force them to retreat to Veracruz, and wait for fever to ravage the invaders. Santa Anna chose a narrow mountain pass just east of Jalapa, close to the village of Cerro Gordo. The American assault on Santa Anna's fortified positions lasted all day and into the next. Scott captured more than 3,000 soldiers along with their equipment and supplies. Three days after Jalapa fell, American forces occupied Perote without resistance. At that point seven volunteer regiments, their enlistments over, left, as their contracts specified. Scott, now with an army of 7,000 mostly regular army troops but also some volunteer troops, decided that rather than wait for reinforcements, he would move on to Puebla and use that city as the staging point for the assault on Mexico City. Faced with a shortage of men, Scott took the risky step of abandoning his line of communication with Veracruz. He began sending one division at a time toward Mexico City even before reinforcements had disembarked in the port of Veracruz.[8] Subsequently, 5,000 fresh troops arrived, but after the fall of Mexico City.

General Santa Anna organized the defense of Mexico City. A series of hard-fought battles testified to his military skills. Scott chose to attack Santa Anna at the convent of Churubusco on the outskirts of the capital. Determined resistance would be overcome, but to enter the city, Scott had to capture a string of fortified positions, including El Molina del Rey (a series of buildings for milling grain) and the large building known as Casa Mata just to the west, then the high ground around Chapultepec Castle, and finally the castle itself. The battle for El Molino del Rey alone cost 25 percent of the attacking force. The brigade that took Casa Mata lost a third of its men and half its officers. The American assault on Chapultepec Castle, preceded by an artillery barrage, required scaling ladders and hand-to-hand combat. After an hour and a half of vicious struggle, General Nicolás Bravo, Guadalupe Victoria's former vice president, who had returned from exile in 1829, surrendered to an officer of the New York Volunteer Militia.

The capture of Chapultepec Castle cleared the way for an attack on the city proper. General William J. Worth led the attack on the San Cosmé Gate. Santa Anna, believing that the Americans would not choose an entrance so far north, had not prepared an adequate defense. The defenders fought well, but in the end, the Americans broke through into the city.

Even as General Scott entered the outskirts of Mexico City, an army of 4,000 commanded by General Joaquín Rea began a twenty-eight-day siege of the remaining American forces in Puebla. Eventually, after a number of potentially disastrous setbacks, American reinforcements from Veracruz relieved the trapped units. If General Rea had succeeded at Puebla, Scott's supply lines would have been cut, and the war's outcome might well have favored Mexico.

For Mexicans, a defining moment of patriotism came at Chapultepec Castle. Cadets, too young to serve on active duty, decided that national honor required them to defend the castle. They battled the Americans until only six cadets remained, then took down the national flag, which one cadet wrapped about his shoulders, before they all plunged to their death from the fort's parapet. The Mexican government subsequently honored them with statues and plaques as the Boy Heroes.[9]

The successful breeching of Mexico City's defenses could well have led to the destruction of the capital. Santa Anna had some 12,000 men inside the city, more than the number available to Scott. Municipal authorities convinced Santa Anna not to engage the enemy and to withdraw from the capital and regroup. Despite the withdrawal of Mexican troops, civilian defenders resisted the American army for two days. In one case, a priest on horseback gathered spontaneous followers to battle the invaders. Another militia unit composed mainly of physicians pinned down General William J. Worth's attacking forces with artillery fire. General Scott publicly insisted that the defenders consisted of street people augmented by prisoners. Privately, Scott understood that his relatively small force could be overrun in the event of a general uprising. Fortunately for the Americans, guerrilla activity within the city died down, with only occasional sniper fire to contend with, until that also petered out. The American command understandably encouraged the normal functioning of the government. Outside Mexico City, the situation remained more problematic. Guerrilla bands in the countryside continued to sporadically harass American troops.

For the American army, concluding a peace treaty became a pressing matter. Battle casualties represented only part of the cost. Inadequate sanitation, polluted water, poor food, and lack of personal hygiene took a terrible toll. In camps scattered around the country, deaths from disease exceeded those inflicted by the enemy. Mumps, measles, intermittent fevers (malaria), typhoid, cholera, smallpox, yellow fever, and diarrhea turned many encampments into hospitals with soldiers too weak to perform minimal duties. Some 11,000 soldiers died from disease, and army surgeons discharged several thousand as too debilitated to serve. It took at least a year for soldiers to gain some immunity to camp diseases.[10] For some of those well enough, lack of discipline and boredom led to drinking, fighting, petty crimes, and desertion. Locals reacted with understandable hostility and did their best to avoid unnecessary contact with unruly soldiers. More disciplined units however, appeared to have had reasonable relations with townspeople, posed with them for daguerreotype photographs, and attended weekly dances. Nevertheless, a long occupation would not be so well tolerated. By the war's end, General Scott's army had been stretched to its breaking point. A war won but defeat not accepted had the potential of reigniting the conflict. A similar sense of urgency motivated Mexican officials worried about the possibility of losing political control and legitimacy. The only course appeared to be to conclude the war under the best terms possible.

Over ten months the terms would be agreed on. The Treaty of Guadalupe Hidalgo formally ended the war against Mexico in 1848. Its provisions forced Mexico to recognize the loss of Texas and agree to the Mexican Cession (New Mexico, Arizona, California, and most of Nevada and Utah), together representing approximately half of Mexico's territory. The United States assumed $3 million in claims against the Mexican government and paid $15 million in reparation.

As in many lost wars followed by a humiliating treaty, looking for explanations preoccupied the political elite, both Liberal and

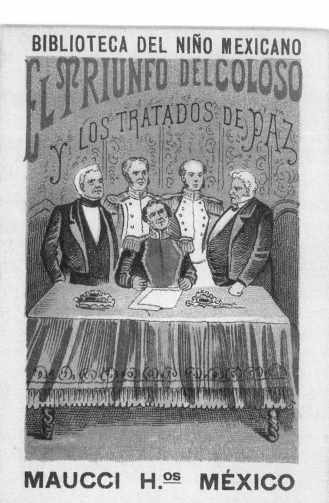

"The Triumph of the Colossus and the Treaties of Peace" The Treaty of Guadalupe Hidalgo in 1848 marked a disaster in which Mexico lost nearly half its national territory, for which the United States paid $15 million and $3 million in claims. After the invasion of Mexico, the United States became known throughout the Western Hemisphere as "the Colossus of the North," a moniker it has not yet shed. Jean Charlot Collection, University of Hawaii at Manoa.

Conservative. While they bore much of the blame, they accepted almost no responsibility for the defeat. The elite understood that the Mexican people had not rallied to the cause and driven out the invaders. Revolts—some of them still to be resolved—and desertions made that evident. Much of the still rural nation had little exposure to the invaders and seemed unaware of the impact and unconcerned about the consequence for the future of the republic. Urban Mexico, the home of the political elite, had been traumatized by the war, but rural Mexicans continued on as usual or resisted wartime measures imposed by the government in Mexico City. For the elite, the war and the American military occupation increased their sense of being a rational island in the midst of a sea of backwardness. They concluded that urban Mexico had been masquerading as the nation, with the still overwhelmingly rural population not yet accepting national responsibilities. Mariano Otero, a politically important Liberal intellectual, enraged at the judgment of many foreigners that Mexico's defeat resulted from "decadence and feminization," explored the reasons as he saw it. He concluded that "in Mexico there is not, nor is there a possibility of developing a national spirit, because there is not a nation."[11] Other Liberals concluded that Mexico lost the war because of the enemy's superior political organization and an economy that had built up unstoppable expansionist momentum of the backs of European immigrants.

The massive loss of territory in the north eliminated the territorial cushion between the Mexican heartland and the United States. The border had moved closer to the core, and might well move again, perhaps eventually extinguishing independence. Another influential Liberal, José María Mata, who had been taken prisoner at the battle of Cerro Gordo and sent to New Orleans, studied the enemy at close range. He returned convinced that Mexico had to follow the American political and economic model. Liberals, with the support of the American occupation authorities, made some tentative reforms at the municipal level.

In contrast, Conservatives explained the failure to ward off a predatory United States as the only possible outcome. Mexico, having abandoned its heritage of hierarchical rule under a monarch, its legacy of Spanish culture, and the social cement of the Catholic Church, had weakened itself fatally. The Conservative explanation laid the blame on the Liberals. The Treaty of Guadalupe Hidalgo ended the war, but more than anything else, the reaction to defeat shaped the course of Mexico for the rest of the century.

Postwar Mexico: Santa Anna's Palace Government

In the post–U.S.-Mexican War period a gaggle of Conservative presidents held office. In keeping with their explanation for the defeat in the war with the United States, Conservative leaders tried to mobilize support for a monarchy. A few plotted to find a European prince willing to govern, but without success. Of more immediate consequence, the influential Conservative Lucas Alamán elaborated a virtual monarchist regime to be ruled by an uncrowned president for life. Alamán viewed the planned regime as a transitional one until some more acceptable arrangement could be made. Meanwhile, Alamán turned to Liberal economist Miguel Lerdo de Tejeda to develop an economic strategy. Lerdo recommended the creation of a Ministry of Development (Fomento) in 1852 to encourage the creation of a transportation infrastructure to serve as the backbone for development. Lerdo advocated a wider distribution of wealth to give the lower classes a greater stake in society and the means to participate in the economy. Alamán and other Conservatives accepted the new ministry but rejected Lerdo's social notions. To head his quasi-monarchy Alamán chose Santa Anna, then in exile on Long Island, New York, for the role. Santa Anna returned in 1853 to form a national unity government. Alamán dismissed the need for a constitution, arguing that "Santa Anna, well advised" would suffice, making clear that he would serve as the adviser.

The general-president recognized that the nation had fallen into a postwar psychological depression. His emotional understanding explains in part his use of ritual to build confidence in the future of the Mexican nation. He invited the Catalan composer Jaime Nuño to come to Mexico as the inspector-general of military bands. Nuño composed the Mexican national anthem and organized modern military bands throughout the country. While Santa Anna sought to restore the national morale, Miguel Lerdo attended to the economy and Lucas Alamán handled the political details.

Lerdo established the parameters within which foreign investors and contractors functioned in Mexico. Those accepting contracts had to agree to be subject to national laws. If they refused to do so, or if they appealed to a foreign government for protection, their concession legally ended. Lerdo extended contracts for the rail line from Veracruz to Mexico City and on to the Pacific coast, and began the construction of a tramline from the city to the Villa of Guadalupe, which was completed in 1857. Gas lighting in the port city of Veracruz added a touch of modernity. Many of these contacts initiated by Lerdo took years to be completed. During the 1850s, development along the Pacific coast as a result of the gold rush in California transformed Mazatlán, Guaymas, San Blas, La Paz, and Manzanillo into viable maritime ports.

Lucas Alamán reserved for himself the position of minister of foreign affairs to explore protective alliances with European nations. He called in the French ambassador to Mexico and laid out his hope for assistance from Napoleon III. Ambassador André Levasseur reported that Alamán believed that with French help, a geopolitical balance could be established that would protect Mexico from the United States. Alamán indicated that he spoke for many others. While he suggested that he spoke for Santa Anna also, it is not clear that the president shared his agenda.[12]

France sympathized, but not to the extent of jeopardizing its trade with the United States. Meanwhile, Spain discussed the idea of a secret mutual defense pact with Mexico as a way of protecting Cuba. Then, the Spanish government had second thoughts about the difficulty of keeping an agreement secret, fearing that such a pact might provide a pretext for an American seizure of Cuba. An approach to Prussia to secure military training for Mexican troops failed. Then disaster struck: Alamán abruptly died. Without direction, Santa Anna's struggle to perpetuate the regime became his only agenda.

(*Previous page*) "The Siege of Querétaro and the Hill of the Bells" The Liberal troops of Benito Juárez placed Querétaro under siege and ultimately defeated the Conservative army (which included European forces) in the spring of 1867. Following the victory, Juárez ordered the trial of Emperor Maximilian, who was sentenced to execution, along with Conservative generals, on the Hill of the Bells. This ended the French intervention in Mexico. Jean Charlot Collection, University of Hawaii at Manoa.

Liberals explained the political debacles of the first half of the nineteenth century as the result of vestigial colonial attitudes and institutions. They argued that the Church hierarchy kept people in superstitious ignorance and that the misdirected paternalism of officials allowed the lower classes to sink into poverty. Moderate Liberals (*moderados*) saw Santa Anna as an individual caught between the ideas of the past and certain new ideas that appeared to be the future, and believed he could be prodded into making necessary reforms. The hard-line Liberals (*puros*), aware that Alamán had had only limited success controlling Santa Anna, wanted to drive him out of office. Their intransigent opposition to Santa Anna forced them into exile. A group of Liberals, including Benito Juárez, went to New Orleans, where they worked on the docks, did menial jobs to survive, and plotted their return. Impressed with the economic vitality of New Orleans and well aware of the relative boom in Texas under U.S. rule, they charted a course for their nation. They believed they would again control the government once the nation tired of Santa Anna. Meanwhile, they bided their time.

The exiled Liberals agreed with Lerdo that transportation and technology appeared to be essential for economic development. Railroads, roads, and even canals became topics debated in New Orleans and in Liberal circles in Mexico. Well aware of the transformative impact of nineteenth-century technology in the United States and Europe, they hoped to stimulate its utilization in Mexico. Collecting the newest machines and gadgets became a hobby for those Liberals who traveled abroad. Ignacio Comonfort, Melchor Ocampo, and José María Mata all bought Isaac M. Singer's advanced (1851) sewing machines virtually the moment they became available. Promotional literature and an amazing variety of small machines and devices filled the trunks of returning travelers. Some Liberals, including Miguel Lerdo, urged the risky strategy of an alliance with the United States as a means of accelerating modernization.

At the same time, in the United States, politicians and business leaders were discussing a Mexican protectorate.[1] Several schemes, including that of the All Mexico movement's call for annexation and proposals to purchase selected territorial assets, had their supporters. Others suggested a controlling economic arrangement, in effect a commercial union. Franklin Pierce, soon to become president, had served in the U.S.-Mexican War as a brigadier general and believed he had a grasp on the value of selected parts of Mexican territory. The appointment of John Forsyth, editor of the *Mobile Register* and son of a well-known politician, as the American minister to Mexico brought both Liberal and southern fantasies together. A close friendship developed between Forsyth and Miguel Lerdo to the extent that the Alabama editor supported Lerdo's attempt to replace President Comonfort.

President Franklin Pierce's administration (1853–57) had a bulging treasury, but Mexican leaders resisted selling off bits and pieces of the republic. The remaining option of a commercial arrangement had possibilities. American interest in Mexico had strong support in the South, especially in the commercial hub of New Orleans. Business leaders in that city worried that railways linking New England with the Pacific would leave New Orleans isolated, an internal colony of the industrial North. A business conference in Montgomery, Alabama, in 1858 suggested that an as yet to be exploited Latin America could be dominated economically by the South.

Significantly, the last territorial loss for Mexico involved a plan to link New Orleans by transcontinental railroad to California and open the possibility of Asian trade.[2] Army surveyors decided that the most accessible route lay just south of the newly established U.S.-Mexican border in the Mesilla Valley. How much land might be necessary for the right-of-way seemed unclear; the instructions to the U.S. minister and those of railway promoter James Gadsden lacked exact requirements. The original treaty proposal of December, 30, 1853, set a $25 million purchase price, with $5 million held back to settle claims, and included navigation rights in the Gulf of California. President Pierce had some reservations but submitted the proposal to the Senate. Bumbling in Washington and a defeat in the Senate led by anti-slave, anti-Democratic Party senators seemed to conclude the affair. Nevertheless, a strong reaction at the commercial convention held in Charleston, South Carolina, rallied southern and western support and forced it through the senate on April 25, 1854, with a reduced offer of $10 million for much less land than Gadsden had in mind. In addition, it provided for right of passage across the Isthmus of Tehuantepec, but not access to the Gulf of California. Santa Anna's desperation led to reluctant acceptance of the price offered, and ratification by the U.S. Senate followed on June 30, 1854. The Mesilla Treaty, or the Gadsden Purchase, as it became known in the United States, proved to be the last straw for opponents of Santa Anna.

Resurgent Liberalism: The Revolution of Ayutla

Exiled Liberals, eagerly awaiting the overthrow of the Santa Anna regime, saw an opportunity in a revolt that broke out on the Pacific coast. Juan Alvarez, whose autocratic rule was centered in the state of Guerrero, led a revolt that became known as the Revolution of Ayutla. The threat to the port of Acapulco's commerce from an arbitrary and unpredictable president lay behind the revolt. Liberal Ignacio Comonfort reworked the language of the original Plan of Ayutla into his Plan of Acapulco. Comonfort's plan emphasized the need for progress and free trade, converting the revolt of Juan Alvarez into a Liberal manifesto, although not necessarily one that had popular support throughout the republic.

The plan as reworked by Comonfort drew Liberal support, including from those exiles in New Orleans. Predictably, Santa Anna led an army into Guerrero to capture Alvarez. In a major battle, the two fought to a standstill. Santa Anna, after sending messages announcing a great victory, returned to the capital, and before anyone could assess the results of the stand-off fled to Veracruz and on to exile in Venezuela, not to return until 1874.[3]

Meanwhile, the New Orleans exiles moved to the Texas border city of Brownsville. On the border they established a revolutionary junta in May 1855 and discussed plans to establish a Liberal political party to move beyond personal regimes such as that epitomized by Santa Anna. When the Liberals returned to the abandoned presidency, they undid the damaging decrees of Santa Anna, established a new tariff of 30 percent, and removed trade restrictions to revive commerce. In addition, new ports of entry along the northern border with the United States, the Gulf of California, and the Isthmus of Tehuantepec provided increased trade possibilities. Other economic measures, including declaring foreign coins legal tender and establishing the same property rights for foreigners as for Mexicans, created new incentives for investors. As an enticement for immigrants, ownership of real estate conveyed citizenship.

The Liberal regime crafted three transformative degrees, the Iglesias, Juárez, and Lerdo laws, issued in 1856 and 1857. The Iglesias Law (Ley Iglesias) created civil registries, ordered the mandatory recording of births, marriages, and deaths, and transferred supervision of cemeteries to civil authorities. The Juárez Law (Ley Juárez) suppressed separate Church and military courts except for issues of internal discipline, thereby reasserting the Constitution of 1812's commitment to equality before the law. Perhaps the most important of the three laws, the Lerdo Law (Ley Lerdo), attacked corporate property, including the Church's agricultural and urban properties, as well as Indian communal land. The law ordered that the properties be sold to individuals or the government would arrange to auction them. The Church viewed these laws as direct attacks on the economic well-being of the institution. The Lerdo Law's provisions lacked clarity and could be interpreted in different ways, which necessitated a series of clarifications. Uprisings in several states against its enforcement followed. Villagers in Cuernavaca and Cuautla attacked sugar plantations to recover land, a response · repeated by Emiliano Zapata in the early twentieth century.

The opportunistic demands of small landowners, the *rancheros*, for Indian land politicized what had been envisioned as an economic issue. In Oaxaca, then governor Benito Juárez promulgated the Lerdo Law in this state and within days faced a revolt. An important sugar producer, Estéban Esperón, requested that the state government transfer ownership of communal land that he rented from an Indian community, citing the provisions of the law. Juárez requested clarification from Lerdo as to whether he could divide the land among the Indians as private holdings instead. Lerdo responded that the intent had always been to favor the original holders of communal land.

When Juárez became president, he issued further clarifications to avoid the unjust acquisition of Indian land. The softening of the Lerdo Law occurred elsewhere as villagers used various means to retain property.[4] In some regions the National Guard, often mainly indigenous guardsmen, blocked unfavorable outcomes. In addition, lawyers and local judges responded with notarized statements of missing land titles or with a fresh set of legal documents.[5] That changed in the 1890s, when the national regime of Porfirio Díaz favored the agricultural oligarchy.

Meanwhile, President Ignacio Comonfort hoped to make rapid progress in implementing secularization and economic objectives. Everything depended on what the national government lacked: tax revenues and investment capital. Any hope of development required the active cooperation of foreigners, perhaps a protective alliance with the United States, already a topic of discussion. A French-language newspaper in the capital understood the potential implications and raised the specter of economic cooperation leading to an informal colony or a protectorate. Rumors and the alleged texts of treaties providing for an economic protectorate circulated throughout the capital.

The Rise of Benito Juárez

Liberal policies and national politics increasingly became identified with the person and the career of Benito Juárez. Born in the
small Zapotec village of Guelatao, Oaxaca, in 1806, in a region
that engaged more in commerce than in agriculture, he avoided
the ethnic isolation that characterized many Indian villagers.
Nor did Oaxaca's self-governing indigenous communities have
to confront a dominant landholding class. Merchants, priests,
and state officials set the tone of a state accustomed to absorb-
ing reasonably educated Indians, mainly Zapotecs and Mixtecs,
into their ranks.

Juárez, tutored by the village priest, acquired a rudimentary
education. The traditional next step up in social mobility required
entering the seminary to study for the priesthood, but Juárez had
another option. A Liberal governor established a new secular
Institute of Sciences and Arts of the State of Oaxaca. The young
Benito immediately transferred, took up the law, and prepared
to enter politics as a Liberal. Subsequently, with a salary as a
civil judge of the first instance, he married Margarita Maza, the
seventeen-year-old daughter of an Italian merchant. Latter-day
mythmakers suggested that the union between a Zapotec and a
creole demonstrated Juárez's ability to overcome racial barriers,
but as the illegitimate daughter of a man who still had a wife in
Europe, Margarita had little status to bestow or lose.

Benito Juárez's complex background made him an unlikely
national politician, but he had a driving ambition. Taciturn, he
preferred to listen, saying little in return. He spoke with cau-
tion, reflecting a basic distrust of his colleagues. Nevertheless,
he enjoyed the pursuit of power, understood the game, and took

satisfaction in his successes. An indifferent public speaker, he compensated by cultivating an image of gravitas and a distinctive style of dress that served him well. His politics, while Liberal, did not run to ideological rigidity. He made tactical alliances to gain his objectives, then just as easily dropped them. He appeared to be able to maintain long-term relationships with politicians on the left and the right.

While impressive intellectuals and theorists, rather than politicians, dominated Mexican Liberalism until the 1860s, Benito Juárez represented a notable exception. He understood the unifying task of politics and distrusted those Liberals who rejected reasonable accommodation in favor of ideology. His political tracts avoided the extremes and in general could be claimed by any Liberal faction. Nevertheless, he should not be seen as a man for every season. Juárez's principles appeared to be structural rather than abstract. In his view, a government had to be constitutional, a civil, not military, regime, presiding over a society that respected and obeyed the laws. Political flexibility meant that he laid aside principles when he believed the good of the nation required him to do so. His concern for the progress of the Mexican Republic overrode other considerations. Toleration, however, did not extend to those Conservatives he considered to be champions of backwardness and obstacles to national progress.

His approach became evident as governor of Oaxaca in the pre-French intervention years. Oaxaca's Liberals divided along factional lines—the moderates, known as *borlados* (academics), and the radicals, predictably called the *rojos* (reds). Juárez, tolerated by both, employed his political skills to keep them together. His pragmatism allowed him to side with the dominant faction when necessary, but he remained fluid and situational.[6] The mythological image of Juárez, fabricated after his death, obscured the path of a talented politician.

The Constitution of 1857

The political confusion of the postwar period, aggravated by Santa Anna's aborted virtual monarchy and the absence of a working constitution, logically required a fresh charter and a new start. The Plan of Ayutla called for an effective federal charter able to guide the nation. That it would be a Liberal constitution seemed obvious, although few anticipated that it would polarize the country and lead to civil war. The general constitutional template would be that of the United States, not in every detail but with the notion that the American constitution had set the stage for that country's remarkable economic progress in the nineteenth century. The Liberals saw a direct connection between material progress and constitutional forms. Work on the new constitution began, symbolically, on July 4, 1856. Predictably, Conservatives charged that the Liberals had become subservient to Washington.

The signing of the Constitution of 1857 on February 12 represented an important moment in the nation's history. It constituted a bold strategic plan to clear away perceived obstacles to economic development and put a structure in place to accomplish the task of modernization. It provided for a federal republic, but with more central authority. The Iglesias, Juárez, and Lerdo laws, because they were incorporated into the constitution, became constitutional provisions. The document abolished the office of vice president, long a source of conflict, and set up a succession ladder in its place. It included a bill of rights for all Mexican citizens and protected free speech, freedom of the press, freedom of assembly, and other privileges of citizenship, but it stopped short of declaring religious toleration. Unfortunately, the failure to develop a supporting consensus in advance of the elaboration of the constitution resulted in a backlash from conservative elements, including the Church, and uncertain support from moderate Liberals. Regional political bosses went along with the constitution but expected to continue to arrange things as usual. In an effort to institutionalize the Liberal constitution, the government required all government officials to swear allegiance to the constitution or be dismissed.

Election under the new constitution elevated Ignacio Comonfort to the presidency and Juárez to chief justice of the Supreme Court. As such, he would be first in the line of succession in case of a presidential vacancy.

While the Liberals elaborated the new constitution, work on an economic protectorate advanced. Ezequiel Montes, the new minister of development, continued negotiations with U.S. ambassador Forsyth. They reached an agreement, which was signed by the Mexican government and sent to Washington on February 10, 1857, just ahead of the adoption of the 1857 Constitution. As specified, all parts of the treaty had to be accepted by the United States. Assumption by the United States of Mexico's European debts represented the key requirement, for it removed the threat of foreign intervention. Had President Pierce been renominated for the presidency, the agreement would have had a chance, but incoming president James Buchanan thought in terms of territorial expansion, not assisted development, no matter how mutually advantageous it might have been to both republics. The rejection came as a shock to Liberals, aware that the French had been encouragingly sympathetic to monarchists after the Plan of Ayutla. The collapse of the scheme, coupled with the negative reaction to the Constitution of 1857 by Conservative elements, fatally weakened the Liberal government.

President Comonfort believed that radical Liberals, the *puros*, had recklessly driven the country to the edge of civil war. The Conservatives, aware of the significance of the Constitution of 1857, reacted forcefully. When an attempt to negotiate revisions of the constitution failed, they resorted to insurrection. High Church officials, encouraged by the Pope, urged sympathetic military officers to seize power. A coup occurred, but one obscured by the creation of a national unity government. Comonfort, a moderate, agreed to remain at the head of a coalition government. Angry Liberals charged that he had abandoned liberalism and the nation and betrayed his office and countrymen. Conservatives dissolved Congress, arrested Juárez, and issued their Plan of Tacubaya calling for a new constitution. General Félix Zuloaga, elected by the Council of Representatives of the Departments, which replaced the federal Congress and state legislatures, claimed the presidency in January 1858. Before being forced out, Comonfort released Juárez, relinquished his presidential office, and embarked for New Orleans.

The War of the Reform

Once free, Juárez prudently fled the city and established a parallel government in Guanajuato, subsequently moving to the Liberal stronghold of Veracruz, where he could draw on customs revenues to support his government. Meanwhile, President Zuloaga annulled the Lerdo, Juárez, and Iglesias laws and ordered the reinstatement of government employees who had refused to swear allegiance to the Constitution of 1857. The U.S. minister recognized the Zuloaga government, assuming that the Conservatives might be more ready to sell territory. Forsyth ignored the danger that the Conservatives, using the nation's resources as the bait, might be able to attract European help. He soon broke off relations with the Zuloaga government and used recognition as a tool to negotiate with the Liberals—recognition in exchange for selling territory in northern Mexico. The desperate Liberals indicated that with recognition in hand, it might be possible. Both sides played a crafty poker game, with territory and diplomatic recognition as the chips.

With considerable difficulty, the Liberals reestablished their government in the port city of Veracruz and began a protracted civil war lasting from 1858 to 1861. Both Liberals and Conservatives borrowed money at ruinous interest rates in a mad scramble to survive. The most notorious debt, the Jecker loan, provided the Conservatives with minimal operating funds in exchange for 15 million pesos of debt. Meanwhile, the U.S. representatives pressed the Liberals to sell more territory. President Buchanan, a crude expansionist, offered to buy Baja California at a bargain basement price. To make his southern constituents happy, he attempted to secure transit rights across the Isthmus of Tehuantepec, as well as the option to use troops to guarantee free passage. In addition, the United States pressed for transit rights from the New Mexico territory (now Arizona and New Mexico) to the Sea of Cortez, to provide the landlocked Southwest with seaports. Hard-pressed Liberals did their best to fend off Washington, but agreed to a Tehuantepec transit treaty (1859) without the provision for American troops. Fortunately for Mexico, the U.S. Senate did not ratify the McLane-Ocampo Treaty.

The War of the Reform dragged on until 1861, exhausting the nation. Endemic violence and banditry in the countryside spread the misery far beyond cities and towns. It evolved into a vicious civil war, punctuated by atrocities and senseless destruction. The country appeared to have turned on itself in frustration. Church wealth suffered as Liberals seized funds and sold valuables to finance the war effort, while the Conservatives secured Church loans that could not be repaid. In 1860, in the midst of the war, a defiant Juárez declared religious toleration. Liberal generals eventually pushed back the Conservative forces, and on New Year's Day, 1861, the Juárez government returned to the capital. Pope Pius IX reacted to the Liberals' victory by listing article after article of the Constitution of 1857 that the Church could not accept.[7]

The civil war left a staggering foreign debt at high interest rates that Mexico could not service or repay on schedule, if ever. Juárez ordered a suspension of debt payments to give the economy time to recover. Rather than attempting to reconcile moderate Conservatives, perhaps through some modifications to the Constitution of 1857, Juárez humiliated his Conservative opponents. Consequently, while the Liberals won the War of the Reform, they failed to consolidate the peace, a failure that endangered the continued existence of the republic.

The government required that everyone doing public business in the courts, buying or selling real estate, recording births, deaths, and marriages in the public registry, and graduating from the university swear loyalty to the constitution. Conservatives, defiantly backed by Pope Pius IX, who ordered excommunication for anyone who accepted the 1857 Constitution, refused to concede defeat. High Church officials together with diehard Conservatives lobbied at European courts and the Vatican for troops and financial support to defeat the Liberals and a prince to establish a Mexican monarchy.

They found their European champion in Napoleon III of France, who was convinced that a French intervention in Mexico would be welcomed both by a grateful Church and by a relieved population. The timing appeared propitious. The United States was already plunged into its civil war and could not block the French emperor's impending adventure. Several fantasies fused together to challenge the survival of republican Mexico.

The Imposition of Emperor Maximilian

Emperor Napoleon III envisioned a coalition of those nations that once had been united under Rome (those that spoke languages derived from Latin) and their former colonies in the Western Hemisphere. To separate the Spanish American republics from their Anglo American neighbor, Napoleon adopted the arguments of François Guizot, who warned that the Anglo Saxon United States verged on destroying the hemisphere's Latin peoples. The prospect of being culturally associated with Europe as part of a Latin world fell on fertile ground in what became, at that moment, "Latin America." The emperor planned a monarchist revival, perhaps in conjunction with Dom Pedro, the emperor of Brazil. A monarchist Mexico would confine the United States to the north of the Rio Grande, to wither in isolation. All that remained before the grand scheme was to be put in motion was to choose a pretext that would justify intervention. Mexico's foreign debt served as that pretext.

Meanwhile, President Benito Juárez presided over a bankrupt government with angry creditors in England, Spain, and France. The French government had taken over the outrageous Jecker loan, floated in 1860 by a desperate Conservative government on its last legs as the War of the Reform drew to a close. Jecker, a Swiss banker resident in Mexico City, advanced the tottering regime $750,000 in return for bonds to be issued at a future date. It is probable that most of the bonds remained in Jecker's possessions, but some had been sold in Europe. The victorious Liberal government of Juárez immediately canceled the contract. Other bond defaults, combined with the Jecker loan, justified pressure to collect overdue debts by Britain, Spain, and France. The French government lodged a claim of 27 million francs, only partly based on Jecker bonds. The three creditor nations agreed to send naval vessels to blockade the port of Veracruz and force collection of Mexico's debts.

France's agenda combined a number of objectives not immediately apparent. The Liberal assault on the Church's role in civil society offered Napoleon III a chance to work on behalf of Pope Pius IX, with whom he had been at cross purposes in the struggle over Italian unification. Moreover, he got to play kingmaker, and decided to strengthen European alliances by choosing Maximilian, the younger brother of the emperor of the Austro-Hungarian Empire, and his wife, Charlotte, the daughter of the king of Belgium, as the new emperor and empress of Mexico. Perhaps most satisfying, he enjoyed the prospect of restoring the prestige of monarchies at the expense of two republics—United States and Mexico.

In January 1862, Spanish and British ships unexpectedly encountered a full-fledged French invasion force of 30,000 men in Veracruz harbor under the command of General Élie Frédéric Forey. The British and Spanish commanders, once they grasped the plan, sailed away in protest, while the French commenced the invasion of Mexico. General Forey did not fully agree with the war aims of Napoleon III. He accepted the command only after the monarch made it clear that a promotion to Marshal of France depended on his acceptance. When Forey landed in Veracruz in January 1862 he issued a proclamation pledging respect for property and order, but also declaring that Mexicans should choose their form of government. Napoleon III reprimanded him and threatened to remove him unless he followed imperial wishes.

French officers anticipated brushing aside defenders, occupying the country, and placing the designated royal couple on the throne. The invasion force made short work of Mexican troops as they advanced toward the capital city until they arrived just outside Puebla, "the City of the Angels," well known as the most Conservative city in the country. The French expected to be greeted as saviors who would restore the Church, remove the Liberals from power, and reestablish traditional values. They would be disappointed.

Liberal defenders, commanded by Texas-born General Ignacio Zaragoza, prayed for rain to bog down the advancing French troops as they prepared for the May 5, 1862, battle. The French line, overconfident and casual, moved forward in single file. Zaragoza and Porfirio Díaz, in command of an infantry brigade, turned the flank of the French and began the slaughter of the stunned French troops. In the brief battle, the French soldiers broke and scattered. The Mexicans pursued but could not complete the destruction of the French army because they became mired in the deep mud caused by sudden, heavy rains. Nevertheless, the victory of Cinco de Mayo went down in history.

The Mexican victory over what at the time Europeans recognized as the world's most powerful army stunned politicians across Europe. In France, an embarrassed and outraged emperor ordered 5,000 troops, veterans of the Algerian campaigns, to reinforce the army and complete the conquest. Throughout Europe, leaders began to rethink French leadership and military strength.

French troops prudently marked time in Veracruz until reinforcements arrived, then renewed their advance on the capital city. Their new respect for the Mexican soldier made them more effective and cautious warriors. At the second battle of Puebla, in 1863, after a prolonged siege, French general Forey forced the unconditional surrender of Puebla, opening the way to Mexico City. Once the capital had been secured, General Forey created a three-man provisional government that included the archbishop of Mexico. A relieved Napoleon III granted his reluctant warrior's request to return to France and, as promised, elevated General Forey to the rank of a Marshal of France.[8]

The Juárez government retreated to the north and for the next four years survived by constant movement from one town and region to another. Mexicans who caught a glimpse of the coach transporting their leaders called them the sick family. The north—decidedly federalist—equated the empire with centralism, although that perception did not mean they unconditionally supported Juárez and his beleaguered government.

The French arranged for the new rulers to journey from their Mediterranean palace to their new country. Even before the imperial couple arrived, Napoleon III requested a report on Sonora's mineral wealth, as well as an assessment of whether or not the region could be pacified. He anticipated that at least a portion of northern Mexico would become part of the French empire, providing a buffer zone between the republican United States and a monarchist Mexico.

The glamorous couple traveled to Mexico armed with ambitions, good intentions, and misinformation provided by high Church informants and Mexican exiles. Ignorance compounded by their disregard of troublesome reports about the political situation and the people set the stage for eventual disaster. Both the emperor and the empress intended to Mexicanize their monarchy. They sought to make Mexicans into Europeans and themselves into Mexicans. Charlotte Hispanicized her name to Carlota, and the royal couple publicly paid homage to Our Lady of Guadalupe. In a surprise move, Maximilian made it known that he planned to bring individuals of all political persuasions into the government. Moreover, the emperor issued an open letter to the Mexican people declaring that he intended to ratify the Liberal Reform Laws and guarantee individual rights, an unexpected announcement that stunned the Church and Conservatives.

The principal supporters of the empire, about 100 individuals, including moderate Liberals and Conservatives, belonged, with a few exceptions, to a transitional generation. Most had been born in the fading days of the viceroyalty or just after the formal independence of the country. They grew up in violence and political confusion but entertained nostalgic notions of a colonial past of peace and tranquility. Their ages ran from forty-four to seventy-two years, with only five under thirty years. In general, they came from the provinces rather than the capital. For many, their defining experience had occurred during the U.S.-Mexican War. They had fought the Americans and bitterly resented the subsequent peace treaty and its harsh terms. They viewed the consolidation of the nation as extremely urgent, if Mexico was to have any hope of surviving. For many, a centralized government, backed by a powerful European monarchy, seemed the best hope.[9]

Imperial officials studied the possibility of a massive highway project, port improvements, and canals. Maximilian toured factories and workshops, inaugurated tramlines, and distributed prizes to encourage productive activities. The government published useful information on the latest technical breakthroughs in the hope they would be employed by industry. In 1865, imperial officials authorized sixteen concessions to introduce new industrial machines into the country. Construction material for railways entered the country duty-free. A life insurance company and another one for fire benefited individuals, but also served to create pools of capital. Combining monarchist paternalism with an understanding of the need for microcredit at the lowest levels of the economy, a *banco de avío* (lending bank) offered credit to small-scale artisan and industrial shops, merchants, and farmers. The Imperial Ministry of Development drew up regulations for a lending society (*sociedad aviadora*) for impoverished artisans and laborers. Maximilian's macroeconomic objectives differed only slightly from those of the Liberal republic but would be pursued in a more conciliatory manner and with attention to the lower classes.[10] Meanwhile, the military situation favored the empire, but complete pacification continued to elude the French and imperial troops.

Physical control of Mexico depended on French troops, including the Foreign Legion. The Imperial Mexican army, still in its formative phase could not be relied on to offer much assistance. On the Liberal side, Juárez had few reliable commanders and an indifferently armed and trained army. Prudently, republican soldiers offered weak resistance before falling back to fight again when the moment seemed more advantageous. As a result, French forces controlled the country's core, but not its fringes. The war became a test of endurance, money, and will. A significant number of Liberals favored negotiating with the French and came to see Juárez as the main obstacle to peace. President Juárez, however, refused to open negotiations, insisting that Mexico could not accept neocolonial subordination to Europe. To ensure that the struggle continued unabated, he decreed his continuation in office for the duration of the war, a decision that blocked Jesús González Ortega, the president of the Supreme Court, from automatically becoming the president of the republic and perhaps making an accommodation with the imperialists.

In the midst of a war, with the outcome uncertain, Juárez embarked on internal political struggle. The president demanded financial and military support from Santiago Vidaurri, the powerful *caudillo* of Nuevo León and Coahuila. Vidaurri responded that such a request violated the rights of the states and moreover, without his Army of the North, he would be defenseless. The

Confederate cotton boom in his state relied on the security provided by Vidaurri's army patrolling the border. Juárez reacted harshly by separating Coahuila administratively from Nuevo León, then ordering his forces to attack Vidaurri. The once powerful *caudillo* fled to Texas, but returned after the French occupied the city of Monterrey, subsequently becoming a councilor to Maximilian and minister of the treasury. After Mexico City fell to the Liberals, he faced a firing squad on July 8, 1867.

A different outcome, but one making the same point, occurred in Chihuahua. Juárez, once in control of Nuevo León, turned his attention to the governor of Chihuahua, Luis Terrazas, whom Juárez suspected of disloyalty. Rather than wait and see, the president declared a state of siege in Chihuahua and suspended constitutional guarantees. A prudent Governor Terrazas fled the state capital just ahead of forces loyal to Juárez. Nevertheless, when the French army arrived in northern Mexico, Terrazas led the battle against them—certainty the right choice, given the eventual victory of the republic.

Mexico remained fragmented: the emperor ruled in French-occupied territories but faced constant attacks. Juárez ruled close to wherever his black coach stopped, and military commanders and regional strongmen were in power in the rest of the nation. At one point, imperial forces nearly cornered Juárez, forcing him to El Paso del Norte on the Chihuahua border with the United States. The president reached the point of preparing to cross into the United States and go into exile, but his troops held, and gradually began to win small but significant battles. The prolonged and costly pacification effort inevitably became a concern.

Napoleon III had anticipated that the Mexican emperor would

be able to organize the nation financially to support most if not all of the cost of war. An annoyed French emperor grumbled that if Maximilian built fewer palaces and theaters and concentrated on bringing honest men into his government, he could curb wasteful spending and allocate sufficient funds to the pacification effort. In 1865 he dispatched a new financial adviser, reputed to be a talented financial master-mind, to take charge of affairs, but this administrative change came too late.

Emperor Maximilian became a victim of European and American events. In 1865 General Ulysses S. Grant defeated the Confederate army of General Robert E. Lee, ending the American Civil War. Shortly afterward the American secretary of state William H. Seward, pointing out that the French presence violated the Monroe Doctrine, demanded to know when the French would withdraw. Seward, hinting in the newspapers that a little war in Mexico might be just the thing to reconcile the Union and the former Confederacy, obliquely threatened France. In Europe, Otto Von Bismarck established the foundations for a stronger Prussia that began to concern and alarm Napoleon III. In France, critics such as Victor Hugo who opposed the Mexican adventure doubled and redoubled their demands for withdrawal in response to mounting costs and increasing deaths without victory, honor, or profit for the nation. Napoleon III reconsidered his commitments to Maximilian and Carlota and turned inward to save France and himself.

Maximilian Stands Alone

In late 1865, Maximilian received official notification from Napoleon III that the French troops would be recalled because the Liberals allegedly had been defeated. French military commanders argued that the resistance consisted only of guerrillas and bandits, both of which they considered outlaws not entitled to the rights of soldiers. The French general badgered Maximilian until the latter issued a statement that repeated this conclusion, and ordered the penalty of death without trial for these renegades. Ironically, the poorly considered decree subsequently justified the emperor's execution.

Changing international opinion and expectations that Washington would soon be in a position to engage the French, diplomatically or in some other fashion, reinvigorated the Liberals. American secretary of war Edwin M. Stanton ordered veteran cavalry units and shipments of surplus arms and ammunition to the Rio Grande region. Cavalry officers received orders to protect the war surplus from marauders, Indians, and ex-Confederates, but in the event that Liberal troops crossed the river, the officers had orders to retreat, leaving the surplus for the Mexican soldiers.

In this mounting crisis, Empress Carlota, fearful of the outcome, traveled to Europe with the hope of renewing support and securing additional military assistance. Emperor Napoleon III refused to receive her and ignored all talk of treaties and promises. Carlota, frantic with foreboding, went to the Vatican in search of the Pope's assistance in pressing the French to keep their troops in Mexico. Pope Pius IX received her but refused to intervene because Maximilian had not restored Church properties. The empress brought with her a draft concordat to regularize Mexican Church-state relations, but it failed to sway the pontiff. Carlota collapsed when she received the decision. She recovered physically but not mentally and took refuge with her father, the king of Belgium, where she lived until 1927, sane only in patches. News of his wife's collapse and insanity added to Maximilian's impending sense of doom as the French began to depart and Conservative troops faded away. Many advisers urged him to return to Europe. Maximilian compounded his poor decision to execute Liberal troops as bandits by listening to the counsel of a shadowy character posing as a German priest, Augustín Fischer, who argued that Hapsburg honor and Carlota's sacrifice demanded that he remain. The emperor, an avid amateur biologist, went butterfly hunting to escape the contradictory advice and reach a decision. When he returned, he announced he had decided to fight on.

Following the French withdrawal, two veterans of the War of the Reform, Miguel Miramón and Tomás Mejía, commanded the emperor's army. They held the city of Querétaro against the advancing Liberal troops, with Juárez and his civilian regime in their wake. Fierce fighting enabled the Liberals to surround the city. The two armies dug in for what appeared to be a long siege. Maximilian, filled with new resolve, decided to march with additional reinforcements to take command of the army at Querétaro. The relief column managed to fight its way into the city, but the Liberals slammed the door behind it and restored the siege. Weeks dragged on, with both soldiers and civilians beginning to suffer from food shortages, limited water, and edgy nerves. The emperor ordered one unit to fight its way out and go to the capital for ammunition, supplies, and reinforcements to break the siege. Wanting to show that he could carry on as normal, his bravado included ordering wine and sheet music along with gunpowder and rations. Many saw this as proof that he had lost touch with reality. It mattered little, because the commander and his troops, after reaching the capital, made no effort to return.

The Liberals ended the siege on June 1867, after they struck an agreement with imperial troops to allow them into the city in exchange for permitting them to escape. Liberal soldiers surprised the high command and the emperor and quickly placed them under arrest to await the arrival of Juárez. The seizure of Querétaro inspired Liberal General Porfirio Díaz to storm the capital. After fierce resistance, Mexico City once again returned to republican control.

There remained the emperor and his two commanders, Mejía and Miramón. Across Mexico, voices demanded retribution, while others urged magnanimity. From Europe and the United States, national leaders such as President Andrew Johnson and celebrities such as Victor Hugo pleaded for the emperor's life. President Benito Juárez ordered treason trials for the generals and a murder trial for the emperor for ordering the execution of Liberal troops. Once the guilty verdicts had been returned, Juárez announced there would be no clemency. A firing squad escorted the three to the top of the Hill of the Bells on June 19, 1867, where Maximilian offered the place of honor in the center to Miramón and gave each of the riflemen a gold coin not to shoot them in the face. The squad executed the three. Juárez issued a manifesto claiming that Maximilian had attempted to assassinate the "Anáhuac nation," and therefore his execution represented a just and necessary act.[11] Mexicans expressed some sympathy for him, although many believed that the republic required his death in order to end once and for all the notion of a monarchy. Subsequently the government returned Maximilian's corpse to Europe, where, as it landed at Trieste, the guns of warships thundered a final salute. Tributes to Maximilian in music, poetry, literature, and painting swept across Europe, attempting to excuse him as a well-intentioned but misguided nobleman. Juárez remained unmoved by the notion of a well-meaning military conquest.

Seemingly anxious to blot out the imperial episode from Mexico's history, he erased many physical aspects of the empire, and those he could not he turned into republican symbols. Maximilian had constructed his own Champs Elysées, the Calzada de la Emperatrz, to connect Chapultepec Palace with the city. When the Liberals retook the city, Juárez renamed it the Paseo de la Reforma and made it into a ceremonial avenue for civic parades. Juárez refurbished the imperial residence, and after stripping the palace of its imperial trappings and selling then at auction, occupied Chapultepec as the presidential residence.

Of more consequence, Juárez, the *benemérito* of his country, understood that the imperial interlude had fatally weakened and discredited conservatism, now linked to foreign intervention. He realized also that an exhausted liberalism had triumphed, but at a cost he did not want to repeat. Economic development and political stability, the goal of both sides, offered the possibility of unifying the country and proceeding peacefully toward long-standing goals. The release of Conservative prisoners and a conciliatory approach toward those Liberals who had collaborated with the French made the point that executions for treason would not be widespread. The three who died in front of a firing squad on the Hill of the Bells appeared to be enough.

Although somewhat overlooked in the euphoria of victory over the French, the internal struggle for control in the north had strengthened the federal government and changed the nature of the republic.[1] The republican regime that returned to Mexico City differed from the prewar government. Juárez had fought two different wars, one against Maximilian and another, transformative conflict against powerful state *caudillos*. The latter war established the presidency as the country's center of authority, with consequences evident far beyond Juárez's lifetime. The federal structure remained, but the states had become subordinate politically to the presidency.

Juárez made it evident that he intended to restore civilian rule and reestablish the rule of law within a civil society. As his advisers and associates he chose from the Liberals who had surrounded him during his exile in New Orleans, the War of the Reform, and the French intervention. As for the army, he thanked his commanding officers but indicated that his government's gratitude had limits that did not include political and financial rewards for everyone.[2] In a reorganization of the military, he proposed slashing the size of the army and its officer corps by two-thirds from the 60,000 men at the end of hostilities. Minister of War Ignacio Mejía had the task of ensuring the loyalty of the army while attempting to cut its numbers down to 20,000. By 1868 he had reduced troop levels to 47,000, but the army still absorbed

45 percent of the budget. Eventually troop levels fell to 32,000, but violence in the countryside and opposition within the army hindered further significant reductions. A highly critical General Porfirio Díaz became the self-appointed champion of veterans and the insecure officer corps. Dealing with veterans and an army still too large and expensive represented both a structural problem and a potentially dangerous political one. Less obviously, President Juárez faced a generational issue that shaped much of the politics of the restored republic.

Juárez may have been a hero to the patriotic masses, but many politicians believed that his task had ended with the reestablishment of the republic. General Porfirio Díaz and others of his generation wanted their turn in power. Nevertheless, a determined President Juárez had an agenda that he intended to accomplish. Those Liberals opposed to the president had sufficient strength to blunt Juárez's initiatives but not enough to break his grasp on the presidency. Meanwhile, a pragmatic president sought the middle ground between the radicals (*puros*) and *moderados* as a step toward national reconciliation and what he believed to be a responsible Liberal party and government.

His plan involved co-opting the Church as a way of reassuring the peasantry and the Conservatives that he understood the cultural role of religion. The president hoped to use the Church as a conservative balance to the radicals and in the process neutralize both *puros* and the clergy. Consequently, Juárez's electoral law of 1864 recognized the clergy's right to vote and hold public office as Mexican citizens. The call for elections in 1867 included that provision. Archbishop Pelagio Antonio de Labastida y Dávalos returned from exile, and the Vatican signaled its tentative acceptance of the arrangement by appointing six new bishops to vacant positions. Of course, Juárez made it clear that the government continued to support freedom of worship. Subsequently Porfirio Díaz elaborated on Juárez's strategy to neutralize the Church almost totally.

In 1868 Juárez, after serving as president for a decade, faced his first election for the presidency. He had assumed the office by succession when ousted President Comonfort fled Mexico, and because of the incessant civil and foreign wars had continued in the position. During the election campaign, the president suggested amendments to the Constitution of 1857 to incorporate his pro-clerical initiatives as well as others designed to make the federal government stable, including ending residency requirements for federal deputies, the creation of a senate, increased presidential power, and a new succession arrangement.

Juárez's effort to reach out to moderate Liberals and Conservatives appealed to them, but it displeased radicals and many municipal leaders, who feared losing local autonomy. As consequence, the proposal ignited small, local revolts in a handful of states, ironically reinforcing the argument that the country needed more central control. Juárez publicly withdrew his proposal, but most of the changes occurred later through legislation. Nevertheless, he laid the foundation for political compromise between the Liberals and the discredited Conservatives. Juárez easily won the presidency.

While Juárez maneuvered politically, the chaotic situation in the countryside threatened to undermine the regime's legitimacy. In the 1860s the *plateados*, bandits who dressed in trim-fitting clothing with silver buttons and used studs on their clothing and saddles, developed regional reputations and political power. In the aftermath of the French intervention, unemployed veterans on both sides of struggle constituted a pool of potential bandits. Technological changes also created uncertainty. Construction of the Mexico City–Veracruz railway, the most important transportation route in the country, even before its inauguration in January 1873 threatened the livelihood of Mexico's estimated 4,670 muleteers and 1,300 large wagon handlers.[3] In addition, other technological advances began to displace workers skilled in traditional forms of agriculture and mining. Even though new jobs were created, the transition unsettled many. Uncertainty and disorder resulted in demands for government action.

Juárez responded to the perceived challenge to order by issuing a decree in 1869 that suspended many of the 1857 Constitution's legal procedures and authorized summary justice. The funding of seven new rural police units constituted the first major expansion of the *rurales* corps since its establishment in 1861. Federalizing existing state police organizations and recruitment brought the force up to strength quickly and at the same time strengthened the federal government.

Recasting the Past

The need to rethink the past three quarters of the century became evident with the triumph of liberalism over monarchism. At a higher philosophical level, the time had come to tabulate the heavy costs, as well as to assess the benefits arising from the events of the turbulent decades since independence. Benito Juárez began the process, but it required fitting Mexico's experience into a broader global context. Fortunately, the French philosopher

Auguste Comte offered an explanatory context seemingly applicable to Mexico that justified its troubled past.

Mexican students in France became followers of Comte and introduced his philosophy to a Mexico more than ready to embrace it. Pedro Contreras Elizalde, considered the first Mexican positivist, studied medicine in France, knew Comte, and became a charter member of the Société Positiviste in 1848. When he returned home, he married one of Juárez's daughters and served in the government. Gabino Barreda, the educator responsible for the spread of Comte's philosophy in Mexico, also studied medicine in Paris, attended Comte's lectures, and knew Contreras Elizalde. Barreda organized the National Preparatory School, which opened in 1868. An important generation of the national elite passed through the school, including José Yves Limantour, who would later serve as Porfirio Díaz's powerful secretary of the treasury.

Barreda's other contribution, perhaps equally as important, involved a psychological recasting of national history to give value to a traumatic past. Employing Comte's theory of stages, he portrayed the nation's history as an epic struggle between darkness and superstition, and suggested another era had begun. The valiant battle against the French ended with a victory for all humanity, one that saved the republican ideal from a monarchist resurgence. Barreda's historical analysis made it all seem worthwhile, in spite of the suffering—a view endorsed by former U.S. secretary of state William H. Seward, invited by President Juárez to visit Mexico. Seward echoed Barreda's interpretation and placed the U.S. Civil War and the French intervention at the center of the epic struggle against archaic monarchies. He predicted that both republics would now be free to demonstrate the material advantages of republicanism. Juárez, the principal hero of the struggle, stood as the benevolent ruler-director that Comte suggested, although the president did not consider himself to be a positivist.

Challenging the self-congratulatory, restored republic was a counter-movement that emerged in the countryside. Julio Chávez López, an Indian instructed in the school of Enlightenment founded by Europeans, posed a reasoned critique of Liberalism. Well grounded in anarchist theory, he opposed state-supported exploitation and called for the abolition of the government. After issuing a manifesto, he mustered his followers to attack haciendas in the Chalco region, not too distant from the capital. Juárez dispatched troops to suppress the rebellion. The president ordered the execution of Chávez López on September 1, 1869. As he faced the firing squad, he reportedly shouted, "Long live socialism!"[4]

Education in the Restored Republic

The restored republic experienced a wave of forward-looking debates that were stimulated and reported on by newspapers. Lively discussion among intellectuals and others anxious to transform the country through education echoed the early decades of independence. Mexico's needs and how they should be addressed elicited suggestions, some of which appeared utopian but foreshadowed many of the programs initiated during the Mexican Revolution. As all understood, the ability to read and write opened the door to civilization, culture, and civic responsibility, while ignorance made it possible for the politically ambitious to field armies and control personal fiefdoms. Some suggested that certain elements in society had an interest in keeping the population uneducated and subservient. Such notions during the initial consolidation stage of the new oligarchy should have been seen as a warning.

Articles dealing with transformative educational issues appeared particularly bold. Suggestions for Indians' and women's education indicated that many understood that restricted access to education perpetuated ignorance and subservience. A thoughtful article proposed a common curriculum for both genders that would transform the family into an important site of education. Commentators demanded that parents make every sacrifice necessary to provide for the instruction of their children. Others suggested stiff fines for those who did not send their children to school, as well as for *hacendados* who hired illiterate children as laborers. Realistic observers suggested that the government pay attention to clothing and the nourishment of students. Looking ahead, perceptive critics noted that to carry on as usual threatened to create an aristocracy of knowledge while condemning the rest of the nation to ignorance and inevitable economic and cultural misery.

Free and obligatory education existed in theory, but whereas Mexico City and state capitals had a number of schools, few could be found in the countryside. An estimated 2,424 primary schools functioned in 1857, with some 185,757 students in an age cohort of 1,250,000 potential but unschooled students. Nineteen years later 8,103 primary schools operated, a number that excluded some 1,500,000 eligible children, indicating that population growth outstripped the expansion of primary education. Most primary schools, some 65 percent, depended on municipal support, while federal and state governments financed only 7 percent. In the northwest, only Mazatlán, Sinaloa, with its port and a budget of 80,000 pesos (in 1871), could afford several primary schools and a secondary school. Mazatlán's revenues relied on property and commercial taxes. The state of Sinaloa in 1875 had 215 primary schools, most of them private. Municipalities supported only forty-three of that number. In the state of Sonora a special education tax was levied in 1869, but not all could pay. Smaller towns and villages at times closed primary schools for lack of funds. Nevertheless, Sonora in 1870 had 103 primary schools with 3,737 students. In the state capital of Hermosillo, the state government provided funds for two secondary schools.[5] Primary education, the first step on the educational ladder, depended on the most impoverished level of the political structure. In more prosperous cities across the republic, private primary schools made up 20 percent of the total available, with a surprisingly low proportion, 1 percent, supported by the Church. An accurate count is not possible, but in light of a population of around nine million, it is clear that most children did not have access to formal education.

Liberal intellectuals such as Gabino Barreda, Justo Sierra, Ignacio Altamirano, Ignacio Ramírez, and others pressed for a massive effort to extend primary education in rural Mexico. Ignacio Ramírez called for a new generation of teachers who would be better trained, better rewarded, and appreciated. As he saw it, education should include the study of two or three Indian languages, with a preference for Nahuatl as a way to dispel the destructive notion of indigenous barbarism. Justo Sierra, with some exaggeration, noted that in the United States, every community provided access to education, reinforcing general knowledge and stimulating prosperity.[6]

The curriculum of the National Preparatory School, founded in 1867 in the capital, served as a model for the nation. It included extensive courses in advanced mathematics and ancient and modern languages, with some attention to fine arts and emerging scientific disciplines. Preparatory schools of various quality appeared in many states, although few came close to duplicating the national school in quality or extent of offerings. Attracting qualified professors to provincial state capitals presented a major problem. A number of states provided scholarships and attempted to attract students from outside the state capital to create a suitable academic environment, with limited results.

Separate schools of commerce and administration, engineering, medicine, law, and fine arts maintained a professional focus. The colonial-era Academy of San Carlos became the Escuela Nacional de Bellas Artes (National School of Fine Arts) in 1867, open to students of both genders. Its curriculum included architecture and mathematics as well as fine arts. Scholarships were available for promising students to travel and study in Europe, broadening their intellectual and professional perspective and making the school a stimulating cultural center. Admirably, the school's faculty and students rescued and restored many colonial-era paintings. Mixed-gender institutions, however, did not meet the demand for women's education.

Liberals had long insisted that women should be educated to make direct contributions to society beyond the family, but at the secondary level only a handful of institutions existed to educate girls. Basic science and mathematics, taught through the prism of domestic arts, perpetuated traditional restrictions on women's education. Mexico City's Girls School opened in

1869 with forty students, and by 1874 enrollment was still only a modest 100 girls. A request by the Mexico City Girls School for permission to offer pre-professional preparation in medicine, pharmacy, and agricultural sciences fell on deaf ears, but nevertheless indicated pressure for the professional training of females. In addition to the Federal District, seven states had secondary schools for women.

The educational debate conducted by the restored republic indicated a coalescing of public opinion around core state responsibilities beyond maintaining order. Few saw education as a panacea, but most pointed out the fundamental connections between education and civil society. Unfortunately, insufficient financial and human resources hindered expansion.

Prelude to the Porfiriato

President Juárez governed from the moderate center but failed to build an inclusive Liberal party sufficiently united to agree on the direction of the republic. Generational impatience as potential successors jockeyed for position may have been the major obstacle. As the end of his presidential term approached, it became clear that after years of battling for survival, Juárez had concluded that his ultimate task remained to be achieved. He decided to run again for the presidency. Many felt his fourteen years in office had resulted in increasingly autocratic behavior that bordered on the dictatorial. He remained a formidable candidate, but more as a patriotic icon than a politician.

Two plausible candidates opposed the *beneméritos* reelection. Sebastian Lerdo de Tejada, the brother of Miguel, represented middle-of-the-road civilian Liberalism, while General Porfirio

Díaz presented himself as the candidate of veterans, who felt their service had been ignored. In a disputed election, Juárez again won. Nevertheless, the tally indicated that support for Juárez had weakened. Benito Juárez won with 5,837 votes, while Díaz received 3,555 votes and Lerdo de Tejada 2,874 votes. Juárez assumed office with a plurality of 48 percent; over half the electorate had abandoned him. Sebastian Lerdo de Tejada joined the government, but Díaz, from his Oaxacan hacienda La Noria, announced a revolt to overturn the government. The odds appeared to favor Díaz. His brother, Felix Díaz, served as the governor of the state of Oaxaca and had succeeded in displacing Juárezista Liberals from power. Moreover, in view of a military force of some 3,000 under the command of the governor of the state, coupled with Porfirio Díaz's connections with disgruntled army veterans as well as with the active army, success seemed possible. As a first step, Governor Félix Díaz published the Plan of Noria and decreed the withdrawal of the state from the federation. The plan listed real and imagined grievances but offered no remedial proposals. Juárez stood accused of imposing himself on the nation, using force against the states, and ignoring the army's contribution. Porfirio Díaz dispatched his old comrade-in-arms, General Manuel González, to attempt to enlist northern states in the rebellion. In Nuevo León, Governor Gerónimo Treviño followed Oaxaca's lead and withdrew from the federation, proclaiming himself leader of the Army of the North. Nevertheless, forces loyal to Juárez, including most northern governors, ended Treviño's revolt. Felix Díaz died a horrible death, and efforts to enlist more support floundered. Díaz ended his revolt.

A complex political situation became more complicated after

just a few months, when Juárez died. A new manipulated election gave the presidency to Sebastián Lerdo de Tejada. Díaz accepted the results, deciding to try again when a new term began in 1876. Under President Lerdo the reforms earlier suggested by Juárez became law, including the creation of a senate. Perhaps unwisely, President Lerdo reinvigorated anticlericalism with a prohibition against wearing clerical robes in public and imposed further restrictions on religious displays. Nevertheless, President Lerdo remained committed to Juárez's insistence on civilian rule. In 1873 President Lerdo presided over an economic milestone when he inaugurated the completed Veracruz–Mexico City system's trunk line and branch extensions, including the one from Apizaco to Puebla, which had been constructed earlier, in 1869. Lerdo remained opposed to rail links with the United States because, as he explained it, "between strength and weakness, a desert should remain." By 1876 the country had 416 miles of track, with plans for a more extensive network. The restored republic's years of relative peace resulted in a general economic recovery, noticeable in mining.

The 1876 elections matched the incumbent, President Lerdo de Tejada, against a persistent General Porfirio Díaz. The general campaigned and made promises that addressed a wide range of complaints, from the northern borderlands to disgruntled federalists upset with the centralism of Lerdo. When the election's result indicated another term for the current president, Díaz issued his Plan of Tuxtepec, demanding effective suffrage and no reelection. This time the country rallied behind Porfirio Díaz. Joined by army veterans and disenchanted Liberals, Díaz plotted his revolution from the safety of Texas before leaving Brownsville by ship for

Tampico to launch his assault on the capital. It almost did not happen. Suspicious authorities halted and searched the vessel but failed to discover the well-concealed Díaz. Subsequently Díaz learned that the crew protected him because one of the ship's officers had noticed his Masonic ring. Díaz landed safely and took personal command of his soon-to-be-successful revolt.

The victorious leader of the Revolution of Tuxtepec entered the capital on November 23, 1876, ousting the Lerdo administration and its supporters. A beleaguered Lerdo fled to New York. Despite Díaz's initial victory, however, the viability of the revolt remained in doubt. Lerdista resistance regrouped in Guanajuato, hoping to draw on silver revenues to finance a counterstrike. Meanwhile, in Mexico City a desperate Díaz pleaded with wealthy citizens to lend him 500,000 pesos to keep the government functioning at a minimal level. They raised less than half that amount. Díaz eventually resorted to temporary taxes to raise funds.

The Struggle for Recognition

Diplomatic recognition of Díaz's government posed yet another critical problem. Without recognition by the United States, loans at acceptable interest rates would be difficult to arrange. Moreover, enforcement of American neutrality laws could not be assumed, perhaps encouraging opponents to buy weapons in Texas and bring them across the border to challenge Díaz. In addition, Mexico's diplomatic corps in Washington, appointed by the previous government, posed a potential political and diplomatic problem. Their willingness to cooperate with the new regime remained to be tested. Moreover, lacking recognition, Díaz could not appoint new ones.

To complicate matters, Treasury Secretary Matías Romero and U.S. Secretary of State William H. Seward had signed an agreement in 1868 to resolve all outstanding claims for monetary damages dating back to the Treaty of Guadalupe Hidalgo. A method of determining valid claims had been settled upon, and Mexico had agreed to pay the first installment of 300,000 pesos in gold starting on January 31, 1877. The agreement, made by the Juárez administration, now became a problem for the financially pinched Díaz, who had earlier declared all contacts and concessions made by the Lerdo government null and void, ignoring the potentially negative reaction in Washington. Convincing the United States to accept the legitimacy of Díaz's regime required backtracking, and above all paying the first claims settlement installment as agreed upon in 1868. A harried and desperate General Díaz needed to find the money without delay.

Eventually, a loan yielded 200,000 pesos, and that, together with other resources, gave Díaz sufficient money for the interim. Other issues now became important. Washington worried that acceptance of the money implied recognition, and Mexico City expressed concerns about the cooperation of Mexican diplomats in the U.S. capital. Fortunately for Díaz, the American representative in Mexico, John W. Foster, ascertained that the Mexicans did not see recognition and payment of the claims installment as directly related. In fact, both sides understood that failure to abide by the claims settlement agreement would derail the recognition process.

Delivering the money to Washington became a major ordeal. With 300,000 pesos in cash, José María Mata and Ciro Tagle boarded the train to Veracruz, intending to take a Mexican warship to New Orleans. On arrival, they found that the ship needed repairs before it could go to sea. After paying for repairs, the hapless duo ended up short by 32,000 pesos. Fortunately, the Veracruz customs house had some funds, and the United States agreed that expenses could be deducted from the first installment. After a six-day voyage to New Orleans, Mata bought gold and then ordered it sold in London, where it would earn a premium. Mata arrived in Washington on January 31 and, accompanied by the Mexican ambassador, still theoretically representing the deposed regime, took the draft to the U.S. Treasury Department and departed with a receipt and, no doubt, a sigh of relief. News then arrived that the SS *Bavaria* had burned at sea, with the loss of all its cargo, including the Mexican gold. An almost tragicomic adventure could have ended badly but for the foresight of Mata, who had insured the shipment with Lloyds of London.[7]

With the first installment paid, the issue of recognition remained. Washington understood that it had to recognize Díaz's government but wanted to exploit the situation to prod Díaz to address problems along the border. The international boundary, stretching from the Gulf Coast to the Pacific Ocean over miles of uninhabited, poorly marked land, had become a haven for Indian raiders, smugglers, bandits, drifters, and others with little respect for authority. Forcing Díaz to clean up his side of the border ignored the reality of a transnational zone. American intransigence dragged out the issue until every other nation represented in Mexico had recognized the Díaz government. Belatedly, the United States accepted the legitimacy of the government, and Foster so informed the minister of foreign affairs on April 9, 1878.

Convergence on the Border:
Mexican Americans and Anglo Mexicans

The conclusion of the war with the United States marked the beginning of a process that became obvious only much later. The relative isolation of each republic from the other had been broken permanently, with consequences few could have imagined. The idea of cultural fusion and the creation of a hybrid culture that served as a bridge across the border in both directions, the formation of what today is greater Mexico, did not enter into the thinking of Mexicans or Americans. Both governments thought in terms of establishing a protective presence on the border able to repel the other, not only politically but also economically and culturally.

The Treaty of Guadalupe Hidalgo ending hostilities between the two warring parties required Mexico to cede the vast northern stretches that today constitute most of the American West. Mexico assumed the largely underpopulated territory as the successor state following the collapse of the Spanish empire, in a manner similar to the acquisition of territory by the United States from the British after 1776. Both republics approached the ceded territory as a physical and cultural vacuum, without regard for existing peoples and cultures that might be present.[8]

Almost immediately after the signing of the treaty, the Mexican Congress passed legislation, to strengthen the new border. The legislation envisioned a build-up of population along the border with a series of military colonies. The legislation, *Colonias militares: Proyecto para su establecimiento en las fronteras de oriente y occidente de la república* (1848), authorized the establishment of border settlements from the Gulf of Mexico to the Pacific

Ocean. The immediate objective, to stop the Indian raiding that threatened to drive settlers completely out of northern Mexico, seemed necessary to avoid the loss of more territory to the United States. Separatist sentiments in the north, along the lines of Texas earlier, were a further incentive to maintain as strong a presence as possible on the border.[9]

After the Mesilla Treaty (Gadsden Purchase) in 1854, which transferred the presidio of Tucson and its settlers to the United States, a distinct border population emerged. The setting up of a new international boundary created an economic magnet that relied on different opportunities, depending on one's side of the river, or, further west, a line drawn in the sand. Fort Bliss, established in El Paso in 1854, as well as federal troops in the settlements of Brownsville and Eagle Pass, added to the American presence on the new border and became an economic engine across the region. Agriculture and ranching mixed easily with smuggling, Indian raiding across the boundary line, rustling cattle, and other activities that rounded out local economies. Manipulating different laws and moving from one sovereign jurisdiction to the other as convenient and profitable became characteristic of the border population.

Unexpectedly, San Diego, California, played a key role in the transformation of an imagined border into a socioeconomic reality. A boom began with the gold rush of 1848–49. With the news, some 10,000 would-be miners rushed northward, depopulating parts of northern Mexico. After the easy placer mines played out in northern California, gold mining in the north became capital intensive and no longer attracted individual prospectors. Attention turned to Baja California as another boom began in the region in 1850 with deposits discovered on both sides of the border. San Diego at the time consisted of a cluster of adobe and wooden buildings with a scattering of Indian huts in the surrounding countryside. With the development of significant mines in the northern portion of Baja California, a Mexican military outpost and a customs house soon appeared, the start of a permanent presence that eventually became the municipality of Tijuana. Miners from Mexico, Chile, and the United States purchased supplies and equipment in San Diego and transported them to Baja California. Guidebooks to Baja California published for miners and settlers encouraged population movement into the border region. The space between San Diego proper and the border filled in with smaller settlements.[10]

The gold rush had a ripple effect all along the border. A series of twin settlements on each side of the border and divided sovereignty became a characteristic of the international line. On the Mexican side of the river, El Paso del Norte (now Juárez), already a substantial settlement dating back to the eighteenth century, adjusted to the new economics of an international border with ties to Franklin (now El Paso) on the American side. Fort Bliss infused federal money into both settlements.[11] Infrastructure developments north of the border began to knit the cross-border region together. Mail service from San Antonio to El Paso, Texas, and on to Santa Fe, New Mexico Territory, began in 1851. A monthly passenger stagecoach from San Antonio to El Paso served customers from the both sides of the border. The trip took sixteen days from San Antonio to El Paso, with another twelve days to Santa Fe.

Laredo, a Mexican settlement that extended to both sides

of the river, barely survived the 1842 flood. By 1848 it had not revived, and consisted of dilapidated huts and a small number of impoverished inhabitants. With the transfer of part of the settlement to the United States the American side retained the old name, while the Mexican side became Nuevo Laredo. With the 1848 treaty, federal forces from Rio Grande City arrived in Laredo to establish Camp Crawford, subsequently Fort McIntosh. The new fort, garrisoned by the entire Fifth Infantry in 1853, consisted of more than 400 men and the regimental band. Federal troops required annually 140 tons of hay at $16 a ton to support the horses and mules of the garrison. Corn grown by small farmers along the river sold for 83 cents a bushel to meet the demand of well over 600 bushels a month. Local beans at $2 a bushel and onions along with beef rounded out basic needs. In addition, employment, from washing to wheelwrighting, brought a degree of prosperity previously unknown.[12] A few hundred yards theoretically determined nationality but did not cut family ties, friendships, or commerce, as people crossed the border in either direction at will and changed residences from one side to the other as convenient.

Eagle Pass, Texas, originally a minor outpost at the beginning of the U.S.-Mexican War, became the site of Fort Duncan in 1849. The Anglo contractor responsible for hauling supplies to Fort Duncan convinced seventy Mexican families to settle around the fort. Eagle Pass became a way station for gold prospectors disembarking at the Mexican port of Mazatlán and traveling overland to the California gold fields. In 1851 a stagecoach linked the settlement and its recently established Mexican twin settlement of Piedras Negras with San Antonio.

The transnational border zone had become a unified region before the railroads arrived. In 1858 the Butterfield Overland Express began service from St Louis to San Francisco through El Paso. A competition between mail carried overland and that dispatched by sea ended in favor of the Butterfield Pony Express, which made the dash to California from the end of the railway in St. Louis in twenty-three days, six days faster than the sea route.[13] Subsequently, the sunset railway route from New Orleans to Los Angeles, completed in 1883, provided the trunk line for subsequent branch rail connections to the border.

The U.S. Civil War firmly established the border economy. The Union blockade made it immensely profitable to smuggle Confederate cotton from Eagle Pass and Laredo into Mexico. The Piedras Negras customs house on the other side from Eagle Pass collected some 50,000 pesos a month, with similar amounts paid at other border crossings. The Union occupation of Brownsville in 1863 could do little to hinder the illegal trade. Bagdad, a boomtown at the mouth of the Rio Grande on the Mexican side, became a port with a population of 15,000. After the war it disappeared into the sand and was declared nonexistent, and the land returned to its natural state. Other tiny settlements along both sides of the river eventually became permanent towns. Matamoros briefly became an important port, receiving and exporting some 7,000 bales of cotton a month and vast quantities of arms, ammunition, food, and clothing to the Confederacy. Merchants, speculators, and laborers enjoyed boom-time earnings and wages. Merchants completed $500,000 worth of transactions a week. The British maritime insurance firm Lloyds of London, with an office in Matamoros, did a brisk business. Contraband cotton provided the capital that transformed Monterrey into the informal capital of northern Mexico and fueled its industrialization. Eight textile mills used 1.5 million pounds of Confederate cotton a year. Evaristo Madero, the founding patriarch of the clan, dispatched family members to England to study the latest production methods, and soon had the largest textile mill in the north.[14] The boom ended with the defeat of the Confederacy, but by then Monterrey had self-sustaining economic momentum. Although the Mexican northern states made positive use of the border, not all went smoothly.

Commercialization of border resources forced some difficult adjustments. The border zone on both sides also experienced the negative onslaught of commercialization. The reaction of the population often became violent. The Salt War in 1877 in the transborder El Paso area drew in individuals across the region. Salt deposits met the needs of most villages along the Rio Grande, and merchants packaged it for sale in northern Mexico. When an Anglo laid claim to deposits traditionally used in common, Tejanos, supported by some 200 cross-border Mexicans, took up arms to preserve free access to the salt deposits.

An even more violent reaction to commercialization known as the Cortina Wars in the Brownville region, led by Juan Nepomuceno Cortina, roiled the border. The Cortina family's extensive land grant in the area around Brownsville came under pressure to the extent that almost any incident could have set off a violent reaction. In July 1859, Cortina responded to an unnecessarily brutal arrest in Brownville by shooting the officer and freeing the Mexican prisoner. Several months later Cortina and his men rode into Brownsville, shot the city jailer and a few others, and took control amid shouts of "Death to the Americans!" and "Viva Mexico!" Convinced to withdraw, Cortina subsequently issued a proclamation demanding that Governor Sam Houston protect the legal rights of Mexicans in Texas. In the second Cortina War (1861), he captured the county seat of Zapata County, Texas. Local sheriffs and the Texas Rangers headquartered in Waco, Texas, must have been relieved when Mexican authorities arrested him in 1875 and confined him to Mexico City.[15] Less sensational than border violence but of more consequence in the long run, the two cultures came in close contact, with results that shaped the nature of the border and its population.

Tucson, then still a small town, provides an example of the cultural hybridization process that accompanied the economic and cultural consolidation on the border. In 1860 Tucson had a Mexican population of 346 males and 307 females, while Anglos numbered 160 males and 8 females. Twenty years later Mexican males numbered 2,368 and Mexican females numbered 2,101, while on the Anglo side there were 1,693 male and 330 female residents.[16] With this kind of demographic mixing, American men married Mexican women and raised their children in Mexican households and within important kinship networks. Their children, often bilingual and having an understanding of both cultures, functioned as cultural bridges.

The unique border culture has remained remarkably stable into the present. Population circulation between northern Mexico and the American Southwest and a similar circulation of Anglos into the region has refreshed the hybrid culture from one generation to the next.[17]

The movement of Mexican labor into the borderlands and

beyond accelerated in the 1880s. The industrialization of Monterrey and the railroads drew people northward, but the underlying attraction, better wages in the United States, resulted from the aggressive exploitation of natural resources. Grasslands from the upper Midwest to Texas made it possible to supply Europe with beef. Upper Midwest iron ore, copper in the Territory of New Mexico, and other industrial ores fueled eastern factories. Timber across the Northwest and the Gulf South and cotton from Texas and across the southern cotton belt did the same. Infrastructure from railways to irrigation ditches expanded the economic possibilities, and the demand for labor often outstripped the supply. Mexican labor drawn into northern Mexico by development would soon be pulled across the border by higher wages. A two-step process that involved seeking employment in the northern Mexico, then saving sufficient money to purchase a train ticket to El Paso, Laredo, or other border towns served by railway lines became a pattern.

The same geology and climate on both sides of the border meant that skills learned in northern Mexico could be used in the American Southwest. Irrigation techniques learned in La Laguna could be applied in Texas at higher wages. Experienced miners familiar with pneumatic drills, air compressors, dynamite, and safety fuses carried their skills with them, as did railway men and track hands. Even unskilled workers went across the border in search of better wages. While workers went north, American capitalists began to move south into Mexico. Guggenheim operated smelters in Monterrey and Aguascalientes. Mexican workers earned three-quarters less in silver-backed pesos than the two dollars in gold that Guggenheim paid workers at the Pueblo, Colorado, smelter.[18]

The Authoritarian Consensus, 1876

Porfirio Díaz, born in 1830 in the state of Oaxaca, the same state as Benito Juárez, represented a generation that came of age in the 1840s. Both men played important roles during the war with the United States and the French intervention. Juárez achieved his political dream and intended to bask in his achievements. He became a national icon, admired for his ability to survive and for his perseverance, which made it possible to prevail over his enemies. His life, the stuff of myth and flattering reinterpretations, infuriated his opponents but thrilled the people anxious to enshrine him as a true national hero. His triumph and death in 1872 at sixty-six years closed one era and marked the start of another, whose promise had to be the work of a new generation. Díaz, forty-two years old when Juárez died, emerged as president four years later at age forty-six, at the height of his physical energy. With an unsurpassed military record and confident that he could provide the order and administration the country needed, he had the support of his generation.

The new president set out to build a national constituency, not within a party but rather around himself as a personal symbol of stability and progress. Like Juárez, he understood the importance of image and gravitas. He projected stability and faith in progress with firmness and conviction. When necessary he appeared in military uniform, but more often he wore the civilian clothing preferred by traditional liberalism. A political elite already supportive of his objectives and anxious to experience liberalism's full flowering needed little persuasion. Much of the new president's aura rested on the camaraderie of liberalism's armed struggle. Patriotic men could be trusted—soldiers of liberal convictions, who had fought in the war of the French intervention. He intended to reward veterans as Juárez had not, and, with a soldier's respect for other soldiers, he planned to redeem those veterans of the war with the United States, the War of the Reform, and the empire who chose the wrong side. He understood officers—their commitment to the nation, their loyalty to fellow soldiers, and their discipline and obedience, under the right circumstances, to their superiors. With men such as these, Díaz believed he could defend national honor, achieve progress, and claim international esteem.

General Díaz's commitment to the nation could not be questioned. He manipulated his daughter's birthday to fall on the anniversary of the defeat of the French at Puebla. The proud father registered the appropriately named child, Luz Aurora Victoria Díaz, on May 5, 1875. He also held his own birthday celebrations on the anniversary of Hidalgo's cry for independence. Few could doubt his attachment to the republic. To many, he personified the victorious military struggle to preserve the nation. He had fought against the French in the battle for Puebla and had been captured, but had escaped to fight for Juárez against the forces of Maximilian. He entered Mexico City as the conquering general days in advance of the return of the Liberal government to the capital. His revolt against President Juárez could be excused as frustration with an icon in decline.

Díaz's first presidency focused on creating national unity to legitimate his seizure of power. Forging unity within the states required working with the various state political camarillas.[19] Díaz used his considerable personal skills to convince people to trust his intentions. The president demonstrated his commitment to maintaining order through firmness and prompt attention to challenges to federal authority. Rural revolts between 1878 and 1884 tested his policy.

Uprisings occurred in twelve states, including México, Puebla, and Querétaro, in reaction to the seizure of land by railway speculators and claims under the Lerdo Law. The agrarian leader Francisco Zalacosta and other agrarian chiefs formed an anti-Díaz alliance. Over a year and a half, Zalacosta and a few hundred men fought the federal army and *rurales* across several states as they burned and sacked haciendas. Their proclamation, the *Ley del Pueblo* (1879), revealed the growing sophistication of the agrarian movement. Agrarian leader Alberto Santa Fe called for the distribution of land to every rural family that possessed property valued at less than 3,000 pesos. Plans for the confiscation and distribution of land by village committees indicated the strong commitment to local control. The proposal required that those who received land repay the value of the land over a period of years. A special agrarian bank with at least one branch bank in every state would make low-interest loans for seed and other expenses directly related to agriculture. Machinery and agricultural processing devices would be authorized by municipal authorities but financed by the agrarian bank. Many of these proposals would be implemented during the Mexican Revolution in the 1920s.

General Miguel Negrete, another prominent agrarian rebel of the time, pressed for sovereign municipalities able to deal decisively with the distribution of land thus by passing the federal and state governments. An avid supporter of the *Ley del Pueblo*, he continued to foment revolt until old age forced him to abandon the struggle in the 1890s. As for Zalacosta and his rebels, Díaz's army and the *rurales* defeated them and executed the survivors.

Administratively, Díaz began the task of clearing away financial, political, and economic obstacles to foreign investment. International diplomacy changed as it became obvious that the United States had replaced Great Britain as the dominant economic power in Mexico. In the year of the Plan of Tuxtepec, the downward trend of British commerce had already become evident. The upward trend of the United States, while based on long-term economic factors, received a push when Juárez in 1867 ended diplomatic relations with all countries that had recognized the Maximilian regime and declared void all conventions and treaties in existence with those nations that had supported the French intervention. To complicate renewal of relations, the offending nations had to make the first step toward reestablishing diplomatic relations. France did so in 1880, but Great Britain, by far the largest holder of Mexican debts, remained without formal diplomatic relations until 1885, leaving the field open to the United States for a period of eighteen years. As early as 1880 Mexico turned to the United States for more than 50 percent of its imports, and looked to Wall Street for direct foreign investment. New York banks also served as a channel for indirect British, European, and Canadian participation. Proximity and diplomatic ties shifted the economic focus decisively from London and Paris to New York and Washington. Porfirian plans for future development relied increasingly on luring American investors and exporting minerals and commercial crops. Order coupled with political stability became an immediate priority.

Díaz offered the option of *pan o palo* (bread or the stick). The carrot-or-the-stick policy worked well enough for the regime to survive its entire term—something that had happened only twice before since independence. Firmness and force made it possible to establish reasonable control in the countryside, but foreign investors needed more.　·

Stability lay at the heart of Díaz's message to his countrymen as well as to foreigners. The fact that Díaz had pledged to uphold the principle of no reelection disturbed many who had little confidence that the institutional structure would be able to guarantee peace if he stepped down. They urged President Díaz to ignore his promise and remain in office. In a message to the Mexican Congress in 1877, Díaz characterized his pledge as one of the most solemn he had ever made and one he must honor. At the same time, he indicated his intention of submitting a constitutional amendment that would permit reelection. To honor his word, the amendment stated that the incumbent could not accept another presidential term or assume the office for any reason until the passage of a period of four years. After that period, resuming office would be up to the electorate. He anticipated that the states would choose to apply the same terms to the governors. Congress approved, and Díaz promulgated the amendment on what had become his favorite day, May 5, the date of the victory over the French.

The Interim Presidency of Manuel González

Despite Díaz's protestations, few among the political elite believed he would relinquish the presidency. He remained the popular choice, particularly among those who believed that only a military man of Díaz's stature could guarantee stability. Nevertheless, a number of presidential aspirants entered the race, although all of them recognized that without the president's blessing they could not hope to win. Of a half dozen serious candidates, two individuals stood out, General Manuel González and Justo Benítez. General González had the right qualifications, except for the mistake of having fought on the Conservative side during the War of the Reform. Nevertheless, his candidacy appealed to reconciled Conservatives, and to the military in general. Benítez, a native of Oaxaca, private secretary to Díaz during the French intervention and considered a close adviser of the president, had became an important congressional leader. He lacked military experience and had developed an independent power base in Congress, all of which made Díaz reluctant to trust him with what he saw as an interim presidency. Nevertheless, rather than immediately announcing his preference, Díaz professed to be neutral, a technique that kept contenders vying for his favors. Only after he announced his support would the candidate be publicly identified as Díaz's candidate. The trick, to find someone strong enough to hold off potential competitors while willing to step down after one term, seemed a difficult one and risky to try.

A calculating President Díaz ordered General González to the north, along with a substantial military force, to deal with disorders there and to bolster the idea that only a military man could preserve public order. Even then, supporters of Benítez did not give up hope, and ambitious *caudillos* such as García de la Cadena and Ignacio Vallarta reportedly stockpiled arms. In the end, Díaz arranged for his general, Manuel González, to be president. The two men had long-standing ties.

Their friendship went back to innumerable battlefield camps and the camaraderie of soldiers who had faced the enemy together.

González had served as Díaz's chief of staff during part of the struggle against the French. He supported his old comrade in the aborted La Noria revolt, and subsequently backed the Revolution of Tuxtepec. He served as governor of Michoacán and took a leave from that post when Díaz offered him the cabinet position as secretary of war. Nevertheless, Díaz carefully pondered the extent of González's political ambitions before making the selection.

A disturbing indicator of a resurgence of political violence occurred in Guanajuato when candidate González survived an assassination attempt, allegedly mounted by the state militia and the city police. The formal election results, announced in the Chamber of Deputies, gave González 11,528 votes and the runner-up Benítez 1,368, about 300 more than García de la Cadena. Ignacio Vallarta received only 165 votes. A total of 15,026 votes cast indicated the small size of the electorate. Manipulation of the vote to ensure that the right candidate won could be taken for granted. Most governors responded to Díaz's wishes as the electorate understood.

Much of the country appeared uninterested in the electoral game of the elites but hoped that stable, normal life would go on. Although most did not cast ballots, they reserved the option of violence if they felt threatened by the new administration. Early fears of an armed uprising faded, although minor disturbances orchestrated by defeated candidates occurred, but did not threaten the social order. Some newspapers trumpeted the election results as proof the nation had moved into a new era of stable politics. Nevertheless, many feared that stability could not be taken for granted, and the general uncertainty undoubtedly influenced politics when Porfirio Díaz sought reelection to the presidency in 1884.

The Importance of the Interregnum

Manuel González, Díaz's trusted friend and colleague, had objectives, but no political ambitions of his own. As a seasoned general, for him the burden of command took precedence, but it did not cancel out loyalty and respect for his old comrade-in-arms. The assertion that he functioned as a puppet misinterprets his support for Díaz's return to office following his term. With the tacit approval and support of Díaz, González implemented constitutional and legal changes that created a framework favorable to economic growth. His policies promoted mining, commercial agricultural, and telegraph and railroad construction by entrepreneurs financed with foreign capital.

Financial restructuring of debt and reassuring investors depended on international diplomacy. President González found a diplomatic mess awaiting attention when he assumed the presidency. Juárez had broken off relations with those countries that supported Maximilian's regime and imposed conditions on them that made it difficult to balance the growing influence of the United States. During his first term, Díaz focused on internal order, recognition by the United States, and meeting the expenses of his bankrupt administration. His payment of financial obligations to the United States created a reasonable climate for subsequent investments, but it required follow-through.

When Díaz left office, scarcely one peso remained in the treasury. President González inherited a bankrupt administration and pressing economic issues. Tariffs remained the principal source of revenue for the national government until the 1880s. Consequently, financing budgetary needs forced tariffs higher, with no direct intention of protecting nascent industries or economic interest groups but upsetting Mexico's trading partners. The Díaz administration no longer found the 1831 Commerce and Navigation Treaty between Mexico and the United States useful. On the final day of his administration, Díaz abrogated that treaty and similar commercial arrangements with Germany, Italy, and several other countries, leaving it to González's administration to negotiate new treaties.

The most urgent treaty was with the United States. The American ambassador observed that the United States could destroy Mexico's export trade if Washington levied duties at the same rate as that imposed by Mexico on American goods. In reality, both nations understood that archaic tariff policies had to be modified to accommodate changing economic circumstances. Railroad transportation shifted trade channels away from long, time-consuming and costly maritime trade routes. Falling transportation costs between the two neighbors expanded trade possibilities as the two rail systems moved inevitably toward border rail connections.

The proposed replacement treaty permitted the duty-free importation of agricultural production and primary products into the United States and the tariff-free entrance of American finished goods into the Mexican market. The idea proved so bold that it galvanized special interests on both sides of the border to oppose the proposed treaty. In the United States, opponents delayed ratification as long as possible, then blocked legislation to implement the treaty. The treaty lapsed in May 1887 without going into effect when a series of last-minute complications, including the failure of the U.S. Congress to pass the legislation to implement it, ended the affair. Economic relations between the two nations remained unsettled.

Border issues had an indirect link to economic relations, particularly the issue of rail connections with American lines at the border. Many individuals inside and outside the Mexican government feared that a railroad connection would allow U.S. expansionism to ride the rails into Mexico, in a manner similar to the settlement pattern in the recently acquired western territories of the United States. As a result, the Mexican Congress voted against the construction of a new line from Nuevo Laredo to Mexico City during Díaz's first term. The González government revived the project by astutely resurrecting the immigration issue, allegedly to counter the possibility of American migration along the proposed rail link to the United States. President González signed contracts with several immigration companies to attract Spanish, Italian, and French immigrants, predictably with limited results, but he nevertheless succeeded in getting congressional approval of the border rail connection. Subsequently, subsidies totaling more than a million pesos spurred construction of two rail links to the United States. Taxes imposed on railroads offset much of the cost of such subsidies but did not render a significant surplus, if any.

Mexico's sensible and slow expansion of its rail system made technical and economic sense. Most of the capital and technology came from the United States. By the 1870s that technology had matured. Advances in track, bedding (wooden cross ties, compacted gravel, lipped spikes), control (the Westinghouse air brake), efficiency (automatic coupling of cars), and many other innovations cut costs, from construction to maintenance to operations.[20] The availability of capital improved as railroad construction in the United States reached a saturation point, but with many investors still hoping to strike it rich.

To speed up railway construction, the Ministry of Development (Fomento) issued an order in 1882 permitting the expropriation of private property for public projects and an administrative procedure that allowed nineteen days to complete the transfer of ownership, although it required prior payment. The Tehuantepec Railroad quickly tested the effectiveness of the regulation. Two villages, Santa María and Guichivere, faced the expropriation of 131 small lots, with thirty-one parcels subject to immediate transfer. In violation of the law, railroad officials seized the lots without prior compensation to owners. Reacting to such high-handed behavior, protesters blocked construction for five months. The episode alarmed other owners along the projected rail route, making it difficult to secure cooperation. In the end, the railroad and Fomento compensated individuals more generously than they had anticipated. Officials learned what should have been obvious, namely, that attracting local labor and supplies depended on good community relations, and even after a segment was completed, constant repairs and upkeep required willing labor. Railroads also became aware of the possibility of sabotage of vast stretches of unprotected track, signals, and roadbeds. Attempts to placate the local inhabitants involved ignoring foot traffic through tunnels and other informal uses of the right-of-way, as well as transporting material needed for municipal projects free or at minimal cost.[21]

Laid track surged from 1,000 kilometers in 1880 to 6,000 by 1884. Less spectacular but equally as important, the government elaborated an effective regulatory framework and laid out plans for future expansion. Construction plans had to be approved in advance, safety requirements agreed to, and schedules set, and all employees in contact with the public had to speak Spanish. An earlier law of 1881 placed government representatives on corporate boards to ensure attention to regulations.

The government emerged as the winner in the railway business. Besides stimulating commerce, the extension of lines into isolated areas strengthened federal and state control. The losers tended to be investors, who typically underestimated the engineering difficulties and overestimated the returns on investment. Traffic on new lines increased slowly, while up-front expenses burned through cash. Railway construction based on speculation rather than on existing economic factors inevitably failed or struggled to survive by cutting costs, including needed maintenance, beginning a slow but certain decline into bankruptcy that injured investors and threatened to discourage further investments. The Mexican Central did not declare a dividend in the nineteenth century. The Mexican National went into bankruptcy and reorganization in 1886. Lesser lines floundered as foreign investors refused to recapitalize struggling operations. Nevertheless, railways in conjunction with maritime routes made it possible for the United States to absorb 70 percent of Mexican exports by the early 1890s.

Railway wages and related activities drew more of the rural population into the money economy and in some cases shifted peasant agriculture from self-sufficiency to broader regional market exchange. The effect would be to elevate prices and spur economic activities at the microlevel. Unskilled laborers, from water carriers to ditch diggers, as well as passengers, provided customers for trackside vendors, including women and children. The many bridges, tunnels, and right-of-ways needed along the route served as shortcuts through difficult terrain for burros and individuals who transported goods on their back. Formerly all-day treks could be completed in a matter of hours. The isolation of villages along the routes ended with the railways. The intrusion of railways had positive as well as negative effects, exposing villagers to external influences and, perhaps, the attraction of a larger town.

In addition to stimulating railway construction, the González administration simplified mining regulations and taxes. The Federal Mining Code of 1884 required that state regulations conform to federal law, providing a workable degree of uniformity. It divided tax revenues, with 25 percent going to the federal government and the remainder to state governments, while eliminating nuisance taxes on the industry. Miners paid one tax based on the value of ores. Most important, the Mining Code allowed private ownership of subsoil rights, with the proviso that mines be continuously worked for at least twenty-six weeks each year by a minimum of six miners. Mines that did not do so could be denounced and purchased by others. The new code providing ownership made it possible to use the title as collateral—an important change in an increasingly capital-intensive industry—while allowing the state to insist on active exploitation of deposits. Large-scale operations using up-to-date technology and minimal labor made it possible to mine low-grade deposits. To protect workers, companies theoretically had to meet safety standards and provide appropriate working conditions in the mines. The enforcement of labor regulations remained weak, but the obligation had at least been imposed. Coal, iron, and mercury (used in silver refining) enjoyed a fifty-year tax exemption. Under the new rules, U.S. investments in mining went from $3 million in 1884 to $55 million in 1892.

Another law dealing with land ownership had social, political, and economic consequences. The land law of 1883 sought to identify and survey unoccupied lands and encourage its purchase and active cultivation. It followed the pattern of previous laws to encourage occupation and productive use, as well as attract immigrants. The law of 1883 placed the burden of proof of title on the current occupant. Small landholders found it difficult, and at times impossible, to demonstrate ownership as did indigenous tribes occupying ancestral land. Many in the north had settled the land informally, perhaps several generations in the past. In the south and center, established local institutional structures, such as village committees and judicial officials able to provide legal documentation based on affidavit, posed more of challenge to surveying companies. Central Mexico experienced major displacement only after the 1894 modifications to the land law. Between 1883 and 1889, companies surveyed some 32 million hectares of actual and at times theoretically unoccupied land and received 27,500,000 hectares in compensation, equivalent to 14 percent of the nation's land area. The land law set the stage for large-scale commercial agricultural operations. Irrigation and new cultivation methods made previously marginal land productive. Displaced occupants moved into small towns and cities or became rural laborers.[22]

Despite increasing economic momentum, the financial structure lagged behind. Accumulating capital in sufficient amounts to extend long-term credit required a modern banking system. On the national level, only two institutions served the republic. The British-capitalized Bank of London and Mexico, established in 1864, provided international contacts, and the colonial-era

Monte de Piedad (National Pawnshop) allowed the poor to raise money on their merger possessions, but it also received deposits, discounted collected bills, and issued banknotes. A handful of state-chartered banks also functioned but served a smaller number of clients. Often state-chartered banks served one extended family's credit needs. Moneylenders extended loans, advanced wages, and provided short-term credit for weddings and other mandatory social expenditures. The Church placed limited funds in trusted private hands to finance some property mortgages. Collectively, the system functioned inefficiently and inadequately. Moreover, money in circulation could not be easily regulated, and unexpected contractions caused unnecessary damage in the absence of readily available credit.

In an effort to modernize the financial system, the González administration issued national bank charters, including that of the Banco Nacional Mexicano in 1882, a branch of the Paris-based Franco-Egyptian Bank. The bank issued banknotes in the ratio of three pesos to one in capitalization. The bank also functioned as the government's fiscal agent, providing an annual open line of credit to the federal government of four million pesos. At the urging of the government, the Banco Nacional Mexicano merged with the Banco Mercantil Mexicano to form the Banco National de México. The government's line of credit increased to a maximum of eight million pesos. The Banco Nacional de México became the depository of public funds, with a monopoly on emissions. Its banknotes alone circulated as legal tender. Together with the new commercial code of 1884, the administration laid the groundwork for an efficient modern banking system. Bank assets jumped from approximately three million pesos to 30 million by the end of

González's term. In tandem with the creation of a central bank, the government Ministry of Development (Fomento) functioned with a budget larger than the Ministry of War. By González's final year in office, the development agency absorbed a third of the federal budget.

The president's willingness to take chances, even long shots, to develop the republic verged on recklessness. He acted in an entrepreneurial fashion, throwing government revenues into schemes that worked and others that failed, often embarrassingly. Newspapers did not give him much credit but quickly pointed out his mistakes. Throwing money into oversold schemes resulted in waste and exaggerated charges of corruption and raiding the treasury.

Nevertheless, at the end of González's term, the nation had cleared away major obstacles to progress, including recognition of the British debt and establishing diplomatic relations with Great Britain. Railway expansion and banking reforms made it possible for his successor, Díaz, to continue modernization and development. Díaz, like González's opponents, did not publicly credit the successes of the administration, preferring to pose as the rescuing successor, straightening out a messy situation left by his predecessor.

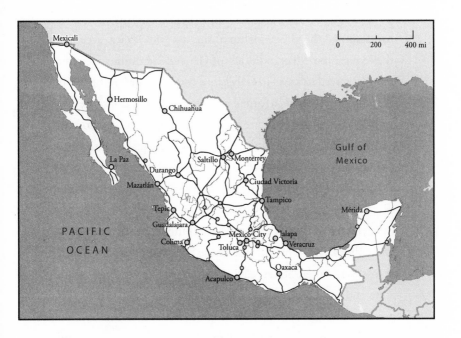

Mexicali

0   200   400 mi

Hermosillo

Chihuahua

Gulf of
Mexico

La Paz

Saltillo   Monterrey

Durango

Ciudad Victoria

Mazatlán

PACIFIC

OCEAN

Tepic

Tampico

Mérida

Guadalajara

Colima

Mexico City   Jalapa

Toluca   Veracruz

Oaxaca

Acapulco

(*Previous page*) Map 2. Mexico's Major Roads

As the end of González's term approached, Porfirio Díaz, who had assumed the governorship of the state of Oaxaca, accepted the request to be the godfather of General Gerónimo Treviño's son and agreed to travel to Galveston, Texas, for the baptism. City officials suggested that a formal visit be considered. Consequently, in 1883 the Texas legislature unanimously invited Díaz to visit Austin, to be received with full honors. Further invitations to visit St. Louis, Chicago, New York, and Washington required an extended visit. General Díaz, who had remarried the year before, decided to take his wife, Carmen Romero Rubio, on a railway honeymoon to the United States combining pleasure, business, and politics. As the private cars of the honeymoon party traveled across the United States, each evening featured a dinner with state and local authorities. At business dinners the new bride acted in the dual role of charming hostess and, because of her fluent English, effective salesperson. In St. Louis, a militia band escorted the visitors from the railway station to the hotel. Three days of receptions followed, during which Díaz was introduced to virtually everyone of importance in the city. Chicago welcomed Díaz and his party in an equally extravagant fashion. A short, romantic side trip to Niagara Falls before the party continued on to Washington allowed for some relaxation. In the American capital, President Chester A. Arthur and his cabinet informally received Díaz, stopping just short of a formal state visit, reserved for actual heads of state. Dinner with former president General Ulysses S. Grant in New York capped the triumphant tour. The only disappointment came when Carmen attempted to visit her godfather, Sebastián Lerdo de Tejada, the president deposed by Díaz, in the hope of reconciling with him. The former president refused to receive her and turned down an invitation to return to Mexico.[1]

Díaz's odyssey, while providing an opportunity to meet with eager businessmen and politicians and establish useful personal ties, took on aspects of a political campaign. Prideful Mexican journalists noted that the receptions of the Prince of Wales and the emperor of Brazil on their visit to the United States paled in comparison to the ceremonial reception accorded Díaz. Mexico City newspapers reported with awe the honors paid the former Mexican president and presumed successor to President González. Díaz could not have failed to appreciate the political impact of his tour on supporters and possible opponents. The political momentum of his American tour alone would have been enough to carry him into the presidential palace. Nevertheless, that the ever-cautious general continued to take steps to diminish President González's reputation provides an insight into the political man.

While Díaz went from one reception to another, his subordinates in Mexico City made certain that González did not entertain thoughts of remaining beyond his term, or of returning to the presidency later. Questionable charges of fiscal misconduct against González dragged out until 1888, making it impossible for him to run again for president, although it seems clear that he had no desire to do so. In addition, Díaz's agents kept González's adulterous behavior and his civil divorce in the newspapers. Everyone understood that one word from Díaz would terminate González's public agony.

Once reelected in 1884, Díaz launched initiatives to strengthen public order, improve Church-government relations, and attract foreign investments. Campaigns to suppress agrarian unrest, ubiquitous banditry, and political upheavals laid the foundation for the illusion of unshakable stability that made Díaz the indispensable man. The long-standing struggle between the civil government and clerical authorities would be manipulated to the extent that the Church became an informal but supportive pillar of the regime. Díaz took action to broaden exports, strengthening national finances, and, most important, attracting foreign investors—in short, building on González's efforts.

Positive results, fused with calculated presidential image building, created a personal regime centered on the strongman. The president made decisions, usually in the form of administrative law or through a compliant Congress, but judiciously, so as not to jeopardize cooperation between state camarillas and the federal government. Politics had internal and external components that meshed. For Díaz, a master politician, Mexico, the United States, and Europe formed one political canvas.

The Conquest of Order

Díaz understood that much of his legitimacy depended on state camarillas, which in turned rested on important families. Politically, the oligarchy functioned as extended family units, so that the number of influential individuals, usually acknowledged patriarchs, was around 400 at most, representing various extended families that collectively made up state oligarchies. The families knew each other, often personally but certainly by reputation. Thus, camarilla politics involved attending to the interests of a relatively small group spread across the federal states. In exchange, state oligarchies supported the federal regime in Mexico City and negotiated mutually acceptable arrangements. In the event of disagreements between camarillas, the president tipped the balance as he judged best. Ideally, governors represented the interest of their state's oligarchies as a whole and transmitted their needs to the president. Díaz preferred that political power rest on a broad base of families. Individual members of camarillas might approach Díaz or one of his cabinet ministers over an issue, but the state governors played an essential role. A governor's readiness to cooperate with Díaz ensured an orderly election, with results that mirrored the president's instructions. Governors might suggest candidates for the federal Senate or the Chamber of Deputies, but Díaz did not tolerate individuals he disapproved of for any reason. A governor who pressed issues that Díaz found unacceptable could not interact with the president in the interests of his elite constituency, and soon left office. National congressmen had to be compliant and in agreement with the president. State oligarchs and their camarillas, managed by Díaz, ensured reasonable political tranquility and order across the republic.

Actual order at times depended on the application of federal force. Nevertheless, Díaz preferred not to use the army unless necessary. He created a public perception that his ruthless response made any challenge to order bound to fail, with harsh consequences for those involved. Díaz recognized the fundamental role of the *jefes políticos*, municipal administrators appointed by state governors, as the first line of defense against disorder. As the primary official in contact with local inhabitants, the *jefe político* had responsibility for the smooth functioning of the municipality, the basic unit of the organized state. Díaz in his early career served as the *jefe político* of Ixtlán in his home state of Oaxaca and fully appreciated their ability to fuse authority with social accommodation and the restrained use of force to maintain order.

These officials became increasingly important as development touched previously isolated areas, with unpredictable reactions. *Jefes* exercised authority over local land and taxes, as well as suppressed informal militias. A successful *jefe* balanced local, state, and national demands in a fashion acceptable to all parties, corresponded with governors, and discussed federal matters with President Díaz. Important *jefes políticos* expected to be invited by the president to attend the independence day celebration in Mexico City.

If local officials failed to defuse a challenge to authority, the next step might be a police unit dispatched from a state capital, followed by the federal *rurales* and finally the local army garrison or a combination of forces. Díaz eliminated local and state militias, leaving states with police powers but without military force. In the event of a major revolt, national army units had to be deployed. The army, however, had the potential to upset the political balance, and had to be handled prudently.

Force and Illusion

Liberals, ambivalent about a standing army, theoretically preferred a citizens' militia. Unfortunately, the Mexican experience since independence convinced Liberals that state militias posed more of a political danger to the republic than the federal army. Nevertheless, they understood that the national army potentially threatened the federal government. In the absence of centralized training facilities each military unit trained its men, a process that cemented ties to a particular unit and possibly to a favorite commander. Soldiers felt close to their officers and stood ready to obey their orders without questioning their intentions or the legality of their actions. A distant Ministry of War had some influence over the officer corps but little direct control of them and their soldiers.

General Díaz as a military man understood the dangers posed by the army, but also the necessity of military force. Díaz began restructuring the army almost immediately after he seized power in 1876. President Gonzáles during his term continued to implement changes. To balance the threat with the need, Díaz scattered garrisons around the republic to make it difficult to organize a unified military challenge to his regime, while maintaining what he hoped would be sufficient strength to deal with emergencies. The president assessed an officer's political ambitions, influence, and personal loyalty before assignment. Senior officers had to be monitored carefully.

The organizational plan divided the republic into military zones, *commandancias*, and *jefaturas de armas*. A zone covered several states commanded by a general. Within a zone a subordinate designation, the *jefaturas de armas* (subregional or district headquarters) provided an actual military presence in a state, territory, or single city, often a port. *Commandancias* in sensitive areas took orders directly from the minister of war. The number of such divisions depended on the president, as did the size of the force in any particular garrison. The presence of army units reminded state oligarchies that the federal government had military force at its disposal, and a fuzzy chain of command acted to complicate plotting. While Díaz claimed that the reorganization provided flexibility, political concerns rather than military considerations determined the configurations. A sudden reassignment or a change in designation could leave a politically ambitious officer isolated. Equally as important, it provided opportunities to reward loyalty.

In the absence of a centralized army supply structure, the government allocated funds based on the number of men on unit rosters. Inflated numbers and the skimming of payrolls provided a bonus much appreciated by commanders at all levels. The extent of the extra income depended on one's position. Corruption had the advantage of making officers too comfortable to contemplate revolt. Díaz understood the system and did not trouble himself with the financial lives of the officer corps, nor did he worry much about the quality of recruits. States assigned to supply a set number of recruits seldom met their quotas. Impressments swept up individuals that communities sought to rid themselves of for various reasons. Although the quality of the soldiers remained low, the army had superior firepower, including modern rifles and artillery. In 1882 the government imported 18,500 Remington rifles, along with the equipment to manufacture ammunition. Another purchase in 1897 included German Mauser rifles, machine guns, and artillery. A fighting force of reluctant soldiers, no matter how well equipped, and contented officers had its disadvantages, as would become evident when the regime faced the Mexican Revolution in 1910. The army would not be deployed casually.

The government used calibrated force and police powers before deploying the army. Nevertheless, when army deployment became necessary, Díaz preferred overwhelming force. Quickly putting down an incident minimized troublesome repercussions from foreign investors and preserved the illusion that troublemakers inevitably faced destruction.

The *rurales*, the rural police, usually provided sufficient force to deal with disorders that fell short of a rebellion, in which case the army would be deployed. They attended to their duty with ruthless efficiency, eliminating banditry and armed agrarians and other challenges to the regime. The *rurales* brought few bandits or individuals to town for trial. Notorious criminal perpetrators generally fell victim to an administrative order that authorized the *rurales* to shoot anyone who attempted to escape. The law of flight—*ley fuga*—added to the *rurales'* reputation for general disregard of judicial practices. Often their very presence appeared enough to maintain the peace.

The corps of *rurales* under Díaz received a glamorous new image with uniforms modeled after the dress of nineteenth-century bandits, the *platereos*. The *platereos* studded their clothes and saddles with silver; in effect, they wore their success for all to see. Over time they became a romantic stereotype usefully employed by President Díaz. The *rurales*, outfitted in light gray bolero jackets, tight-fitting suede leather trousers braided and decorated with silver, and heavy gray felt sombreros, made a distinctive and impressive display. They paraded in civil celebrations in towns and cities as guarantors of peace and order in the countryside and internationally as a symbol of an orderly nation.

To reinforce the message, an annual banquet honoring the *rurales* took place at Mexico City's finest restaurant, the Elysian Tivoli. Guests on the way to the ceremony passed mounted *rurales* in dress uniforms lining a three-mile stretch of the Paseo de la Reforma. The highly selective guest list included diplomats, intellectuals, prominent foreigners, investors, and other influential individuals. At noon, Porfirio Díaz reviewed mounted units from the restaurant's balcony. After an elegant dinner around a horseshoe-shaped table the guests joined the president in a champagne toast to the corps of *rurales*. Such a highly civilized event glossed over the reality. If the guests at the dinner honoring the *rurales* knew about the methods employed by the corps, as they likely did, they treasured order above the niceties of law. Foreigners delighted in repeating the old saw that one could carry a gold bar from one end of Mexico to the other in perfect safety. In fact, the distribution of detachments blanketed the areas where the most economic development occurred. Large operations often maintained their own units to guarantee security. The positivist's slogan, "Order and Progress," rested symbolically in the hands of the corps of *rurales*.

After the ceremonial dinner the guests may have tried their luck at the casino or enjoyed a stroll through the lovely garden. When they walked out of the Elysian Tivoli they encountered the *Gendarmería*, the modern police force of the capital, some 3,000 strong dressed in blue uniforms topped with Parisian-style kepis, almost indistinguishable from the French *Gendarmerie*. The gendarmes made sure that only acceptable people entered the best parts of town, thus creating a façade of safety and modernity. Impressed diplomats and foreigners, carefully attended to by the president, reported it all to their foreign ministers, friends, and acquaintances.

All the elements of force and illusion came together during the ritual celebration of independence day. Army and *rurales* units, parading through the streets on September 14, began a celebration that climaxed on the 16th, the actual date of independence. Beautifully mounted units engendered national pride and demonstrated the government's power. Meanwhile, the caped and kepi-topped *Gendamería* circulated among the crowd to ensure their personal security. On the 16th, Díaz on horseback, in military uniform, recalled previous victories and suggested Mexico could confidently face future challenges. Garbed in a general's attire, complete with medals and foreign decorations suggesting order and stability, Díaz convinced Mexicans and foreigner observers alike that he personally represented order.

A less public but perhaps politically more important event took place on September 15, on the eve of independence day. A ceremony in honor of the president's birthday had all the aspects of a public act of submission to the paramount ruler. Officials throughout the republic attended the dinner and presented gifts, usually associated with their region or state. Important members of the oligarchy also sent presents. At the 1905 celebration, Serén Palomar García Sancho of the town of Cocula, Jalisco, arranged for the newly formed musical group, the Mariachi de Justo Villa, to be conveyed to Mexico City to play for the president.[2] Newspapers carried laudatory coverage of the president, the dinner, and—most important—the list of guests. To make sure foreign investors understood the network of loyalty and submission that bound local, regional, and national administrators to President Díaz, the Ministry of Development published a detailed account of the banquet and other events in honor of the president.

The Porfirian Economy

The Porfirians, like the Liberals earlier in the century, sought modernization through economic development, but unlike their predecessors they enjoyed demand-driven momentum for Mexican raw materials. Recovery, combined with the end of ideological conflict and an almost complete railway system, created a favorable environment. Population resurgence and a Gross Domestic Product (GDP) of 2.7 indicated accelerating growth, with an estimated 66 centavos of every peso invested in development by 1911, mostly coming from foreigners. Between 1877 and 1911, Mexico's exports of raw materials of all sorts grew by 6.1 percent on an annualized basis. The convergence of high demand, transportation, technology, and foreign capital set the pace of development until 1900. In the decade from 1890 to 1900, exports grew 144 percent. Demand then tapered off in the last decade of the regime, rising only 75 percent.

Demand for industrial ores, particularly copper, zinc, lead, graphite, and antimony, diversified mining activity beyond the traditional silver and gold. Around large-scale mining operations there sprang up small settlements with hospitals, schools, electric plants, water systems, and services owned and operated by the company. Cananea, transformed by copper mining, was a city of 14,841 by 1910. The introduction in 1881 of a mechanical knotting device that used twine, an inexpensive substitute for the wire binding introduced earlier in 1874, made the McCormack reaper much more efficient, lowered costs, and created heavy demand for Mexican henequen. Henequen plantations in Yucatán returned on average profits of 50 percent, and in times of extraordinary demand as high as 600 percent. Profits went into private rail and tram lines to make the industry more efficient and created the modern, aptly named port city of Progreso.

Railways continued to attract American investors, while British capital concentrated in public services and the urban infrastructure needs that accompanied the modernization of cities. French investments followed the lead of French merchants resident in Mexico, who gradually turned to manufacturing. French capital channeled through the Sociedad Financiera para la Industria de Mexico, organized in Paris in 1890, accounted for 55 percent of all capital in the industrial sector. The Compañía Industrial de Orizaba (CIDOSA) established the largest and most modern textile factory in the republic in 1892 in Río Blanco. Textile production cut imports down to an insignificant 3 percent in 1911. In the industrial sector, mainly textiles, profit margins ran from 10 to 15 percent. Domestic investment primarily went into agribusiness, which by 1910 accounted for 70 percent of all land holdings. Export agriculture grew by 6.29 percent between 1877 and 1910. The Laguna, an ancient lake bed that spans Coahuila and Durango, became a major producer of cotton as a result of the rechanneling of the Nazas River.

In 1903, the Fundidora de Acero de Monterrey, Mexico's first iron and steel operation, met some of the needs of the mining industry, in addition to producing tracks for rail and tram lines. The domestic production of concrete, glass, processed foods, beverages, including beer, tobacco, textiles, and an assortment of other products grew substantially. In the period from 1886 to 1910, an estimated 40 percent of all investments in industry came from Mexican sources, while foreigners accounted for 60 percent of the 131 million pesos.

High import tariffs, the traditional sources of federal revenues, virtually eliminated foreign competition in light industrial goods. Duties ranging from 50 percent to 200 percent of value protected selected domestic production, and the falling price of silver made imports even more expensive. Meanwhile, industrialists enjoyed tax exemptions and subsidies, and negotiated state and local deals that ensured a profitable return on capital. Duty-free importation of machinery and inputs of all types stimulated new industries. The Cuauhtémoc brewery, established in 1892, enjoyed the standard seven-year tax exemption and subsequently a 75 percent tariff on imported bottled beer, which sold for $25 a barrel over the $8 cost per unit in St. Louis, Missouri. Further enhancing the national market, the federal government succeeded in cutting many of the transaction costs imposed by individual states, thus creating a relatively tariff-free internal market. Railways lowered the cost of distribution by cutting the time and the expense of transshipment from field or factory to market. Between 1877 and 1910 the cost of shipping a ton of textiles from Mexico City to Querétaro, some 130 miles away, dropped from $61 to $3. Nevertheless, railways did not reduce expenses for all industries. The cost of Mexican cement increased by the mile to such an extent that its use became prohibitive beyond 250 miles. The need to attract a continuous flow of foreign investments required constant promotion by officials, the president, and exposition organizers, and a steady outpouring of commercial propaganda.

The government trumpeted the country's progress in informative books, often published in French and English in addition to Spanish. Lavishly illustrated and bound, and distributed to businessmen's libraries in Europe and the United States, they presented investment opportunities to tempt even the most cautious investors. Foreign expositions and world fairs provided concrete demonstrations of progress. Mexico could be relied on to participate in such events, as it did in Paris, Berlin, Chicago, Buffalo, St. Louis, New Orleans, and other cities. A working model of the proposed Tehuantepec Ship–Railway delighted visitors to the Cotton Exposition in New Orleans in 1884. A Mexican military band so delighted listeners that it received an invitation to perform at the presidential inauguration in Washington, D.C.[3] When the band returned home, President Díaz personally congratulated the musicians and appointed its conductor head of the National Conservatory of Music. At the 1889 Paris Exposition on the centennial of the French Revolution, the organizers awarded Mexican exhibitors twenty-five grand prizes of honor and a host of lesser awards. Crafting positive representations of Mexico became a major objective of the regime.

The other side of the coin did not shine as brightly. In 1894 a series of laws building on the 1883 surveying law made it even easier to displace occupants and concentrate holdings. The south and center now experienced displacements similar to those in the north under the 1883 law. In the state of Morelos, sugar growers expanded their plantations, appropriating land that had been communally owned for centuries.[4] In central Mexico only 10 percent of villages retained some communal land on the eve of the revolution. Displacement of the original occupants, those unable to produce acceptable proof of ownership, forced Indians and peasants into the labor market or into marginal share cropping arrangements with landholders. Nevertheless, land concentration and efficient utilization did not increase per capita production sufficiently. Between 1877 and 1907 agriculture grew at an annual rate of .07 percent, half the rate of the population growth. Domestic food production fell at an annual rate of 0.5 percent.

The profitably of domestic agriculture and industry and the displacement of some imports may have been a source of official gratification, but it obscured the larger problem. A shift in tariff policy away from the former emphasis on revenue to include protection of emerging industries resulted in upward tariff revisions in 1892, 1893, 1896, and 1906. Government officials ignored the reality that protected manufacturers, in the absence of competition, had little incentive to lower prices and develop a mass market. Rising prices and falling wages limited consumption and industrial employment. Real wages fell over the course of the century, but between 1898 and 1911, wages fell by 25 percent. Consequently, producers expanded only slowly so as not to overwhelm limited but profitable demand. While the production of raw materials for domestic industry grew by 2.5 percent, indicating growth, urban and rural job creation lagged. Population growth and the large numbers of displaced peasants drove down wages and depressed consumption.[5]

The City Beautiful and People Made Presentable
By the late 1850s the elite had begun to abandon the city center and move to newer, less crowded and more modern subdivisions. The colonial model of a city with districts that remained socially static gave way to the movable urban environment that left older housing to decay, a pattern repeated into the present. Real estate speculators soon developed both sides of the Paseo de la Reforma. Much of its beauty mirrored that of Paris. Newspaper editor

Ignacio Cumplido visited Paris in 1860 after Baron Georges-Eugène Haussman had recreated the city under the inspired direction of Napoleon III. When Cumplido returned to Mexico, he served on the municipal council in charge of boulevards. Following the French model, he planted trees on both sides of La Reforma. In the 1870s, railway man Antonio Escandón added *glorietas* (circles) to La Reforma, along the lines of the *étoiles* in Paris. Soon statutes, trees, gardens, and grand *glorietas* swirling around impressive monuments rivaled their Parisian inspiration. Parks and gardens scattered throughout the modern sections of the capital added peaceful elegance. On holidays and Sundays military bands played as well-dressed people ambled on the delightful paths that looped around landscaped grounds. Mexico City served as a showcase for Porfirian civilization and provided the new urban model.[6]

The impact of the city beautiful could be observed across the nation. State capitals and secondary cities began adopting urban improvements and beautification projects. Cities such as Mérida, Puebla, Guadalajara, and Querétaro, and to a lesser extent smaller cities and towns, developed urban programs. Meanwhile, the rural population, usually hidden from view, could not be tolerated in the city beautiful. They belonged to a different Mexico, one the political elite hoped to transform.

Municipalities, following the lead of Mexico City, attempted to clear the streets of beggars, vendors, and rural people in general. Poverty, unemployment, homelessness, and daily life in the streets would be redefined by new laws as the state assumed the task of determining an appropriate urban appearance. Requirements specified European-style trousers and dresses, rather than the raw cotton peasant dress and indigenous clothing. In Guadalajara, the authorities levied fines on those wearing large-brimmed rural sombreros. Workers in various lower-class occupations linked to modernity required special hats or clothing, including hack drivers, newspaper salesmen, and porters, among others. Those who resisted the new laws encountered the urban gendarmes charged with enforcing modernity.

Being modern also required lifestyle changes, including sustained labor in factories and commercial agriculture and other modern labor practices. The tyranny of the clock conflicted with traditional customs, and adjusting to the new rhythm of work posed difficulties. What happened after work received attention. Modern, healthy European and American sports such as soccer, baseball, bicycling, and roller skating opened the possibility of creating a lower class dedicated to thrift, sobriety, hard work, and modern hygiene worthy of the city beautiful. The middle class and the elite enthusiastically endorsed social rules that implied their right to modify lower-class behavior based on a presumed superior understanding of virtue and its fruits. On a policy level, public welfare became a federal responsibility when Díaz placed it under the Ministry of Gobernación (Interior). Reformers employing rational methods and the latest management techniques reconstituted hospitals, orphanages, night schools for workers, and other institutions to reproduce the scientific results supposedly achieved in advanced societies.

Rats and *Rateros*

The Porfirians viewed the city as a civilizing force, both in its physical presentation and in its behavioral impact on the citizenry.

Consequently, antisocial behavior in public places appeared to be a betrayal and a cause for indignation among the better classes. Most failed to appreciate that in a country undergoing economic change of the sort that results in displaced villagers and an urban economy unable to absorb migrants, social adjustment is difficult. For many without other options, trying their luck in the city streets became a matter of survival.[7] Those better off considered beggars and street peddlers to be actual or potential thieves and pickpockets. Newspapers referred to them as *rateros* and compared their presence to a plague of rats. Antonio Medina y Ormaechea's *Las colonias de rateros* (1895) may have come closer to reality when he wrote that minors without family ties, education, or work became thieves. Police sweeps targeted presumed criminals, with little attention paid to actual evidence. Newspapers urged the police to pay attention to the law as much as possible, but also to use their suspicions based on experience to apprehend *rateros*. Indiscriminate arrests, street conflicts with police, and bribes to avoid imprisonment damaged the legitimacy of law enforcement and engendered widespread distrust of the authorities among the lower classes.[8]

The elite viewed the lower classes in general as uniquely susceptible to alcohol if left to their own devices; thus they had to be rescued from themselves. The use of *pulque* came under attack as a distasteful throwback to ancient times.[9] Fermented pulque, fortified with roots, provided an inexpensive alcoholic beverage readily available in the city. *Pulquerías* attracted a doubtful clientele and could be recognized by their distinctive smell. Mexico City had some 1,600 *pulquerías* around the turn of the twentieth century. The law forced them to close at 6 p.m., but street vendors and individuals who sold *pulque* out of dwellings could be relied on at any hour. Signs of class tensions could be gleaned from the names of *pulquerías*, including, "The Retreat of the Holy Virgin," "The Hangout of John the Baptist," and the promising "A Night of Delight". Women vendors prepared food in nearby doorways and circulated among the clientele. Regulations, generally ignored, barred women from remaining in cantinas and *pulquerías* to avoid scandal. Unlicensed prostitutes found ready clients among the patrons. The laws upheld respectability, and poor enforcement bowed to reality. The authorities, unable to control consumption, made sure that *pulque* establishments remained out-of-sight as much as possible.

Alcoholism and drunken violence occasioned countless editorials in the newspapers complaining about the spectacle. Health issues also caused concern. *Pulque* adulterated with contaminated water had a predictable, immediate impact, followed by long-term damage to the liver and related maladies, and reduced life expectancy to the extent that Mexicans died from alcoholism at a rate four times that of Americans. Significantly, per capita consumption of *pulque* doubled during the Porfiriato, in tandem with urbanization.

Containing the *Rateros*

Mexican Liberals viewed themselves as full participants in a rational world. Nevertheless, they clung to stereotypes and class suspicions. Rational notions conflicted with everyday observations in the streets. As a result, crime became an innate lower-class characteristic. Prison reformers responded to a mixture of stereotypes and rationality. Nevertheless, while life in the streets continued to be a matter for the police, they did not disregard the search for causal factors. Vicente Rocafuerte in 1831 wrote an essay calling for milder forms of punishment and adoption of the Philadelphia system's separation of offenders according to the seriousness of their crimes.[10] A more realistic José María Luis Mora dismissed the Philadelphia system as too expensive, and advocated isolating hardened criminals instead. Most thoughtful citizens accepted the idea of different punishments for juveniles, with the idea that they could be rehabilitated before they became full-fledged criminals. Lack of opportunity or a trade, parental abandonment, illiteracy, consensual relationships, inadequate wages, misery, and a general lack of education all would be discussed. Insufficient tax revenues made many admirable ideas impossible to implement. Consequently, the state settled for symbolic reforms and model projects that touched only a fraction of the population and did not do much to reduce criminal activity. Nevertheless, the new federal penal code elaborated by Minister of Justice and Public Instruction Antonio Martínez de Castro went into force in 1871, bringing Mexico into line with modern notions, at least on paper.

The First National [U.S.] Congress on Penitentiary and Reformatory Discipline, held in Cincinnati in 1870, with Irish prison director Sir Walter Crofton in attendance, led to the popularity of the Crofton system. Crofton developed a three-stage process that placed the burden of reform on the prisoners. Separation of inmates based on gender and age and the isolation of persons convicted of a crime from those merely detained seemed useful concepts but expensive to implement. The morality of the workshop, coupled with primary school education and religion, became the solution to what officials viewed as a lower-class behavioral problem. The government's eagerness to be viewed as modern resulted in President Juárez's appointment of U.S. penologist Enoch C. Wines to represent Mexico at the First International Penitentiary Congress in London in 1872.

When Díaz assumed office, only one national prison existed. The fortress of San Juan de Ulúa in Veracruz harbor received prisoners sentenced to long terms. States paid 25 centavos a day for their maintenance, although the odds of a prisoner surviving his term were slim. Yellow fever and inadequate funding regularly reduced the prison population. In Mexico City, Belém Prison, established in 1863, held some 2,000 inmates in 1873. Prisoners slept in long galleries with two large barrels in the open space, one for water and the other for human waste. As many noted, Belém served as a school where prisoners could brush up on their criminal skills and learn new ones. Mexico City and other urban centers struggled to approach crime from a modern perspective. Guadalajara, the capital of the state of Jalisco and the second largest city in the republic, provided the one bright spot in an otherwise dismal reality. The penitentiary provided sufficient food, vocational training, and clothing. In the countryside, in towns and villages not burdened with modern pretensions, the situation differed dramatically.

Jails in small towns dealt with individuals serving short sentences for minor offenses, such as public drunkenness and brawling, requiring an overnight stay. In villages everyone knew the troublemakers and often the perpetrators of an unacceptable act. Peer and community pressure usually deterred all but exceptional offenses. When a serious crime occurred, those arrested would be sent to the *cabeceras* (municipal seat) for disposition. In cases of notorious crimes, local authorities might administer summary justice under the pretext that the person attempted to escape. The *ley fuga* (killed in the act of escape) avoided expense and met the need for blood revenge. Jails in the *cabeceras* often lacked sufficient security, and escapes occurred with regularity, perhaps another reason for the *ley fuga*. Most prisons at any administrative level provided limited rations. In the state of Hidalgo, regional jails provided two meals a day of tortillas, beans, and chili salsa, but rarely meat. While this reflected the local diet, the quality and quantity differed.

Conflict between reformers and those living life in the streets revolved around the issue of the death penalty. Article 23 of the Constitution of 1857 indicated that as soon as a penitentiary system was established, the death penalty would be abolished. Meanwhile, the death penalty could be applied in cases of treason in foreign wars, piracy, arson, highway robbery, the killing of close family member, and premeditated murder. Those who supported abolition of the death penalty argued that many innocent people had been executed and that once executed, a person cannot be brought back to life. Most of the public remained unconvinced, and one prominent opponent claimed that the finality of the ultimate penalty made it attractive to a long-suffering public. Journalist and federal deputy Querido Moheno calculated that Mexico City, with 500,000 inhabitants, had 400 murders annually, while in France, with 39 million people, only 840 murders occurred; thus, "our lowest classes are forty time more criminal than the those in France." The reason why Mexico figured among the most criminal in the world, according to Moheno, could be traced back to the fact that the lower classes sprang from the "cannibalistic Aztecs." Demonstrating their lack of control, they killed for a glass of *pulque* or a "*taco de carnitas.*" When they entered prison they greeted their friends and enjoyed all the pleasures available, from alcohol to unnatural sex. Moheno conflated criminals and Indians into a single category, expressing the widespread view of the lowest classes as Indian. In reality, poor, uneducated migrants fell into the social category of Indians, as did potential criminals, regardless of actual racial composition.[11]

The conflict between the desire to appear modern and the rejection of elements perceived to be criminal made the notion of penal colonies attractive. Penal colonies along the lines of those established on remote islands by Britain and France enjoyed immense public support. The geographic removal of criminals from civilization seemed just and proper. Penal colonies appeared to be an ideal combination of removal, punishment, and self-redemption. In 1905 the federal government purchased the Tres Marías islands off the Pacific coast of the state of Nayarit for 150,000 pesos and began operations on Madre María, the largest of the three, in 1908. Prisoners and their families functioned in a controlled replica of a normal society, theoretically training to reenter the larger society on the mainland.

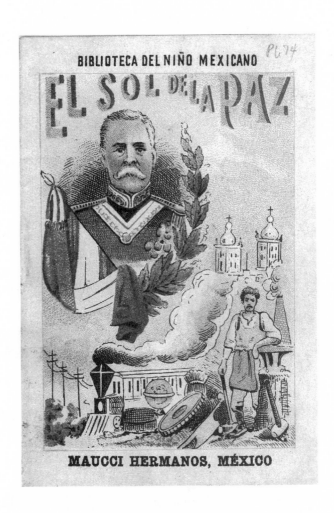

In the last decade of the nineteenth century only 2 percent of the population could be considered wealthy, while 8 percent fell into the middle class, leaving 90 percent of the population at the bottom.[1] In Mexico City the numbers in the upper and middle classes may have been double that of the national distribution, which still left 80 percent in the lower class. The poor selling to the poor or working for the better-off in the cities and towns for low wages accounted for a large part of urban economic activity. In rural areas, with the exception of administrators, the vast majority of workers were from the lower class. Slim profit margins and low wages made it almost impossible to accumulate capital. In the absence of a reasonable distribution of wealth, spending would not be sufficient to propel internal consumption and create economic momentum.

The use of credit indicated potential demand held back by economic factors. Small stores extended minor amounts of credit and in some case lent money on household goods, jewelry, and clothes pawned by individuals. *Casas de empeño*, or private pawnshops, charged more interest than the National Pawnshop (*Monte de Piedad*). The Monte established branch locations throughout the country. Individuals from the middle class on down pawned and redeemed items on a regular basis. Such limited credit could not generate much additional consumption, but it did allow many to manage their finances from week to week.

Several major factors determined the nineteenth-century class structure. The slow recovery from the destruction that accompanied the independence movement, a Liberal ideology that advocated placing resources in the hands of those deemed best able to utilize them, and legislation designed to accomplish those goals that shifted wealth (land and mines) to the top of the structure were among the leading factors stifling the efforts of the majority of workers to improve their lot.

The Oligarchy

The leveling destruction of the independence period, followed by civil strife, a foreign war, and foreign intervention, depleted old wealth. Colonial-era fortunes that survived the turmoil of independence had to navigate the economic collapse and political instability that followed. In the republic's early years, survival depended on chance and luck more than on enterprise. Economic miscalculations compounded by fatal political mistakes ruined many. The downward trajectory of Sánchez Navarro is instructive. The family's wealth owed its origins to an energetic priest in Monclova in the 1760s, with the family eventually controlling land equivalent to the size of Portugal. The family's fortunes began to decline with the Revolution of Ayutla in 1855, when they backed the Conservatives, then plunged after they supported the losing side during the French intervention. After the defeat of Maximilian, President Benito Júarez ordered General Mariano Escobedo, commander of the Army of the North, to seize land from both the Sánchez Navarro and the Zuloaga families in Coahuila. Júarez intended to use the land to reward military commanders and key supporters, and divide the rest for sale. Merchants, politicians, and businessmen added land to their diverse assets. In similar fashion, Escobedo forced the Pérez Galvez family in Nuevo León to cede much of the Soledad Hacienda land.[2]

In Chihuahua, the Terrazas family owed their initial success to the efforts of Luis Terrazas, who began his career as a butcher in the 1850s. Taking a foreign partner, the first of many, he expanded his land holdings. At a critical moment he assisted the Liberals during the difficult days of the French intervention. That key decision enabled the family to flourish during the restored republic. The Terrazas family consequently had the resources to take full advantage of the cattle boom of the 1880s. The family fortune became legendary. Some 400,000 cattle, 100,000 sheep, and 24,000 horses stocked the land of the elder Terrazas. Approximately 15 million acres, some of the best-watered land in the state of Chihuahua, was in family hands. An estimated half a million dollars' profit from cattle exports financed diversification across a number of enterprises, including banks, insurance companies, and textile factories, the state's first flour mill, a brewery, and copper mines. The Guaranty Trust and Banking Company in El Paso, Texas, functioned as a cross-border partnership between Terrazas and investors on both sides of the border. Family members and Americans made up the board of directors of a variety of companies along the border. Politically astute foreigners sought Terrazas's approval before establishing themselves in Chihuahua. Matters could be facilitated if they took family members as partners. The Terrazases' bank provided easy credit for family operations and on occasion lent money to foreigners, including Alexander Shephard's Batopilas Mining Company, as well as Colonel William Greene's Sierra Madre Land and Lumber Company.

Coming from a modest background similar to Luis Terrazas's, Evaristo Madero began his rise to wealth with a train of cargo wagons that linked San Antonio, Texas, with Parras, Saltillo, Monterrey, and San Luis Potosí. During the American Civil War, wagons carried Texas cotton into Mexico to circumvent the Union embargo. High demand and high prices generated fantastic profits. Evaristo founded the first bank in the north, the Bank of Nuevo León. Subsequently the family competed in the copper industry with giant U.S. firms owned by the Guggenheims and Rockefellers. The Maderos became one of the nation's ten wealthiest families. Evaristo's son, Francisco (the elder), became president of a business empire.

In Monterrey, another modest middle-class family began the industrialization of the city, drawing on new wealth generated by Confederate cotton smuggling. The Garza-Sadas laid the economic groundwork for the Monterrey Industrial Group, which became a dominant force in the state of Nuevo León. In central Mexico, a pattern illustrated by Leopoldo Gómez and a cousin (a fictional representation) drew entrepreneurs to a rapidly developing capital. When the Mexico City–Veracruz rail line bypassed Puebla, merchants moved to the capital. As they flourished they expanded into textile factories, tobacco mills, banks, insurance companies, land, and other profitable sectors. Collectively they established an oligarchy of achievement, giving substance to the Liberal emphasis on individual entrepreneurship.

On its surface, the lifestyle of the economically based oligarchy reflected a desire for status, but on a more fundamental level it rested on the oligarchs' ability to organize capital and recognize economic and political opportunities. Families joined their talents with foreigners willing to finance new undertakings, often in return for the political influence of the oligarchy. They developed the skills necessary to deal with international buyers and financial networks in England, France, Germany, and the United States. At times such dealings required personal contact, transportation, and the deposit of specie or currency in order to conduct business. Travel by ship from Veracruz to Havana to New Orleans, then on to New York and Europe, took considerable time away from their enterprises. Elite families as a result developed the practice of making annual trips abroad, using the railroads to reduce travel time. From Matamoros in the 1880s the traveler waited for the weekly ox cart freight operated by the reliable Sada organization to ship silver and gold bullion to the border. On the American side a Wells Fargo stage made the grueling trip to Austin, Texas; then the traveler made the four-day journey to New York by a much more comfortable train. If necessary, one could proceed to Europe by ship. A European visit might last months, and mixed business with relaxation if the family went along.

Presenting a proper modern image abroad and at home made the point that the oligarchy functioned within a cosmopolitan environment and could interact profitably with businessmen and bankers worldwide. Demonstrating their attachment to modernity required an amazingly diverse set of activities and choices. Elite consumers required imported foods, fine European wines, German cutlery, and exquisite dinnerware, along with a French cook, to make the proper impression on guests. In the interior, the arrival of a trunk filled with the latest items shipped by the Army and Navy establishment in London or ordered from a French company provided a family with the latest cosmopolitan goods.[3]

Culture arrived in the form of French books and magazines, including the Parisian *Revue des Deux Mondes*, a biweekly review of European events and letters. Spanish books and periodicals, while not as prestigious as French works, could be obtained. The domestic literary journal, *La República Literaria*, published foreign articles and poems in translation.

The well-to-do idealized Europe, indulging in French food and wines and the latest fashions from Europe; patronized the opera; and traveled abroad. Self-confident oligarchs gambled at the tables of the exclusive Jockey Club (established in 1882) and rubbed shoulders with their well-dressed peers while exhibiting their wealth, political influence, and participation in modernity.

An oligarchy of achievement did not last beyond the period of economic recovery and export expansion. The generations that followed the original entrepreneurs shifted away from risk, preferring wealth conservation and status. They combined economic and political influence to eliminate serious competition and effectively closed the door to all but a few. Consolidation of wealth at the top and risk avoidance slowed social mobility despite favorable terms of trade.

Between 1850 and the outbreak of World War I, export-led development dependent on industrial markets encountered few tariff barriers, but the oligarchy failed to take advantage of a situation that could have raised per capita incomes significantly, thereby restricting the distribution of wealth and the pace of positive change and compromising the oligarchs' political future.[4] Wealth preservation, coupled with repatriation of profits by foreigners, explains the feverish promotional activity engaged in by the president and his cabinet to lure a steady stream of

American and European capital, along with investors to assume developmental risks.

High-level national politicians represented an important subset of the oligarchy. Their friendship could be used to increase the influence of favored families at the state level, and conversely, their disfavor could have damaging consequences. President Díaz and his cabinet set the tone for the elite and tacitly indicated preferred trends. The oligarchy's desire to be modern inevitably clashed with tradition; as a result, they looked to the national elite for direction. Modernization of the role of women had long been a Liberal goal, but little had been accomplished. Díaz, well aware of the contribution of American women, set an instructive example.

Porfirio Díaz's second wife provided an ideal model of a modern woman's role. A young woman of eighteen when she married the fifty-one-year-old general in 1881, she symbolized the new generation that came of age after the collapse of France's adventure in Mexico. She met Díaz at a reception at the American legation, introduced by the wife of the American ambassador John W. Foster. Both Carmen and Porfirio enrolled in the same English class offered at the legation. Archbishop Pelagio Antonio de Labastida y Dávalos officiated at the wedding, while President Manuel González served as one of the witnesses at the civil ceremony.[5] Carmen Romero Rubio, the daughter of Manuel Romero Rubio, a delegate to the constituent convention that crafted the Constitution of 1857 and President Lerdo's secretary of foreign relations, had high social status.

Young, in the full flower of her beauty, optimistic, cosmopolitan, charming, fluent in English, socially confident, and from one of the most prominent families in the nation, Carmen had all the skills and attributes of a political wife. She gently nudged women to adopt modern attitudes and consumption practices that mirrored those exhibited by foreign women. American and European investors saw Carmen as symbolic of the emerging modern Mexico. Her political role became important to the success of the Porfiriato. In what appeared to be a tacit political bargain, Díaz, after he returned to the presidency in 1884, appointed his father-in-law to the powerful cabinet position of secretary of the interior.

In addition to the example of Carmen, foreign women provided a model that their Mexican sisters could observe rather than just read about. At least six prominent Porfirians married American women. Matías Romero, who represented President Juárez in Washington during the difficult days of the French intervention, married New Yorker Lulu Allen. He credited his success in lobbying American politicians to her intelligence and skills. Ignacio Mariscal, minister of foreign affairs, married Laura Smith of Baltimore, and the two often worked as a team. Nevertheless, not all could be convinced that foreigners should be emulated.

Clerics attacked the Women's Club, founded by Americans, as a threat to traditional family values. A newspaper expressed relief that no Mexican women had joined the Women's Club, thereby avoiding contamination. The notion of moral vulnerability as a means to justify control of working women could not be applied to the elite, so upper-class women succeeded in establishing new roles well before their lower-class sisters. An important arena of social interaction for well-to-do women emerged in 1870s. The first department store, Le Bon Marché, established in Paris in 1838, provided a model that depended on high-income customers. The first department store in Mexico City, El Puerto de Liverpool, opened its doors in 1875. Housed in an elegant building downtown, it offered a public space for modern upper-class women to shop and socialize. Another department store, the Palacio de Hierro, opened in 1891. Both stores presented a refined environment that acknowledged the status of their patrons but still functioned as a public space where strangers mingled. The clerks who served the clientele came from the middle class. What the clerks thought privately as they catered to the well-off is unknown. They may have reverted to the subservient behavior expected in a patriarchal system, but the experience would unavoidably have changed their social perceptions and perhaps life expectations.

The Uncertain Class

As part of the numerous celebrations marking the centennial of Mexico's independence in 1910, planners organized a parade that presented the republic's history from pre-Hispanic to modern times. Aztecs, Spanish soldiers, friars, and nineteenth-century heroes, in chronological order, all marched down the parade route, to the delight of the crowds. Of more significance if somewhat pedestrian in the eyes of the onlookers was a civic parade of men wearing business suits and hats, seemingly indistinguishable from their counterparts in New York, London, and Paris. Middle-class individuals engaged in the professions—medicine, law, architecture, journalism—managed medium-sized merchant businesses and distributorships, industrial workshops, and activities that required education and managerial skills. They represented the well-established middle class, though not the middle class in general. Those associated with the new economy had better opportunities. Railway construction and the operation of rail lines required a large number of people with administrative skills, including accountants, schedulers, cargo trackers, timekeepers, labor supervisors and recruiters, and others able to coordinate the activities of a large workforce dispersed across hundreds of miles. A top-down management style could not work in such a complex industry. Decentralized decision making characterized railway operations and increasingly was the model of modern business. Higher wages, management responsibility, and the respect that came with both benefited those in the middle class able to become part of the new economy. The solid middle class lived in the new district of Santa María to the northeast. In addition to the demands created by technology and modern business, most middle-class jobs would be created by the emerging state.

The lower middle class hovered between sinking down into the ranks of poor laborers and rising within their class. Government service, made possible by political stability and rising revenues, offered some opportunities. The bureaucracy expanded from a small base, increasing by 700 percent during the Porfiriato. Some 70 percent of the middle class relied on the bureaucracy for employment as inspectors, clerks, and assorted functionaries. At the bottom levels public employment provided a modest salary and some sense of security, but little respect. President Díaz harshly dismissed bureaucrats as late risers given to irregular schedules who were ever ready to shirk work, had too many children, and remained constantly in debt. More sympathetically, the Catholic newspaper *El Tiempo* called the middle class the solid social layer that encouraged "peace, tranquility, order, and work."[6] Subsequently Díaz, in a 1908 interview by the American journalist James Creelman, overcoming his irritation with the bureaucracy, called the middle class "the active, hardworking, self improving" class that Mexico depended on to "develop democracy and progress."[7]

The lower middle class lived in the older city center in close proximity to the working-class poor. Colonial mansions and palaces, some with remnants of their prior glory, such as archways with coats of arms carved in capstones, but now haphazardly subdivided into apartments overlooking a central patio occupied by washerwomen and tubs of water, provided accommodations. Lower-middle-class families rented apartments, sparsely furnished them with a few chairs, assembled a home altar, and threw straw mats on the cold stone floors. They paid for services that made life a little more pleasant. Collectors picked up excrement daily in those districts without sewers, and in the absence of running water, water carriers filled up large clay jars lining the outer corridors on a regular schedule. They could afford public bathhouses for the occasional needs of personal hygiene.

The middle class in general ate traditional Mexican food, perhaps with a little more meat and chicken, and drank pulque. Food consumed 60 percent of their salary. Moneylenders provided extra money for special occasions. For entertainment they preferred music halls and one-act plays, *tandas*, that addressed their problems, traveling circuses, and cockfights, and avidly attended the bullfights during the season, paying for the more expensive seats in the shade that separated them from the sun-baked masses. In the latter part of the 1890s, movies opened up new entertainment possibilities and, like the *tandas*, perhaps suggested new thoughts.

Modest-quality clothes and inexpensive shoes marked the middle class and separated it at a glance from the elite. In turn, the middle class struggled to find ways to distinguish itself from the bottom social levels. Middle-class families strained to afford a servant to indicate their social status. Household servants in turn constantly moved on when an opportunity to work for a better-off family arose.

Discretionary expenditures such as a family tram ride to Chapultepec, rather than a stroll in the more accessible Alameda Park, or the occasional extravagance of a carriage ride down the Paseo de la Reforma served to reassure them. The gap between the middle class and the elite appeared unbridgeable both economically and culturally, but upward social mobility such as that experienced by those associated with the new economy seemed possible. Meanwhile, for those in the lower middle class, the fear of sinking into the lower class was ever present.

The Industrial Labor Force

Industrial workers represented the future of urban labor. Machines progressively reduced the need for skilled artisans, forcing many artisans into the undifferentiated ranks of industrial workers—a socially disruptive process that would not be completed until the twentieth century.[8] Conflict between master-owners who supplied the capital and their journeymen artisan employees became more frequent as the interests of the two increasingly diverged. Craft production lasted longer in areas well away from the rail lines; however, the leveling trend could not be resisted. The mobilization of workers to counter the negative impact of modern industrial production would be difficult and only marginally effective. Searching for explanations as well as solutions, the same process as occurred earlier in rural Mexico, became evident in the city. Socialist, anarchist, and anarcho-syndicalist ideologies, sometimes mixed with utopian ideas, competed to supply both explanations and cures.

In the state of Jalisco, still in the incipient stage of modernization, a socialist organization, Las Clases Productoras (LCP), formed to bridge the gap between those who supplied capital and the workers. Francisco Bañuelos, a prominent member of the LCP, recognized the movement toward an industrial worker force, although as late as 1880 Guadalajara's industrial workers numbered only around 2,500, many of them women and children, out of some 50,000 workers.[9] The late arrival of the railroads in Guadalajara meant that labor strikes occurred less frequently than in other urban concentrations, but Bañuelos understood that what he observed in other parts of the republic, including the capital, would soon engulf the workers of Guadalajara.

Bañuelos sought to transform the emerging modern state into a republic based on those who labored and produced the wealth that all depended on. The LCP suggested a separate working-class constitution within a Mexican Republic organized by corporate groups, thus broadly anticipating the political divisions of the official party created by President Plutarco Calles in 1929.[10] The mixture of socialist and utopian ideas promulgated by the LCP reflected the generalized fears that accompanied the transformation to an industrial proletariat.

Telegraph line and trains facilitated communications with workers nationwide. The weekly newspaper *El Socialista* provided a sober assessment of the situation of industrial labor read by those concerned throughout the republic. Technology, the driver behind changes in the workplace, ironically helped to develop a consensus on what remedial action needed to be taken by workers. The Gran Círculo de Obreros de México, established in 1872, became the first labor organization to break with the mutual aid model that had characterized earlier efforts to organize.

A virtual last stand for craft workers occurred with the hatters' strike of 1875 in Mexico City. Journeymen workers employed by industrial manufacturers sought improved wages and working conditions. The strike, supported by the master hatters of small independent shops, could not reverse the trend toward impersonal sweatshops and machine-produced goods.

Several events of importance to the industrial working class took place in 1876. On January 10, General Porfirio Díaz announced his Plan of Tuxtepec, which toppled the regime of President Sebastián Lerdo. In April 17 the Gran Círculo de Obreros de México inaugurated its Congreso General de Obreros de La Republic Mexicano in Mexico City. The organizing committee sent letters to state governors requesting they nominate delegates in keeping with their claim to be an apolitical national congress. During the deliberations, the delegates took great pains to indicate their patriotism, including the obligatory homage to Benito Juárez. Nevertheless, worker political pressure on the state would be evident in a veiled warning that the sanctity of the vote made revolution unnecessary. Public accusations that agents of President Sebastián Lerdo had infiltrated the congress caused some outrage. Frequent reminders to avoid politics indicated that it simmered just below the surface. Nevertheless, the workers' congress did not break formally with Lerdo's government.

Evidence of a more confrontational attitude between the working class and the state occurred on-stage. On Sunday, April 22, while the workers' congress remained in session, Alberto G. Bianchi, a journalist and playwright, staged his play, *Los martirios del Pueblo* (The Martyrs of the People). An appreciative working-class audience gave the production a rousing reception. The plot revolved around a debt-stricken shoemaker living in misery with his wife and two young daughters who was forced into the army and subsequently killed. The play ended with his widow and children huddled together crying. The lamented shoemaker's wife cried out to "the government that you call republican—I have your victims." The play's author, jailed by President Lerdo, would be freed when General Díaz entered Mexico City in December 1876. Unbowed, Alberto Bianchi restaged his work.[11] By 1876, working-class consciousness had a recognizable form but had not settled yet on an effective political strategy to achieve its goals. Possible union models appeared as American unionists began to follow the rails into Mexico.

American unions had well-defined objectives and organizational skills. Railway men helped organize Mexican workers just across the border in Nuevo Laredo in 1887. Union organizers moved on to do the same in Monterrey and Puebla in 1889, and in Aguascalientes and Mexico City in 1900. The Brotherhood of Locomotive Engineers established a Mexican local in 1884, and were soon followed by the Order of Railway Conductors and the Brotherhood of Firemen and Engineers. American labor unions, as well as industrialists fearful of low-wage competition, sought to drive up wages south of the border.

Montana congressman (later senator) Thomas H. Carter,

responding to American mining interests, supported a tariff on lead content ores, noting that "pauper" Mexican miners worked as virtual slaves. The McKinley Tariff of 1890, however, obliged American refiners to promptly construct refineries across the border. American Federation of Labor (AFL) president Samuel Gompers correctly viewed Mexico as a low-wage magnet for industrialists fleeing union labor, a situation that required the internationalization of labor.

The Western Federation of Miners (WFM), with a more radical agenda than that of the AFL, established a cross-border presence and organized Mexican miners in Colorado, Arizona, and the copper mines of Cananea, Sonora. Causing even more concern, the radical Industrial Workers of the World (IWW) began to organize workers in the newly developed Mexican oil fields. The IWW sought to create one big union combining skilled, unskilled, and agricultural labor, a combination that frightened the Mexican oligarchy.

For all the concern over the radicalization of industrial workers, agricultural workers made up the majority of the workforce. As late as 1895, only 11.2 percent of all workers worked in industry, compared to 60.3 percent in agriculture. On the eve of the Mexican Revolution in 1910, that percentage declined to 10.9 percent as export agriculture outstripped industrialization, now employing 64.4 percent of the workforce.[12]

Rural Labor

In the nineteenth century, once recovery from the economic collapse that accompanied independence occurred, haciendas modernized and expanded their operations. They did so at the expense of small landholders and Indians. While some unoccupied arid land could be transformed by irrigation, expansion relied on the displacement of peasant owners under the laws of 1883 and 1894, as well as under the provisions of the much earlier Lerdo law, which was applied more harshly than during earlier Liberal regimes.

The size of haciendas varied depending on climate and water. In the arid north they tended to be large, with one very large hacienda in Zacatecas covering more than 2,900 square miles. In the center and south of the country, with more reliable rainfall and fertile soil, haciendas could be modest.

Two general labor systems existed, one traditional, often communal and village centered, the other capitalist and focused on external markets. Yucatán, a notable deviation, developed a capitalist structure grafted on to an archaic labor system akin to slavery. In general, the nineteenth-century hacienda functioned as a business, with an administrative staff of eight to twenty and a permanent labor force of around 250 *peones acasillados* (resident workers), supplemented by temporary labor as needed. Beside field workers, the workforce included cowboys, shepherds, carpenters, blacksmiths, and masons. Around the fringes renters (*arrendatarios*) and sharecroppers occupied plots. They constituted a reserve pool of workers and at certain times they also hired temporary workers.

Wages could be paid in money or in cash mixed with in-kind payments. Resident workers received rations in addition to a weekly salary that ranged from 3 to 6 pesos, while skilled employees received from 5 to 8 pesos. Administrators, in addition to rations, received 10 to 15 pesos per week, enough to afford a solid middle-class lifestyle. Temporary workers could expect around 3 pesos plus rations or, if they chose, extra pay in lieu of daily rations. Renters and sharecroppers could trade labor for rent or an adjustment in their share. Land to graze animals might also be negotiated in return for services.

The role of the company store, the *tienda de raya*, remains a controversial issue. Often the company store was the only option for workers, in the absence of a nearby town. The question of whether or not such stores overcharged their customers is hard to answer. The customers, often illiterate and unsophisticated, could be deceived easily. The record of the Hacienda del Señor San José del Maguey in Zacatecas indicates a more benign possibility. The hacienda's store extended credit and took money on an account that would be drawn down until the next payday, providing a safe place to keep cash. As a way to accumulate money for the purchase of animals or material for small-scale home enterprises by the wives of employees, this system made sense. Most workers carried small debt balances and regularly paid them off. Hacienda administrators appeared to be most heavily in debt, generally borrowing to purchase their own herds.[13] The Batopilas Consolidated Mining Company, on the other hand, held back some 75 percent of wages, 50 percent to pay the labor contractor for the expenses of transporting the worker to the mines and another 25 percent against purchases at the company store. Presumably, once the contractor received his money, the workers could dispose of 75 percent of their earning as they saw fit.[14] In the city of Monterrey, industrialists hoping to retain workers created company enclaves with on-premises housing, schools, medical facilities, and a company store that sold goods at subsidized prices. The use of debt peonage to hold on to workers occurred, but whether it represented a mutually satisfactory arrangement or an exploitive one is not clear. The use of police to track down a worker who fled without satisfying his debts and return him to the workplace seems to support the notion of ownership through debt, although we do not how often employers resorted to such methods, and one presumes that it depended on the amount versus the cost.

The labor situation in Yucatán, however, can only be described as cruel and exploitive. Demand for sisal for use on the McCormack reaper created heavy demand for Mexican henequen. Some thirty families, known as the divine caste, controlled the industry. Henequen plantations required hard and exhausting labor under difficult tropical conditions. The population of the Yucatán Peninsula had declined dramatically as a result of the Caste War of the 1840s when the Maya reacted to encroachment on their land by sugar planters and other extractors. As much as half the population may have perished. Consequently, labor needs could not be met. Each plantation required the labor of least 100 to 250 workers and the larger ones up to 1,000 workers. Disease and overwork rapidly decimated the workforce, requiring constant replacements. The government authorized the importation of Chinese and Korean labor; few survived. Labor contractors known as *enganchadores* (hooks) recruited laborers from the populated regions in the temperate and arid tablelands and transported them to a tropical climate with a different array of diseases. False promises, alcohol, and a cash advance delivered them into semiservitude and often death. An effective police force hunted down runaways, technically chasing a debtor. Conditions became worse as a result of a secret agreement in 1902 between International Harvester and Olegario Molina. Between them, they manipulated the price of henequen, to the disadvantage of other producer. The unit price in 1902 of 21.65 cents fell to 8.6 cents in 1911, while International Harvester became the only exporter and Molina a very rich man. Other producers sought to extract limited profits at the expense of workers. Ironically, Díaz appointed Molina minister of development (Fomento). In the aftermath of the government's war on rebellious Indians in Sonora, Molina arranged for 16,000 Yaqui prisoners to be transported to Yucatán. Even that would not be enough. Henequen plantations consumed people. Nevertheless, for all the horror that labor endured in Yucatán, conditions in the Valle Nacional appear to have been worse.

Valle Nacional, located in the far northeastern corner of the state of Oaxaca, is a deep gorge, about six miles wide at its widest point, that is boxed in by mountains. The Papaloapán river runs through it. Labor-intensive tobacco cultivation in Valle Nacional required outside workers to meet demand. Labor contractors recruited labor with the usual false promises and cash advances. When they arrived in the valley, the contractor then sold the debt, including transportation costs, to eager landholders. The worker followed his debt and had to work it off under miserable conditions. How many survived is unknown. The horrible reputation of the Valle Nacional required the *enganchadores* to conceal the destination of labor recruits until the last possible moment.

Women in the Workplace

The fundamental if idealized role of women in childrearing and family life, sanctified through religion and embedded in culture, made it difficult to accept changes that appeared to compromise traditional roles. Although the Porfirians saw themselves as modernizers, they remained caught in the same web of tradition as most nineteenth-century Mexicans, regardless of class or gender. Urban life required innumerable pragmatic adaptations that collectively altered gender roles but appeared to others to be unacceptable and willful violations of social norms. Technology and urbanization blurred, but not entirely, traditional notions of suitable employment for women. The 1895 census in Mexico City indicated that some 82,000 women made up 33 percent of the workforce. Of that number, 26 percent worked in the commercial sector, mainly as street vendors. Most labored as domestic workers, laundresses, wet-nurses, cooks, or some aspect of micromarketing. Indian women from nearby villages sold produce, pots, and hand-made cotton items. A vocational school for women, established in 1887, offered training in the use of the new Singer sewing machine, as well as instruction in other tasks considered suitable for women.

For new migrants, employment in a private household offered a place to stay, a minimal salary, and long hours at the pleasure of their employers. An established domestic servant might command a slightly better salary and live away from the work site. An estimated 30 percent of women in Mexico City worked as domestics.[15] The number of household servants employed indicated the status level of the employer. Even lower-middle-class individuals and families struggled to employ a servant. Domestic servants conferred status, but did enjoy respect.

The 1879 *Reglamento de criados* (domestic servant regulations) reflected the public's social perception of domestics. The law required that an individual pay 25 centavos for an identity booklet listing his or her qualifications and allowed employers to enter comments indicating their level of satisfaction with the employee's performance. Modified regulations reissued in 1885, justified on the basis of frequent robberies by household servants, required a photograph and threatened fines or confinement in a correctional institution if they let anyone else use their identity book.[16]

Emperor Maximilian, following the example of many European countries, legalized female prostitution, with the rationale that not to do so would lead to even worse perversions. Nevertheless, the existence of prostitution in nineteenth-century cities conflicted with the notion of the city as a positive civilizing force. Its existence appeared to be one of many affronts that the better-off had to endure at the hands of the lower classes. Consequently, prostitution had to be controlled and dealt with in a scientific manner that sanitized it as much as possible.

An 1889 regulation set up what passed for the scientific classification of prostitutes, running from first class to fourth class based on age and presumed desirability. Practitioners also fell into categories depending on where they conducted business, with most first-class prostitutes practicing in bordellos.[17] Unlicensed streetwalkers theoretically risked arrest. In reality, the marginal existence of lower-class rural migrants made prostitution one of many undesirable options. Prostitution, legal, suspected, or potential, threw a pall over the respectability of all urban lower-class women.

Women's alleged moral vulnerability had an institutional reflection in the establishment of El Asilo de Infancia y Regeneracion de la Mujer (Children's Refuge and Women's [moral] Regeneration Asylum) and La Casa Amiga, open to those that had fallen into vice, where they could live, learn a trade, and become "honest" women. Urban centers multiplied the number of occasions that all the classes came in close visual and physical contact. Seclusion by class broke down in nineteenth-century cities as size and complexity increased; thus the upper and middle classes became increasingly insistent that the lower classes be made to conform to what they defined as acceptable norms. The perceived need to control the public conduct of women in the face of change increased as gender roles became uncertain. Moral assumptions in a time of modernization reflected the contradictions between ideal behavior and necessary adaptations forced by circumstances. In Mexico's patriarchal culture, women breaking with tradition, willfully or out of necessity, caused concern. Rural migrants from small villages moved into a dramatically different social context, making both women and men more vulnerable.

One of the fundamental arenas of interclass contact resulted from the need to service massive numbers of urban consumers. New market buildings constructed to provide protection from the elements, with proper ventilation, better sanitation, and supervision by municipal authorities, created a public space. Women of different social levels came in close physical contact as consumers and vendors. An extended field of class contact, filled with women street vendors, surrounded the market buildings, much to the displeasure of the authorities. Nevertheless, women vendors pressed municipal authorities to allow them to continue to sell in the streets in close proximity to centralized markets. Such demands conflicted with approved modernity, but municipal official hesitated to remove them, indicating a reluctant acceptance of the circulation of lower-class women vendors.

Nevertheless, women street vendors in constant contact with the public came under suspicion because of what many believed to be the thin line between selling items and selling their bodies. Street vendors rejected the centrality of morality and pointed out that they were helping to support their families and in many cases were the sole support of their children. They understood that they functioned within a patriarchic society but did not hesitate to challenge it. Moreover, they appealed to their middle- and upper-class sisters, forcing them to confront the presumption of women's moral vulnerability in their lives at a time when new public spaces brought them all into broader contact with general society. The challenge of different spaces extended to factory labor, which, though not public in the same way as a central market, nevertheless brought strangers together.

Factory work in the cigarette, textile, and clothing industries required multiple adjustments with almost no prior experience to draw upon. A factory supervisor, an unrelated male, had to be dealt with differently. Factory work detached women from their families for an extended period during the workweek and modified gender relations within the family.

In the face of employer and work demands, women reacted not as a part of a multigendered village but as a group based on a single gender and female-specific occupations. Attempts to raise production beyond a certain level in factories employing female labor occasioned protests and letters to newspapers and government officials. Although women workers enjoyed few outright successes, their protests contributed to raising the social consciousness of society that women struggled also with the new demands of industrial modernization. They at least established women's right to protest to the political authorities as citizens.[18]

Women's mutual aid societies often approached important

political figures to be their honorary patrons, including Carmen Romero Rubio de Díaz, the president's wife. While a ceremonial ritual, it suggested that political figures had a constituency that crossed class and gender lines. As reported in the newspapers, a symbolic event organized by a group of women workers on the occasion of President Díaz's birthday and attended in person by the president delivered a subtle but important message. The women requested that the president step into a mock cage, while a worker delivered a congratulatory speech that portrayed the "good-humored" Díaz as the "prisoner" of the people.[19] With the exception of midwives, women workers had little occupational status.

Middle-class women entered the work-force out of necessity, usually when their husbands died. They might manage a small store or property directly or through an agent, and lived off rents. Teaching offered a respectable position but a modest income. The new industrial economy offered opportunities acceptable to middle-class women. The 1895 census indicted that the percentage of middle-class positions available to women increased by 46 percent, at a faster clip than for males (27 percent), a trend that continued into the next century as administrative tasks required by modern businesses proliferated. Women made up a significant number of telegraph operators. Only a few women entered the professions.[20]

Nutritional Well-Being and Mortality

Of all the elements necessary for social and political stability, adequate food is a basic one. A full stomach and reasonable social satisfaction are linked psychologically and in the end politically. In

Porfirian Mexico, the degree of well-being went from negative at the bottom, perhaps neutral for the industrial working class, cautiously mixed for the lower middle class, and at a comfortable level for the solid middle class. At the privileged level of the oligarchy, nutritional well-being may be taken for granted. The traditional Mexican diet, inherited from pre-Hispanic civilizations, survived, with significant modifications as one moved up the class structure.

At a basic level, what a person eats, and how much, is determined by income, class, and culture. Supply and demand set prices, but wages determine the quality and quantity of food consumed. Traditional *milpa* (microscale) agriculture production in which a rural family grew and consumed corn and beans and sent a small surplus, if any, to the local market kept staple prices low. That changed in the 1880s with the expansion of the railways. Railways created a national market, draining supplies of food from previously isolated rural areas into urban markets. Moreover, food crops gave way to more profitable agricultural exports such as cotton, coffee, and other items that offered a greater return on capital. In 1906 a metric ton of corn in the port city of Veracruz cost 53 pesos, an increase of 200 percent from the price in 1877. Nevertheless, corn could not compete with returns of 400 percent for coffee and 375 percent for cotton and other profitable export crops. An estimate 60 million hectares planted in corn met a minimal demand of 50 million, a thin surplus easily thrown into a deficit by weather and wastage.

Severe food scarcities occurred in 1884, 1892, 1896, 1900, 1904, 1909, and 1910. Starting in the 1890s, the government imported corn from the United States, but not in sufficient quantities. The distribution of imported staples tended to be focused in urban centers and along rail lines, leaving rural villages and towns to fend for themselves. In 1905 the government sold food at subsidized prices in regions of extreme need, and four years later opened fifty subsidized outlets in Mexico City.[21] Subsidized prices remained physically out of reach of rural inhabitants. In Sinaloa, desperate peasants ate mescal roots to survive, and in Durango, 4,000 people attempted to storm warehouses and break into stores. Flophouses in Mexico City reported that some of their customers died overnight, and many appeared too weak to stagger back into the street. The government and private charities maintained dormitories, bathhouses, laundries, and presumably soup kitchens, which in 1895 served 80,000 on a short-term basis.[22]

Urban Mexico had sufficient food, but at prices that restricted consumption. Lowering the quality of food to drive the price down sacrificed nutritional value and encouraged the unscrupulous to invent all sort of ways to meet demand at affordable prices. After Francisco Madero assumed the presidency in 1911, he authorized the Universal Corn Manufacturing Company to add pulverized corn cobs in amounts up to 25 percent of the content of tortillas. The decree permitted bread to be adulterated also.[23] Food sold to the lower classes often contained dangerous additives. Biscuits baked with lead chromate instead of eggs gave the illusion of nutritional density. Milk adulterated with polluted water and thickened with discarded animal brains contained little nutritional value and posed health dangers.

Meat consumption, an important indicator of nutritional well-being, varied by class. The lower classes reserved meat for special occasions and made do with artfully favored animal parts shunned by the more selective. Chito, goat organs fried in fat, met needs for affordable meat, as did other items of doubtful nutritional value.[24] High meat prices reflected the reality that the cattle industry utilized land in the north, far from urban markets in the south. Cattle cars, common in the United States, came into use slowly. In addition, driving cattle across the border, where a better price could be obtained and the difficulties of distribution avoided, also impacted supply. Finally, an inadequate number of slaughterhouses limited the availability of dressed meat.

A public health official estimated that a family of three living in Mexico City required a daily income of two pesos a day to have a reasonable diet, but earnings often did not reach that threshold. Alfredo J. Pani, a public health pioneer, collected a number of budgets of weekly expenditures by manual laborers in Mexico City earning 75 centavos a day. At the end of the week the workers had either a slim surplus or an equally small deficit. Wages could barely support one individual. An estimated 2 to 2.5 times the prevailing wage would be necessary to support a family of four. Those with skills in demand might at best earn 1.5 times the prevailing wage, still not enough to support a family.[25] Any emergency threw the worker and the family into the hands of moneylenders or pawnshops, leaving food as one of the few items they could squeeze to repay debts.

Ensuring the safety of food relied on smell and luck, rather than on enforcement of regulations. An 1871, reorganization of the Consejo Superior de Salubridad (Board of Health) appeared necessary to meet modern standards. Originally established by Santa Anna in 1841 and charged with supervision of markets and slaughterhouses, the agency took on added responsibilities for public health, such as vaccinations and examinations of licensed prostitutes. An understaffed organization like so many elements of the proto-state, it served more as an official recognition of problems rather than providing functional solutions.

Malnutrition, chronic hunger, and polluted water, coupled with unsanitary urban housing, would be reflected in mortality rates in Mexico City. A significant percentage of the population lived in run-down buildings subdivided into *conventillos*, so named for the tiny chambers occupied by solitary nuns, but now an equivalent space crammed with too many people providing hosts for parasites, lice, fleas, and a variety of worms. Rats and their vermin found sustenance amid the squalor. Efforts to keep the older sections of the city reasonably clean failed in the absence of effective municipal hygiene. Under such conditions, contagious diseases could not be contained. Infant mortality carried away half the children before they reached their first birthday. The annual mortality of children under five years exceeded 8,000 in Mexico City. Among all residents in the capital, tuberculosis, typhoid, dysentery, skin diseases, pneumonia, bronchitis, typhus, and an assortment of other preventable diseases resulted in 11,500 deaths annually. Mexicans had a life expectancy of twenty-four years.[26]

Escaping into an Imaginary World

In 1896 Mexico entered the new imaginary world of film. Those who had little chance of visiting Europe or the United States, or of comparing their life with others', suddenly found that the world came to them. Initially, the audience's sense of wonder focused on the technology. The arrival of the French Lumiere projector made possible the presentation of brief, one-minute films recording everyday events, such as the arrival of a train, a Spanish regiment about to embark to combat the insurrection in Cuba, a view of Berlin or of Bengal tigers in the Paris zoo. Journalist Luis Urbina, who attended the showings at the Cinematógrafo Lumiere, reported perceptively that fantasy would triumph over science. In 1897 a young engineering student, Salvador Toscano Barragán, ordered a projector and camera and created films that offered make-believe scenarios. Enrique Rosas began filming Mexican events in 1905, as well as showing foreign productions, including the *Great Train Robbery* (1903). In Guadalajara, Jorge Stahl opened the Cine Verde with seating for 400 and a player piano to provide sound. The cigarette company El Buen Tono opened a movie salon, collecting a number of empty packets as admission. By 1907 sixteen movie salons were entertaining audiences in Mexico City alone. At least two rental companies supplied equipment to individuals who traveled the country filming local interest events. The first major Mexican scripted film, *El Grito de Dolores* (1908), recreating Father Hidalgo's revolt, opened to mixed reviews. In at least one case, a reviewer pointed out that a scene of the mob responding meekly to the directions of a policeman seemed improbable, although certainly a Porfirian ideal.

More intriguing fare arrived with the screening of a French serial, *Los rateros de Paris* (Thieves of Paris) in 1906. Muted social issues embedded in *The Great Train Robbery* and *Los rateros de Paris*, although presented as disapproved behavior and in the context of different countries, suggested comparisons with everyday life in Mexico. In 1897 a newspaper suggested that criminals had become more skilful and sophisticated as a result of copying the techniques suggested in movies. In 1914 a safecracking gang admitted to imitating the procedures presented in the French-produced movie episodes of *Nick Carter: The King of Detectives* (1908, 1909). The minister of the interior later insisted that the movie *Los misterios de Nueva York* (ca. 1914) taught Mexican criminals how to pull off high-class robberies. While it is impossible to calculate the influence of films on Porfirian audiences, the advent of film marked a new imaginary era. As the journalist and critic Luis Urbina noted in 1906, the masses went to the cinema for an escapist fantasy that alleviated the "sadness of [their] existence" when they returned to their "bare and melancholy abode."[27]

7

Relations with the United States got off to a rocky start with Porfirio Díaz's seizure of power in 1876. The prolonged process of obtaining American diplomatic recognition soured relations, although Washington insisted that it acted in a friendly fashion. Throughout the ordeal an angry Díaz publicly remained polite, but firm. President Díaz understood the utility of reasoned, polite discussion, even if the other side seemed intent on acrimonious relations. Soft diplomacy characterized the Porfiriato's foreign relations, although it required incredible restraint.

President Díaz dispatched Manuel María de Zamacona to Washington during the impasse over recognition. His mission, to explain the difficult situation along the border and pressure the U.S. State Department to recommend establishing formal relations, required cultivating public opinion. Zamacona, a cultured and intelligent man, understood that public opinion in the United States could be used to restrain a heavy-handed American government. He had in mind a two-pronged public relations offensive. Lectures and presentations to clubs, industrial associations, chambers of commerce, religious groups, newspaper editors, and other citizen groups constituted the public campaign. Efforts to win over politicians required informal contacts designed to establish friendships and mutual respect. An elegant and refined embassy to entertain in a suitable fashion seemed a basic requirement. A supply of exquisite Mexican handicrafts provided select guests with tokens of appreciation. Zamacona soon became a popular personality among politicians and newspapermen, even testifying before a House committee at the invitation of Representative Henry B. Banning of Ohio.[1] While other factors played a role in resolving issues, soft diplomacy moved things along.

President Díaz's long-range strategy concentrated on enticing foreign investors to finance the country's development, assume the risks, and, if they succeeded, be compensated with a high rate of return on capital. Foreigners could count on such investor-friendly treatment that annexation by the United States, or even heavy-handed coercion, would not be necessary. The president cultivated entrepreneurs and capitalists over fine food and drink at Delmonico in New York, at dinner parties, and at Chapultepec Castle, his official residence. His aura of a simple, straightforward soldier made it possible to lay aside presidential formalities. Camaraderie drew important capitalists into lifelong friendships. The president spent much of his time enticing individuals with sufficient capital to invest in modernization. Mexico could offer concessions and on occasion subsidies, though not much immediate material help. Just as important, however, Díaz offered friendship and an open door to the presidency.

Díaz's Resident American Constituency

Mexico's open investment climate attracted wealthy foreigners as well as the enterprising. Many of them had ideas but limited money. They used presumed or real expertise and charm to raise the funding they needed to buy land and other resources. Americans began buying land and mines in the 1880s and continued to do so until the outbreak of the revolution. Mexican Liberals had long dreamed of attracting immigrants to its northern territories. The underpopulated north, plagued by marauders and Indian raiders through the 1870s, had underutilized land and resources. Mexican officials had in mind European immigrants, physically separated from their former mother country by the Atlantic Ocean, not Americans. Europeans could be Mexicanized, while Americans, given the territorial proximity of the United States, might Americanize Mexicans. The government's acceptance of American land purchases could be rationalized as a way to facilitate the introduction of technology, but American purchasers could not be considered colonists.

Only Mormon settlers came close to the immigrant ideal—energetic, orderly, and hard-working, and, perhaps equally important, somewhat alienated from the U.S. government over the issue of multiple wives.[2] As a result of heavy-handed efforts to stamp out polygamy beginning in 1862, Mexico became an attractive refuge. After scouting out the possibilities in 1876–77, Mormons purchased land in Casas Grandes, Chihuahua, from the state government in 1885. The first two colonies, diplomatically named Colonia Porfirio Díaz and Colonia Benito Juárez, soon had red brick houses, schools, and irrigated farms. Eventually nine colonias, six in Chihuahua and three in Sonora, prospered in varying degrees.

At Mexico City's first International Exposition of Industries and Fine Arts in 1896, Mormon settlers exhibited canned fruit and vegetables, needlework, and photographs of their colonias; an impressed President Díaz dispatched an official to examine their remarkable progress. Unfortunately, the experiment ended badly, as the colonists fled with the outbreak of revolutionary violence.

Thomas Romney, a thoughtful colonist and historian, explained the ultimate failure of the colonies as the result of fundamental differences in habits and ideals between the Mormon settlers and the surrounding Mexican community.[3]

Investors, mining and railway administrators, a sprinkling of bankers, and commodity agents, rather than settlers, made up most of the American community in Mexico. Thomas Brantiff, among the most influential members of the community, began his rise to wealth in the gold fields of California in 1849. Unlike Collis Huntington, who became a successful merchant in the gold fields before becoming a railway man, Braniff's good fortune began when he met English railway engineer Henry Meiggs. Meiggs's company was involved in constructing railways in Peru and Chile and introduced Brantiff to the profits and risks of Latin American development. After learning the ropes in South America, he arrived in Mexico to work on the Veracruz–Mexico City railway project, then stayed on as its manager. He bought up companies along the rail line, including a textile factory in Orizaba that he later exchanged for stock in a French textile company, eventually becoming the major stockholder. Brantiff had a controlling interest in fifteen mining operations, three railways, several public utilities, and other enterprises. His predictably profitable touch earned him the informal title of "the Midas of Mexico." Brantiff functioned at the center of the domestic economy. A close friend of the president, he played an active role in Díaz's reelection campaigns. His children became Mexicans culturally and married into the Porfirian elite. A founding member of the Jockey Club and the American Club, Brantiff moved in elite circles of Mexican society, as well as in the American community. At his death in 1905 he left what at the time constituted a fortune of $4 million.[4]

Other principal members of the community included Major Robert B. Gorsuch, who first went to Mexico in 1856. Subsequently he served the Confederacy, then found employment with Emperor Maximilian and later with President Juárez on railway projects. He represented the railway entrepreneur Collis Huntington in Mexico. Along the way he became a wealthy real estate developer. Another influential member of the American community, General John B. Frisbie, served in the U.S.-Mexican War as a captain in command of a unit of a volunteer regiment sent to California. He married the fifteen-year-old daughter of Mexican general Mariano Vallejo and went into business with his father-in-law. He rejoined the army at the start of the Civil War and rose to the rank of general in the Union Army. After the war he moved to Mexico City, where he served Collis Huntington in different capacities. Major Gorsuch and General Frisbie facilitated contact between Díaz and investors while providing advice and encouragement. Frisbie supported Díaz unreservedly and became an outspoken critic of the U.S. State Department. John S. McCaughan, hired to manage Collis Huntington's Iron Mountain Company in Durango, eventually went into business on his own. He bought troubled mines, introduced new technology, and made a handsome profit. His land speculation began with the acquisition of 13,000 acres in southeastern Durango for $8,700. He made a specialty of buying low and selling to Americans at a premium. In similar manner, William V. Bachus bought land and planted rubber trees, as well dealt in real estate until his trees matured. He agreed to sell his entire rubber operation to a British investment group for £250,000 (U.S. $500,000), but before the deal could be closed the revolution broke out.[5]

Collis Huntington also had direct personal contact with President Díaz. His interest in Mexico had been encouraged by then foreign minister Matías Romero, who cultivated a circle of bankers and entrepreneurs. Subsequently he developed a close bond with Díaz. The allegedly ruthless Huntington refused the president's offer of a subsidy to construct the 880 miles of the Mexican International Railway, designed to cut 400 miles off the route to Mexico City, expressing concern the subsidies might hinder the pace of Mexico's progress.

One of Porfirio Díaz's favorite Americans seemed an odd choice, but they shared a mutual attraction, perhaps based on Arthur Stilwell's riveting personality and elegance. Stilwell, a former salesman turned railway tycoon, dreamed of building a rail line from Kansas City, across Oklahoma and Texas, into Chihuahua and Sinaloa, to the Pacific port of Topolobampo, to connect the American heartland with Asia. He traveled in his own exquisitely furnished Pullman railcar complete with an organ. On occasion he enticed guests to sing Christian Science hymns along with him. The dream ended in bankruptcy, but his "express route to the Orient" had intriguing possibilities.[6]

The second generation of American residents had less flair than the early tycoons. Largely professionals, managers, and merchants, along with the occasional confidence man, they mirrored the declining importance of the resident American community in Mexico as rail travel and modern communications increasingly interconnected the two nations. Access to the president became more of a ritual exercise, with the American ambassador herding visitors in for an audience. Nevertheless, they continued to be useful to furthering Díaz's financial and diplomatic goals. By then the American community had become a storehouse of flattering but useful myths.

Comparisons of Mexico before Díaz relied on faulty memories and naiveté. Stories circulated, such as one about the American who offered a governor a $5,000 bribe with the promise of complete secrecy. The governor allegedly responded, "Give me $10,000 and you can tell the world."[7] Díaz reputedly eliminated corruption and established an unshakable order, but in reality he used corruption as a political tool. The unshakable Porfirian order as it existed in the American community's mind was an imaginary construct, but one that proved useful.

The American community could be mobilized to instruct potential investors, advise the American ambassador, and convince visiting journalists that Mexico valued its ties with the United States. American residents in the capital provided a quasi-binational lobby assiduously patronized by a genial President Díaz and his charming wife Carmen. They willingly served Díaz's diplomatic objectives and helped defuse the sometimes unwarranted hostility of Washington. The president in turn developed friendships with many in the community, secure in the notion that they did not pose a political challenge.[8]

Border Diplomacy

Díaz dealt with a dangerous situation on the northern border. The Treaty of Guadalupe Hidalgo that ended the U.S.-Mexican War in 1848 created a new, thinly populated boundary whose inhabitants on both sides had little respect for the law. The free zone on the Mexican side, in Washington's view, facilitated smuggling.[9] Weak enforcement along the border encouraged raiders and bandits to plunder from cross-border sanctuaries just out of reach of the authorities. Unauthorized incursions by both Mexican and American soldiers occurred frequently, risking the possibility of an armed clash.

The American representative John W. Foster realized that part of the problem stemmed from the lack of a significant Mexican military presence on the border. Moreover, the absence of a high-ranking Mexican commander risked the possibility that a minor incident could balloon into a major confrontation. President Díaz took Foster's advice and appointed General Gerónimo Treviño commander of Mexican forces on the border. Unfortunately, his entire command consisted of 400 soldiers.[10] Washington failed to understand that Díaz could not afford to maintain a large military force on the border. An empty treasury struggled to maintain a semblance of fiscal solvency.

The United States demanded a formal agreement permitting both governments to cross the border chasing raiders and smugglers. To make such a concession to the United States would have been fatal to Díaz's efforts to consolidate power. Moreover, given the disparity in troop strength, most of the border crossings would have been into Mexican territory. In June 1887 a frustrated United States ordered Brigadier General Edward O. C. Ord, commander of the Military District of Texas headquartered in San Antonio, to enter Mexican territory in pursuit of marauders and to recover stolen property. This unilateral act by Washington caused consternation in Mexico. Loose talk in Texas about the desirability of invading or buying Mexico's northern tier of states in order to control Indian raiders added to the tension, although Washington did not encourage such talk. Ord's border-crossing authorization continued in force for more than three years, until U.S. secretary of war Alexander Ramsey revoked the instructions on February 25, 1880. In an effort to improve relations and demonstrate respect, General Ord ordered that General Servando Canales, governor of the border state of Tamaulipas and an early supporter of Díaz, be received with full military honors on his formal visit to Ord's headquarters in San Antonio, Texas. Although cross-border raiding continued, both parties acted with restraint. Eventually a reasonably consolidated administration negotiated a mutually acceptable border-crossing agreement in 1882.

As border raiding died down, a new threat emerged. The border region in Texas nurtured anti-Díaz revolutionaries. Most disgruntled opponents could be ignored; however, as it became evident that the oligarchy absorbed the lion's share of development, hostility grew. In Rio Grande City, Texas, Catarino Garza and Francisco Ruiz Sandoval recruited men, and on Mexican independence day in 1891 they issued a Plan Revolucionario that demanded a new constitution that included land reform, local political autonomy, and no presidential reelection.[11] The *San Antonio Express* referred to Garza's men as a constitutional army, and the *New Orleans Picayune* published an article laying out the regime's vulnerabilities. Díaz, always worried about bad publicity scaring off investors, pressured Washington to contain unruly border residents and do its best to discourage American newspapers from indulging in alarmist reporting. Díaz's fears of border plotting eventually proved prophetic.

A Reluctant Partnership: Mexico as a Regional Power

Díaz's success in creating the illusion of Mexico's permanent stability and its impressive progress propelled the country into regional power diplomacy. Washington's blatant detachment of Panama from Colombia and the creation of a subservient republic in 1903 disturbed Díaz. Although Mexico recognized the Republic of Panama, it considered the possibility that Washington had a new territorial template in mind. Consequently, General Bernardo Reyes, considered the most competent Porfirian general, became minister of war, and the treasury agreed to finance the reorganization and modernization of the army along Prussian lines. It soon became evident that the budget could not carry the expense of large-scale military modernization. As a stopgap measure, the government organized a military reserve composed of weekend soldiers, recruiting, among thousands of others, Francisco Madero, Venustiano Carranza, and Jesús Flores Magón—all of whom later played high-profile roles in opposing Díaz.[12] A newspaper raised money for the purchase of a pocket battleship, and the government purchased two gunboats. To outside observers it appeared to be an indication that Mexico intended to assume a more aggressive geopolitical role in the hemisphere.

A misreading of events in Mexico strengthened American secretary of state Elihu Root's argument in favor of multinational intervention in Central America. Root consequently urged Theodore Roosevelt to create regional blocs to share the task of ensuring stability.[13] President Roosevelt, never one to think small, suggested that Mexico incorporate Central America all the way to the border of American-controlled Panama. Washington envisioned two subspheres of influence, one centered on Mexico in the north and another, South American sphere managed by Brazil. Washington would advise both, and if necessary dispatch the American Navy to deal with unexpected situations.[14] Brazil responded positively but Mexico declined, though not absolutely.

Mexico elaborated what would be called the Díaz Doctrine, which revolved around the idea of multilateral application of the Monroe Doctrine as decided by the American republics in concert. Behind Díaz's attempt to restrain Roosevelt's interventionist tendencies lay the objective of pressuring the United States to enforce the neutrality laws against Mexican revolutionaries plotting to overthrow his regime from their sanctuary in the United States. In particular, the Partido Liberal Mexicano (PLM), the Mexican Liberal Party, appeared to threaten Mexican stability and the Díaz government. Díaz requested that Ricardo Flores Magón and his close associates be extradited. The U.S. attorney general refused on the grounds that a federal court had ruled that the PLM leaders had not committed a criminal offense. Nevertheless, Díaz managed to focus the attention of American authorities on the group. When the Cananea Copper Company strike broke out on June 2, 1906, the government claimed that the PLM had played a leading role. Díaz's apprehension turned out to be well placed, although the threat would not be immediate. Nevertheless, the United States, at the request of the American ambassador, deployed troops on the border at Eagle Pass to block PLM supporters. The Cananea strike, put down by the *rurales* and volunteers from Arizona, embarrassed a worried Díaz and resulted in investors suspending their financial commitments until they could be assured that the situation had been brought under control. Under the circumstances, Díaz dared not offend Washington, but at the same time he did not want to be maneuvered into acting as a subordinate agent of Teddy Roosevelt's hemispheric schemes.

Despite some disagreements, Mexico and the United States shared similar objectives, if for different reasons. Roosevelt understood that constant violence in Central America risked spilling over into British Honduras (Belize) and might prompt Britain to dispatch troops to punish the offending nation. Such a possibility might compromise the Monroe Doctrine and complicate U.S. control over the projected canal. Mexico, for its part, had interests in Guatemala that could be negatively affected if the British intervened. Both Díaz and Roosevelt did not want European involvement in hemisphere affairs. On the other hand, unilateral American intervention would geopolitically bracket Mexico between two potentially troublesome borders and diminish its influence in Central America.

Consequently, when the U.S. State Department invited Mexico to join with the United States in pressing the warring parties in Central America to settle their differences, Díaz agreed to participate. Subsequently, Mexico and the United States jointly offered their services to end the fighting between Guatemala, Honduras, and El Salvador. The Marblehead Truce (1906), named after the American destroyer that hosted the warring parties, followed by a peace conference in San José, Costa Rica, initially calmed the situation. Unfortunately, conflict between Honduras and Nicaragua threatened to start yet another cycle of violence even before the 1907 International Central American Conference in Washington, jointly sponsored by the United States and Mexico, took place.

Roosevelt urged Mexico to control Central America and privately suggested Mexican military intervention. Díaz, when asked his reaction to an intervention by the United States in Central America, indicated he would not disapprove, a response just short of support. The Washington conference resulted in an agreement to be supervised by Mexico and the United States, but without provisions for enforcement. The warring republics agreed to stop harboring the hostile opponents of other republics. Díaz believed that such a principle set a precedent that could be applied to the PLM in the United States.

In 1907 the future canal's security motivated the United States to request the permanent lease of a naval base in Magdalena Bay on Baja California's Pacific coast. The request followed the schema of former secretary of state James G. Blaine (March 1881–December 1881 and March 1889–June 4, 1892) as part of the proposed canal project. Blaine envisioned transforming the Caribbean Sea into an American lake, but with an outlet through a canal (its location not yet determined) into the Pacific. The Spanish-American War in 1898 and the Treaty of Paris in 1902 that ended it advanced that goal. Acquisition of the Danish Virgin Islands would eliminate any threat to the U.S. Navy's control of the Caribbean, a strategic goal achieved in 1917 with the purchase of the Virgin Islands. In the Pacific, Blaine envisioned a defensive arc of naval bases from Puget Sound to the U.S.-occupied Hawaiian islands (1898) and American Samoa (1899), anchored in the south by a base at Chimbote, Peru. The projected canal lay at the center.

The creation of Panama in 1903, followed by the purchase of the remaining assets of the failed French canal effort and the resumption of construction, indicated a completion date within a decade or so.[15] Defense of the soon to be functioning canal became a priority. Steps to preempt other powers from establishing a naval presence within the defensive arc lay behind the United States' request to lease Magdalena Bay. Rather than refuse Washington outright, Díaz cannily offered a three-year lease, effectively derailing the notion. Subsequently the Japanese proposed buying Magdalena Bay in 1912, ahead of the opening of the Panama Canal in 1914.

In the diplomatic contest with the United States, the Porfirians demonstrated patience and skill but failed to appreciate fully the level of insecurity of the United States as it sought to establish itself as an imperial power. Nevertheless, typical of the careful diplomacy that characterized the Porfirian regime, Díaz in a 1908 interview by American journalist James Creelman for the popular *Pearson's Magazine* praised Roosevelt during the national debate in the United States over a third term. Careful to suggest that only the American people and Roosevelt could decide, he nevertheless declared Teddy Roosevelt to be "a strong, pure man, a patriot who understands his country and loves it well."[16]

Disagreement over Nicaragua and the ambitions of that country's president, José Santos Zelaya López, pushed Washington and Mexico City farther apart. American intervention in Nicaragua became inevitable in early 1910 as rebel forces began to converge on Bluefield. Washington assumed control of customs to collect tariffs and pay debts, and especially to avoid compromising the security of the canal project. Díaz had the difficult task of appearing to be somewhat cooperative while being mildly obstructionist.

A Fine Balance

As Mexico settled into relatively peaceful politics and economic development, foreign diplomats took note. In the 1890s the nation in general basked in unfamiliar praise. Díaz the miracle worker seemed to have reversed Mexico's decline into anarchy by force of personality alone. The international perception that Mexico had found the key to political stability became a mantra, both in the Mexican capital and abroad. Foreign observers did not comprehend the fragility of the regime or the intricate balancing of interests required to make the country function.

Throughout most of the nineteenth century the foreign debt problem had derailed both progress and political stability. Díaz dealt with a bankrupt government in 1876 and understood the dangers of foreign debt. The president sought to strengthen the federal government and concentrate as much resources as possible in Mexico City.

Restructuring of old debts and dealing with currency backed by silver in an era of falling silver prices required a high level of financial competency. Matías Romero began the process of rationalizing the international debt, although the final step fell to Manuel Dublán. Dublán became secretary of the treasury in Díaz's 1884 term and, over a four-year period, restructured the entire foreign debt. The Dublán Convention of 1888 represented a triumph in the history of Mexico's debt management. Bonds valued at £10,500,000, bearing 6 percent interest, were sold to consolidate old debts. Acceptance of the new bonds made it possible to borrow new money at reasonable rates. Although the debt would be refinanced in 1899 and again in 1911, an orderly process reassured bond holders. The government believed with some justification that a nation with an expanding export economy could carry an ever-larger debt, although the rate of increase in exports declined after 1899. To maintain confidence internationally, a balanced budget year after year became a political necessity. Such fiscal inflexibility did not allow for the unexpected, nor did it provide for pressing social needs.

In addition, as power shifted to the center, a national camarilla with political interests that differed from those of provincial camarillas split the elite into two distinct groups. An increasingly powerful federal government allowed Díaz to make decisions with insufficient input from state camarillas. The federal system became dysfunctional as increasing centralization overrode federalism. In the absence of political parties that reached across the republic, it became difficult to coordinate state and national policy objectives and to gauge the extent of political support outside the capital.

8

After returning to the presidency in 1884, Porfirio Díaz remained in office through the election of 1910. The decades of the 1880s and 1890s changed the country but not the regime's basic governing premise. Díaz failed to adjust to the changes his own administration had brought about. His inability to do what the nation needed robbed him of credit for generating the momentum that propelled modernization. The problem came down to two crucial areas, political reform and economics.

Within a decade of Díaz's seizure of the presidency, the country seemed stabilized. Thoughtful but friendly critics suggested how to consolidate the gains. Some of the most useful suggestions came from a loosely organized group called the Científicos, implying a scientific approach to governing. Formed during the presidency of Manuel González, its members included Minister of Finance José Limantour and Díaz's father-in-law the Secretary of Gobernación Manuel Romero Rubio, Secretary of Public Education Justo Sierra, and some of the brightest members of the new generation. They believed that with Díaz's strong leadership, new institutions could be put in place to create a viable constitutional republic.

The Científicos proposed a political party able to develop a civic consensus as well as unite the national and state camarillas into one organization. The Liberal Union intended to move politics beyond the era of strongmen and into that of institutions and laws. The National Liberal Union Convention in 1892 laid out a political platform that called for a strong judiciary with judges independent of executive power. Federal deputy Justo Sierra introduced the proposal as a constitutional amendment in the 1893 National Congress. His bill carried in the lower chamber but failed in the Senate. Newspapers carried extensive commentary for and against the amendment, but its fate came down to Díaz, who opposed the change. The political structure could not accommodate more than one directive force. Newspapers involved in the public debate coined the term "Cientificos" to poke fun at the reformers and their rejected program.

Nevertheless, the voices of reform continued to make rational suggestions. Governor Emilio Rabasa of Chiapas in the 1890s pressed for a less personal presidential regime. He argued for democratic procedures and reforms that would not jeopardize progress but rather broaden the regime's appeal. Journalist Francisco Bulnes observed that, while Díaz's personal rule may have been necessary in the past, changing times and a country now on the path of orderly development required a different approach. Bulnes advocated the formation of at least two different political parties within a constitutional framework. These men thought of themselves as supporters of progress, anxious to preserve its gains and preserve the stability of the government. Their reasoned views, however, while not ignored, could not be translated into action.

The problem of an impoverished peasantry could not be ignored. Andrés Molina Enriquez, a notary and local judge, concluded that the concentration of land, while it produced wealth for the few, had pushed the peasantry down to an insupportable level. Another thoughtful critic, Wistano Luis Orozco, suggested that the government buy and distribute land to rural inhabitants. Other critics, usually exceedingly polite, could be found among the new generation of agriculturalists, miners, industrialists, technocrats, and churchmen who gradually replaced those who had fought with or against Porfirio Díaz.

The Church also began to pay more attention to the well-being of workers. The papal encyclical *Rerum Novarum* (1891) introduced a pro-worker moral element in support of decent working conditions and fair wages, and directly challenged the individualism of Porfirian progress.

Díaz may have considered himself the indispensable man, but for others that moment had passed; however, they hesitated to act aggressively on their convictions. In retrospect, Díaz made fatal mistakes, but perhaps even more fateful, a timid, fearful oligarchy could not relinquish its dependency on Díaz and failed to challenge his obstinacy. The other crucial failure involved economics.

Like earlier Liberal regimes, the Porfirian concentrated on development by those with sufficient capital and expertise to utilize resources. Capital accumulation, vital in the initial stage, occurred at the expense of low wages and minimal consumption. At a certain point in the late 1890s the economic structure needed to be rebalanced and transformed into an engine of redistribution to increase consumption. The economy worked in the first stage but failed disastrously in the second stage. Instead of a rebalancing to expand the domestic market, real wages fell by 25 percent between 1898 and 1910. In agriculture, the largest sector employer, wages fell by much more, while miners did better but still lagged.

Whereas economic development in the early period had increased faster than the population, by 1900 that had changed: the rate of economic growth slowed to .09 percent from 1.6 percent earlier, and the labor force as a percentage of the population declined from 35.4 in 1900 to 34.8 by 1910. These figures suggest that the export sector could not absorb more workers, and the light manufacturing sector, while growing as urbanization increased, did not experience sufficient demand to actively expand the workforce. Several factors must be considered, including the use of modern machinery, electrification, the market calibration made possible by international telegraph and transatlantic undersea cables, and production efficiencies. Nevertheless, the economy needed to expand, but could not do so without a reasonable distribution of wealth sufficient to create consumers and a mass market.

Mexico's silver-backed currency declined in value as developed nations changed to the gold standard and abandoned silver purchases. As demand fell, so did the price of silver and, as a result, the value of the peso. The price of imports went up and consumption by an impoverished population went down, for both foreign and domestic goods. In 1904 Mexico retained the silver-backed peso for the domestic economy and created a gold-backed peso for external use. Exports earned in gold, while producers paid wages in depreciating silver. When the monitory change went into effect the domestic peso immediately lost 50 centavos in value. In the short term, the oligarchy benefited from a monetary policy that favored it over the general population. In the longer term it failed to consider the dangers of Mexico's economic dependency on its northern neighbor that made export-driven prosperity increasingly subject to economic cycles in the United States. This soon became disastrously evident.

Financial problems in the United States began in 1906 with the San Francisco earthquake. The federal mint that supplied the western states lay in ruins, causing an immediate economic contraction. An emergency shipment of coins and currency from the East Coast helped, but the destruction of the center of trade, commerce, and banking in the West shook confidence nationally. The following year New York experienced a financial crisis, stocks fell by 50 percent, and panic-stricken depositors rush to withdraw their funds, forcing banks to call in their loans or go under. Turmoil spread with the speed of the telegraph to engulf the entire credit system and Mexico's export economy. Mexican export producers had banking arrangements in El Paso, San Antonio, New Orleans, New York, and Europe that ceased to function normally. Dependent on credit transactions to fuel demand and production, many faced difficult times. The Mexican government did not have funds available or the administrative structure to extend credit temporarily.

The events of 1907 threatened the well-being of the oligarchy, and politically the foundation of the Porfiriato. In 1906–7, strikes and general economic turmoil disrupted the Porfirian order. To make a difficult situation even more so for laid-off miners and agricultural workers, a series of droughts severely reduced crop yields. An already stretched food supply experienced acute shortages of corn and beans, and the food distribution system drew near the point of collapse. Workers in mines, factories, and fields faced lower wages, unemployment, deteriorating living conditions, and food uncertainty, with no relief in sight. By early

1908 the panic had passed, but the damage had been done. The oligarchy's confidence in the regime had been badly shaken, and the survival of the lower classes remained economically precarious, the people fearful.

Generational Politics

A generational shift changed both faces and attitudes. Those who came of age after the Revolution of Tuxtepec, including Francisco I. Madero, who was born in 1873 and was thirty-seven years old in 1910, and Ricardo Flores Magón, born in 1874 and just a year younger, had little appreciation of the difficulties faced by the Porfirians in 1876. Flores Magón and Madero represented the two extreme outcomes of nineteenth-century liberalism—the disinherited masses and the oligarchy. The tone of the republic changed, but without a leader able to speak for the new generation, it could not be articulated effectively. Flores Magón and Madero, along with other prominent critics of the regime, failed to provide leadership and a commanding voice at a crucial prerevolutionary moment.

Members of the new working class lived in the cities and towns but still had one foot in the rural villages that housed their parents, family, friends, and memories. They understood how much had been lost and how little gained, just as did those who remained in the countryside. The Mexican Liberal Party's anarchism spoke to their sense of angry disappointment and bitter nostalgia.

The Porfirians viewed Ricardo Flores Magón and his PLM followers as plotters and potential revolutionaries. Only later would Díaz understand that the challenge went beyond Flores Magón and the PLM. Nevertheless, the PLM played a subtle but important role in changing the political tone of the republic in the first decade of the century. The seeds of a mass movement could be identified, but only in retrospect.

Initially, the PLM claimed to be the heir of earlier Liberals. Mild socialist rhetoric concealed the anarchism that would become evident over the years. The three brothers Ricardo, Enrique, and Jesús Flores Magón challenged the incumbent regime through a series of short-lived, bitingly critical newspapers. After several stints in jail and the sacking of the newspaper office, Jesús turned to more moderate forms of opposition, but Ricardo and Enrique continued their struggle. Francisco Madero for a time offered the PLM financial support, until its anarchism became evident.

After the brothers faced increasingly threatening measures to silence them, they fled across the border. Ricardo barely escaped assassination by Mexican agents in San Antonio who wrecked the newspaper office. The two brothers moved to St. Louis and focused on distributing their newspaper, *La Regeneración*, and on the organization of the PLM. In Mexico, PLM agents distributed copies of *La Regeneración* and attempted to organize support groups. The St. Louis junta presented their goals in a widely circulated document, the Plan of 1906. Their pronouncement called for justice for workers, the end of starvation wages, and the return of land to agrarians and indigenous peoples, especially the Yaqui, who had been forced from their tribal territory. The plan also called for democratic politics.

The Plan of 1906 obscured the PLM's anarchism and, in the end, limited Flores Magón's influence, turning him into a symbol of resistance rather than a revolutionary leader. The Mexican government hired private detectives to keep an eye on Flores

Magón and the PLM and encouraged U.S. law authorities to do the same. The United States, concerned that dangerous anarchists agitated among immigrants, embroiled Flores Magón and other members of the PLM in the American judicial system. The U.S. attorney general saw the PLM as more of a domestic threat than one aimed at the Mexican government. Ricardo never returned alive to Mexico, dying in Leavenworth Federal Prison in 1922. His corpse would later be returned to Mexico, and Ricardo would enter revolutionary mythology.

The PLM's appeal rested on its potential to provide political expression for the folk liberalism espoused by members of the lower classes. Their interpretation of Juárez and the Constitution of 1857 built on the nationalistic pride that came from the successful expulsion of the French and the escape from the imaginary perils of conservatism. It made Juárez into a messianic figure whose refusal to pardon Maximilian gave him the aura of an Old Testament prophet. A mythological Juárez and Constitution of 1857 became a powerful symbol to those who believed that the Porfirian regime had cast aside its impoverished citizens. Folk liberalism clashed with both reality and the official mythical Juárez fashioned by Díaz.

The Porfirian regime's counter-myth presented Juárez as the foundation of the Porfiriato and Porfirio Díaz as his successor-disciple. Díaz burnished this image as he dedicated Juárez's marble tomb (1880), renamed a main street in the capital (1887), and renamed El Paso del Norte Cuidad Juárez in 1888. The centennial celebration of Juárez's birth in 1906 became a national cult celebration presided over by the government. Díaz inaugurated Juárez's elaborate white marble *hemiciclo*, just off the Alameda

Park in 1910, one of his last official acts. The official version of Juárez confronted the more popular account. Nevertheless, folk liberalism could not be displaced, because it represented hope, if not reality. Turning hope into reality required action.

A strike in 1906, in part under PLM leadership, in the Sonoran copper mining town of Cananea set a pattern. The following year a strike at the Río Blanco textile mill in the state of Veracruz resulted in labor unrest spreading to the adjoining state of Puebla. In both Cananea and Río Blanco workers protested low and unequal wages, as foreigners earned more than comparable Mexican employees. Other secondary issues involved unsafe working conditions and, in the textile factory, child labor. In both cases the companies had foreign majority ownership. Díaz at first saw the strikes as nationalist issues similar to those that motivated his purchase of majority control of Mexican railroads in 1909. His initial favorable disposition toward the workers changed under a barrage of hysterical advice from such cabinet members as Governor Ramón Corral of Sonora, who argued that the workers had fallen under the influence of foreign socialist ideologies promoted by PLM anarchists. The president's political instinct to treat the strikes as motivated by nationalism could well have provided an opportunity to take action to broaden his support among industrial workers. In the end, Díaz, convinced that he faced a workers' insurrection, smashed the strikes. In the case of the Río Blanco strike, a massive overreaction left many dead; rumors circulated that bodies had been loaded on railcars and dumped into the sea. Díaz misread the situation and objectified discontent as the work of the PLM rather than an indication of Mexico's socioeconomic malaise.

Nevertheless, shaken by the economic downturn in 1907, violent strikes, criticism from intellectuals, and grumbling by the oligarchy, Díaz turned to public relations. In a 1908 interview with the American magazine writer, James Creelman, Díaz exuded the confidence investors had come to expect. Creelman described the president as an old but energetic warhorse, complete with "dark brown eyes that search your soul . . . fine ears close to his head . . . fighting chin . . . wide shoulders, deep chest . . . and a personality suggestive of singular power and dignity"—in short, a man who in his seventy-eighth year remained magnetic, charismatic, strong, and able to direct his people. The president's self-congratulatory description of his successes in the remaking of his nation led him to announce that finally, he believed the people had developed sober, self-disciplined habits learned through Porfirian schools, factories, and farms. As a result, they had reached the point that they could organize political parties and choose between candidates.

Demonstrating that he believed himself no longer indispensable, Díaz announced he would not be a candidate in the presidential elections of 1910. He probably anticipated that the elite would clamor for him to remain in office rather than risk their privileges. Inadvertently, Díaz made it possible for others to contemplate running for the presidency without appearing to be disloyal or an agitator. In the wake of the Creelman interview a flurry of new political parties formed, although most appeared to be concerned with presenting a favored candidate rather than building a mass political organization. A handful of plausible candidates considered entering the presidential race based on their convictions of how to preserve social tranquility, expand the economy, and consolidate the progress that had been made since 1876.

In the northeastern state of Nuevo León, General Bernardo Reyes believed that Porfirian success rested on having a veteran military officer at the top. In the Veracruz region General Félix Díaz, nephew of the president, suggested that longevity depended on having a Díaz family member as president. In Sonora, Governor Ramón Corral found Porfirian success in tough-minded administration, such as that of a former frontier governor and as an experienced vice president elected in 1904, and currently in office.

In Mexico City, the Científicos believed social science ideas and the application of technology could maintain the regime, but they remained uncertain of the best candidate to consolidate the gains of the Porfiriato. Others envisioned the continuation of Díaz as president, but with the selection of a suitable vice president groomed for the position as the key to a peaceful transition in the likelihood that Díaz would not live through another full term. An acceptable vice president would inherit the mantle in a constitutional manner in a seamless political succession.[1]

That some reforms would be necessary to preserve Porfirian achievements seemed reasonable. Structural reforms to strengthen the rule of law had been discussed for some time, as well as the formation of independent parties able to compete for public support. Understandably, politics claimed most of the attention, but economics lay just beneath the rhetoric. Andrés Molina Enriquez viewed rural land consolidation and commercial agricultural expansion of the 1890s as the greatest danger. Export agriculture stripped property from smallholders and reduced domestic food crop production. Molina Enriquez did not envision himself as a presidential candidate, but his conclusions, expressed in *Los grandes problemas nacionales* (1909), perceptively examined the issue.

In Coahuila, the powerful but out-of-favor Madero family, like many of their class, believed Porfirian prosperity could be preserved with the peaceful transfer of presidential power to an appropriate vice president. The Madero family preferred Finance Minister José Limantour, a close friend, as their candidate. Others suggested General Bernardo Reyes. His supporters claimed, with some justification, that as governor of Nuevo León he had transformed the state into one of the most prosperous in the republic. Monterrey, the state capital, had become an impressive industrial center, in large part for reasons other than the Reyes administration, nevertheless, he had a role in maintaining its entrepreneurial momentum. His state passed Mexico's first workmen's compensation law, indicating concern for workers at the same time Reyes had a reputation for firmness. The Democratic Party supported Reyes and became the first party organization to establish a national presence outside the capital. Initially the public reacted with enthusiasm to the idea of Reyes as vice president and possible successor to Díaz. It required the potential candidate to encourage what appeared to be an unstoppable bandwagon impossible for Díaz to resist. General Reyes held back at a crucial moment. The reluctance of Reyes to challenge Díaz puzzled his supporters. He appeared anxious to make statements in support of President Díaz, including declaring that the choice of a vice president should be left to the president alone, indicating his preference for a continuation of Díaz in office. Such reticence opened the door for Madero's Anti-Reelection party.

The young Francisco Madero had a bold vision. His book, *La sucesión presidencial en 1910* (The Presidential Succession of 1910), expressed the view, long shared by many intellectuals, that Mexico had reached a crucial point in its political evolution. In it, Madero considered Mexico's political history from colonial times through his, with an emphasis on rebellions, dictatorships, and civic irresponsibility. A few bright spots, such as the formation of the Constitution of 1857 and Benito Juárez's activities, indicated, in Madero's opinion, that latent democratic tendencies needed to be revitalized by appropriate structural changes. Madero echoed the views of others that Díaz's methods no longer appeared to be necessary, although he complimented the president and brushed aside the notion that Díaz had established a dictatorship. Nevertheless, Madero listed Díaz's mistakes, while minimizing the difficulties faced by the president at the time. Subservience to Washington and neglect of education, while partially correct criticisms, ignored the broader economic situation that restricted Díaz's options. Harsh treatment of labor and Indians, an attitude embedded in liberalism, hardly originated with Díaz, and Madero could well have written the same about Juárez.

Madero crafted his book to justify his objectives and to articulate popular complaints against the regime. He concluded by observing correctly that unless the public rallied to make its wishes known, Díaz would select as vice president either Corral or General Bernardo Reyes. Of the two, Reyes might be preferable, but as a general he would continue the absolutism of Díaz should he assume the presidency. Madero stressed the need for a civilian president, who would presumably be more attuned to democracy than an army general. He called for the formation of an Anti-Reelection Party dedicated to the principle of effective suffrage and no reelection. The first printing of 3,000 copies sold out in three months. Its publication elevated its author to national prominence while having little impact on Díaz. It went through several editions, each a little more daring.

Most of the potential challengers circumspectly waited to see whether President Díaz would indeed step down. The frustrated editor of the *Diario del Hogar* wrote Díaz asking him to confirm or deny the important points of the Creelman interview. President Díaz responded that his comments represented his personal desires, implying that other considerations might be in play. Within months he had allowed himself to be persuaded by various groups to reverse his position and accept the nomination for the presidency in the 1910 election. Limantour and others formed the Reelection Party to arrange for Díaz's and his vice president Ramon Corral's continuation in office.[2] Another party composed of friends of Díaz, the National Porfirista Circle, kept their disquiet about the vice president private and dutifully endorsed the president.

In the aftermath of the Creelman interview and the high expectations that followed, Díaz's decision to run with the highly unpopular Corral amounted to a failure of judgment and doomed the hopes of the oligarchy for a smooth transition. Díaz's hubris drew on the uncritical praise of foreign governments as validation that his methods and political judgment were correct. He dismissed dissatisfaction among the provincial elites as a temporary situation that would change when prosperous times returned.

The warning signs that the status quo could not be maintained emerged as Reelection Party speakers encountered angry crowds.

In Guadalajara, a mob stoned the hotel of party representatives. President Díaz blamed Reyes and his supporters and acted to neutralize the Reyistas. Finally, General Reyes resigned as governor of Nuevo León and accepted Díaz's appointment to conduct a military study in Europe.[3] During a stopover in New York, he predicted Díaz would be reelected without difficulty.

Díaz might have been able to ride out the turmoil had it not been for Madero's energetic campaign. The contrast between the two men could not have been overlooked. The difference between an aged, fading president seemingly holding on to the past and an idealist whirlwind intent on galvanizing the population into democratic action was startling. Although Madero remained confident that he could overcome public apathy and the reluctance of the oligarchy to confront the government, even his family sought to discourage Francisco from what seemed an impossible quest. The family patriarch, Evaristo Madero, made it clear he thought the young Madero had lost touch with reality and his foolhardy quest would injure the family's interests. Francisco's parents wanted him to give up his efforts and assist in running the family's enterprises. Significantly, however, the younger generation, in the form of his brother and sisters, supported him.

Establishing Anti-Reelection Party clubs became his immediate objective. He made two extensive tours by rail, usually greeted on arrival at each stop by thousands of people anxious to hear and see the man who had directly challenged President Díaz. He promised a national nominating convention in the summer of 1910. For the most part, Porfirian governors and *jefes politicos* followed the example of the president and ignored Madero. A few of the more autocratic administrators broke up the Anti-Reelection Party organizational meetings, harassed speakers, and in some cases jailed local party officers. To no one's surprise, at the national nominating convention the Anti-Reelection Party selected Francisco Madero as their presidential candidate, and he spent the summer of 1910 campaigning for office. A dismayed oligarchy, out of patience but paralyzed and unwilling to confront Díaz, contemplated the likely possibility of a succession crisis. Meanwhile, the president ignored Madero, whose reputation as a dilettante agriculturalist and spiritualist appeared to rule him out as a serious contender.

Madero defined democracy to mean elections and the creation of political parties with declared principles. He had no quarrel with Porfirian progress, held property rights to be the foundation of Mexican prosperity, respected the rule of law even if it favored the oligarchy, and assumed that the lower classes would follow the lead of their betters. But in assuming that an independent political process would resolve issues of importance to the lower classes, Madero misread the circumstances. He failed to comprehend the issues that underpinned the desire for change. Consequently, he became a victim of expectations he did not recognize and others he had no intention of fulfilling. To what extent rural inhabitants understood the implications of Madero's definition of democracy is difficult to determine.

In the small town of San José de Gracia, Michoacán, residents followed Madero's efforts with interest, believing that a younger man should take over from Díaz, but paid little attention to the changes that Madero had in mind. Immediate local problems, such as the drought that wiped out most of the corn crop and endangered the survival of animals, concerned them more than Madero's political program. Like other small towns and villages, however, San José de Gracia entered into the national debate. In 1906 San José de Gracia for the first time had regular, once-a-week mail service by horseback from the nearest railway station. Newspapers came with the mail, providing details and stimulating discussion. Villagers may not have had a sophisticated understanding of the issues, but they did have opinions. Only after the revolution carried Madero into the presidency did villagers add demands to what before had been the simple expectations of a new but not revolutionary era.[4]

President Díaz gave little thought to Madero's presidential election campaign, confident that he could derail it when necessary. During the summer of 1910 he focused on the organizational aspects of the celebration of the centennial of independence. In the midst of preparations and preliminary events, the presidential elections approached. Díaz decided to take no chances with Madero and placed him under house arrest in San Luis Potosí, effectively ending his campaigning. In addition, trumped-up felony charges made Madero technically ineligible to seek public office. The elections occurred without incident. Electoral officials reported that Madero received some votes that had to be discounted because of his indictment, and announced the reelection of Porfirio Díaz and Ramón Corral with an overwhelming number of votes.

In disguise, Madero fled to Texas, then on to New Orleans. Safely out of the country he issued a statement, purportedly written in San Luis Potosí to avoid a violation of U.S. neutrality laws. The Plan of San Luis Potosí called on members of the Anti-Reelection

Party to reconstitute themselves as revolutionaries and invited Mexicans to join them in overthrowing the Porfirian government. In secret circulars, Madero announced that the revolution would begin at 1 p.m. on November 20, 1910.

Díaz's Magical Moment

For most Mexicans the centennial year meant the dedication of new buildings, or perhaps a fountain or drainage ditch, or some other improvement. The fall of 1910 brought a series of inaugurations of impressive buildings, monuments, and institutions to commemorate independence. Among the array, several became lasting icons. The Monument to Independence, designed by the Italian architect Adamo Boari and erected on a prominent *glorieta* on the Paseo de la Reforma, remains a favorite landmark. The construction of a new national theatre, commissioned in 1901 to mark the glorious conclusion to Mexico's first century of independence and the beginning of a promising new one, appeared to rise along with the anticipation. Architect Adamo Boari, employing the very latest architectural style, subsequently called art nouveau, and modern construction materials supported by steel girders, promised a theater second only to the Paris Opera House. Unfortunately, it would not be completed in time for the centennial.[5] Nevertheless, other symbolic structures made the point that Mexico had made admirable progress since 1810. President Díaz and other important government figures could be counted on to make an appearance and some brief remarks as each tangible monument to progress opened for public admiration. Newspapers printed schedules, reviewed events, and marveled at the progress the country had made during the century.

As the celebration moved toward the September 16 climax, parades and speeches drew official and unofficial visitors from Europe, the United States, Latin America, and Japan. Through it all Díaz, the elderly president, remained slightly remote, a living national symbol, the patriarchal patriot and the man responsible for Mexico's progress. Special trains filled with excited foreign delegations arrived, to be met by distinguished Mexicans. Visitors were spirited off to luxurious accommodations filled with freshly cut flowers, tasty regional treats, and servants to attend to their needs. Carefully pampered foreign journalists reported on the amazing displays that marked the centennial. Much of their attention focused on President Díaz. Great men extolled Díaz's accomplishments, comparing him to history's greatest leaders. The final triumphant celebration in a refurbished national palace amazed and delighted the invited guests.

As the Díaz regime basked in the celebration's afterglow, scattered rebel attacks took place in distant Chihuahua. The administration, including the president, gave little attention to Madero and his revolution beyond sending troops to the north to battle Pascual Orozco Jr. and Pancho Villa. The federal army won a victory at Nuevas Casas Grandes on December 1910, seemingly ending the troubles.

A Persistent Insurrection

Madero and his insurrection persisted, joined by a growing number of regional rebels, such as Emiliano Zapata in Morelos and others across the country who had their own goals but found Madero's name politically useful. Díaz and the Porfirians failed to recognize the tacit alliance, albeit short-lived, between the lower classes seeking a better future and a disaffected elite worried about what might happen after Díaz.

In April 1911, rebels in Chihuahua managed to isolate and besiege the federal army in Ciudad Juárez, just across the river from El Paso, Texas. The event, reported worldwide, represented a nightmare for Díaz, who had long feared that such a situation would undermine the illusion of strength he had worked so hard to foster. The battle for the city attracted sightseeing American tourists, who jostled for a view of the fierce action, crowding onto rooftops and climbing telegraph poles to peer across the border. Fortunately, the few spent rounds that fell on the streets of El Paso did little damage, although they wounded seventeen careless spectators. Madero, worried that an incident might provoke a U.S. intervention, ordered Orozco and Villa, the two insurgent commanders, not to attempt to take the city. In what might have been an early indication of problems to come, they ignored his orders. The rebels captured the city, giving them a border crossing over which to import guns, horses, and ammunition and giving Madero an even greater public relations victory. Following the capture of the city the mayor of El Paso gave a formal banquet in Francisco Madero's honor, with Madero on one side of the mayor and the defeated federal commander, General Juan Navarro, on the other. Villa and Orozco had not been invited.[6]

Hard on the heels of the fall of Juárez, rebels struck deep into the Laguna, the heart of commercial agriculture in the north. In the Laguna, technology and irrigation had transformed an extensive prehistoric lake bed into a vast cotton-producing region. La Laguna was a Porfirian showcase. Along with modern processing factories, the Laguna represented the triumph of developmental capitalism. The new cities of Torreón and Gómez Palacio, established in 1883 and 1884, respectively, had large enclaves of Europeans, Americans, Canadians, and Chinese residents. In the first decade of the twentieth century Torreón had the second largest number of U.S. citizens in the country. Modern housing, wide streets, streetcars, railways, hospitals, foreign diplomatic offices, and international banks set Torreón and Gómez Palacio apart from other Mexican cities in the north. Modern communication tied the region to the United States and the world. The Laguna gave some substance to the grumbling that the Porfirian regime had made its people orphans while showering wealth on foreigners. When the revolutionaries approached Torreón, a demoralized federal army on May 17, 1911, abandoned the city. Madero's followers unleashed their rage on the Chinese community, which had remained in Torreón. The burning, looting, and killing lasted into the next day.

Almost daily, new rebel groups appeared, as many sensed the imminent collapse of the regime. Díaz ordered negotiations with Madero, which concluded in May 21, 1911, with the Treaty of Ciudad Juárez. Hoping to end the revolution, the president agreed to resign and go into exile.[7] Díaz, his family, and his closest advisers sailed for France within the month. The thirty-five-year Porfirian regime had ended.

A Crucial Century Assessed

The hundred years from 1810 to 1910 constituted Mexico's crucial century. Fatal combinations of civil wars, territorial loss, foreign intervention, and economic dislocation came close to extinguishing the republic. The country, materially damaged by the civil war and insurgency that raged from 1810 to 1821, lost much of its economic strength, a reality that could not be reversed until the latter half of the nineteenth century. Infrastructure created during the colonial era had been destroyed, in many cases beyond repair, even if the money could have been found to undertake its restoration. Treasure accumulated from the sixteenth century to the early nineteenth century evaporated. Manufacturing activity, agricultural production, and trade declined disastrously. Formerly productive land lay abandoned, and the deep silver mines of the eighteenth century sat flooded and useless. Government revenues, dependent on import and export taxes, dropped to disastrous levels. An impoverished state turned to foreign loans at predatory rates.

The Mexican Republic emerged from the ruins of New Spain with an untried political structure that had to be consolidated politically, and former subjects of the king had to be transformed into responsible citizens. Liberalism, which drew on enlightened ideas as well as the ideals of the Constitution of 1812, became an aggressively reformist ideology. It was not without powerful opponents. Mexican Conservatives challenged Liberals at every turn, convinced they could protect Mexico's Catholic culture and its traditions in the face of a worldwide movement toward republicanism. Attempting to resurrect what they saw as Mexico's tradition of social harmony based on hierarchy and religion, they reassembled archaic bits and pieces of the past. The Church and the Conservatives fed each other to the extent that the struggle between conservatism and liberalism occupied much of the century. Santa Anna's uncrowned pseudo-monarchy from 1853 to the Revolution of Ayutla exemplified their destructive nostalgia. Emperor Maximilian, their last, best hope, turned out to be unacceptably liberal for Mexican Conservatives and the Church.

Conservatism in the nineteenth century failed not because of ideology but because of a rigid attachment to tradition in a century of technological and social change that altered political and sociocultural expectations. Conservatives' failure to modify their ideology meant that the outcome of the French intervention could only be a political and cultural defeat that demonstrated the bankruptcy of the Conservatives. Had the Conservatives formed a political alliance with the lower classes, the pace and impact of modernization might have been tempered. In the end, the dream of a traditional monarchist-Catholic sociopolitical hierarchy as a replacement for a Liberal oligarchy clashed with modernity. Liberalism became the dominant ideology, but with fatal flaws that led to the Mexican Revolution of 1910.

Time did not favor the Mexican Republic. The realignment of empires in North America posed a challenge that an enfeebled nation appeared ill-prepared to meet. The danger posed by an expansionist United States became evident even before Mexico's independence. The Louisiana Purchase in 1803 suddenly brought the United States hard against the border of a vulnerable Texas. It was the first domino to fall. The new international border created as a result of the annexation of the Republic of Texas (1845) and subsequently the Treaty of Guadalupe Hidalgo (1848), which ended the war with the United States, and the Gadsden Purchase (1854) brought both republics into direct demographic contact along the international boundary's 2,000 miles. The rush by both governments to secure the new border created an economic zone that drew Mexicans northward and North Americans and recently arrived European immigrants to the U.S. Southwest.

Culture convergence became evident in the transnational borderlands almost immediately. The gold rush in California (1849), the knitting together of the region by stagecoach, and the relentless extension of the railways drew people into sparsely inhabited regions. New railway lines facilitated settlements in northern Mexico and encouraged the continuous movement of people in both directions. While greater Mexico extended into the American Southwest, cultural penetration went in both directions, a process that accelerated in the twentieth century. Convergence had its own historical momentum that paid little attention to obstacles or governments.

The industrialization of the United States generated demands for raw materials and markets that altered the world within which all successor states of Spain's American empire functioned. The Liberals correctly assessed the dangers. Economic revival could not wait but had to be propelled forward by reformers with scant resources to draw on. The nation's potential had to be managed by the most capable, a conclusion that excluded those without education and unable to grasp modern economic realities or understand national objectives.

Mexican liberalism, driven by a sense of urgency, demonstrated a unique harshness. Liberals supported a nation, but not the existing national community. The individualism at the heart of their ideology required individuals to elevate themselves in order to contribute to as well as enjoy the fruits of a modern economy. Liberalism's rejection of paternalism did not preclude assistance to the less fortunate, but assistance meant social transformation, abandonment of superstition (that is, the folk aspects of religion), and acceptance of a secular state. An oligarchy emerged in the 1880s that monopolized the fruits of modernization. Its members understood that the destruction of the independence era had allowed them to displace the old colonial elite, but now they sought order to make their possession of wealth and status permanent.

Nineteenth-century liberalism left painful social scars that continue to make it difficult to acknowledge the contributions of its logical extension, the Porfiriato. An ideology rooted in the concept of economic individualism favored a small group deemed able to exploit the nation's resources. Liberalism viewed the great mass of the population as backward and an obstacle to modernization. Liberals' lack of sympathy and disdain led to rural and urban suffering and repression by the army and the *rurales*. The bulk of the rural lower class engaged in subsistence agriculture, sometimes mixed with seasonal work in commercial operations, mining, agriculture, or railway construction. A significant percentage of the workforce became impoverished as new technology rendered traditional skills obsolete and pushed workers into the ranks of ill-paid laborers. Artisans could compete with machines only by offering hand manufacturing and accepting unskilled factory labor at low wages. At the end of the century, two types of production functioned side by side, one modern, machine- and technology-based, with access to capital, and the other closer to its pre-independence roots, with marginal returns.

The answer to the question of what brought down the Porfiriato is not as clear-cut as its vulnerabilities might suggest. The concentration of wealth in the hands of so few, the loss of village communal land, nutritional deprivation, and the shock of urbanization would seem sufficient. Nevertheless, research suggests that land concentration is not as important as the gap between rich and poor, particularly when movement is from rural villages into urban centers, where wealth inequality becomes glaringly evident. Moreover, in periods of rapid development marked by the introduction of transformative technology such as railways, electricity, and other innovations, income inequality is to be expected. When the initial phase ends, the gap shrinks as manufacturing and service sectors become important. This did not happen because of the nature of Mexican development.

Mexico diverged from the development model of nineteenth-century Britain and the United States, which relied on the domestic market as the primary economic engine. Britain at its peak depended on external trade for only one-third of its economy. In similar fashion, the United States as early as 1850 had the largest free trade region in the world. The importance of the domestic market encouraged production and cost cutting to expand consumption at the same time that labor militancy pushed up wages and purchasing power. Transportation, another factor of importance in Britain and the United States, made broad distribution feasible. In Britain, by 1800, waterways and good roads had made domestic regional and national markets possible, even before the arrival of the railways. In the United States, 3,000 miles of canals had been constructed before 1840, and by 1860 there were 30,000 miles of railway tracks.[1]

In contrast, Mexico's domestic economy had been destroyed, along with its roads and finances, in the civil wars. Violence repeatedly stalled recovery attempts. Without a sufficiently large domestic market to build on, Mexico relied on external export markets and failed to move on to the next stage, which entailed a rational distribution of wealth to make mass consumption possible. Accumulated economic and political miscalculations created a tectonic situation that suddenly gave way.

The sudden collapse of the Porfiriato, seemly at its zenith, stunned the world, which was unaware of how the country worked. The political balance established by Díaz required constant and ongoing recalibration. On a tactical level it demanded timely recognition of potential threats and co-optation or repression as necessary. The failure occurred on the macrolevel; Díaz did not expand the government's political base beyond the oligarchy, despite the urging of many worried but friendly critics. The middle class, expected to be grateful for rising above the lower classes, had few incentives binding it to the Porfiriato. The desire for order and stability, which had effectively bound the middle class to the regime in earlier years, had faded. The urban working class, initially forced to accept paternalism, decided that it wanted remedial action to provide better working conditions and reasonable wages. In the countryside, a desperate rural population wanted land to feed itself. In the absence of responsive political parties, the agenda of the discontented could not be ascertained, nor could steps be taken to address their needs. The Liberal oligarchy did not see the need for a party system and rejected suggestions that might have prolonged the stability it cherished.

The extent to which the regime depended on a delicate balance became evident as critics began to chip away at its foundations. The semi-repressive government of President Díaz allowed pseudopolitical participation, symbolized by an acquiescent Chamber of Deputies and Senate and by state governors anxious to please the president by delivering predetermined elections. Moreover, to preserve a liberal façade, Díaz permitted demonstrations and newspaper criticism, but only to a degree. The regime waited to see if indirect means limited anti-regime activity before employing repressive methods to determine the outcome.

Porfirio Díaz prudently undercut potential rivals in a timely fashion, but after the Creelman interview appeared in *Pearson's Magazine*, Díaz felt more constrained. He made the mistake of allowing supporters of General Bernardo Reyes to organize, although in the end, Reyes lost his nerve and withdrew. Francisco Madero, however, began organizing immediately after the interview, incessantly traveling by rail to build a string of Anti-Reelection Clubs into a national organization.[2] Díaz waited too long before ordering Madero's arrest and concocting an excuse to declare him ineligible to run for the presidency.

Once determined revolutionary violence broke out, the illusion of permanent stability shattered. An army organized for political purposes could not prop up the regime. With fewer than 14,000 troops and a military establishment directed by aging generals, the army could not respond rapidly enough. In May 1911, everything unraveled. On May 8 the border city of

Tijuana fell to an assortment of PLM anarchists and adventurers, nominally under the control of Ricardo Flores Magón. Two days later Cuidad Juárez fell to the forces of Madero, and three days later Emiliano Zapata attacked Cuautla in the south center of the country. On May 15 Torreón, the Laguna showcase of northern commercial agriculture, was abandoned by the army and fell, followed by looting and the killing of Chinese residents. Two days later, on May 17, Díaz agreed to resign, doing so formally on May 25 and sailing for a European exile on May 31, 1911. The Porfiriato collapsed like a deck of cards in slightly less than a month. Francisco Madero, who had challenged Díaz politically, became the designated hero and inevitable successor.

The Mexican Revolution began with a disaffected oligarch miscast as a revolutionary but unable to comprehend the complaints of those with a socioeconomic agenda. Madero's Anti-Reelection Clubs focused on political change, ignoring the resentments and urgent needs of the lower classes. Madero saw his movement as a way of making revolutionary change unnecessary.

In Madero's initial roles, first as an opposition candidate, then as the principal anti-Díaz leader, he responded appropriately, but without a guiding ideology. As president, his fatal mistakes stemmed from the reality that he approved of the sociopolitical and economic organization of the Porfiriato, except for its antidemocratic features. Ricardo Flores Magón perceptively called Madero "Díaz the Little." Madero saw no need to replace an administration that had directed Mexico's development and ensured the well-being of the oligarchy. Instead of purging the bureaucracy and the federal army, he left them intact, with fatal consequences for himself and serious ones for the republic.

Madero's successors in office, notably after 1920, drew a lesson from the failure of the Porfiriato to create an engine of distribution and consumption to match the juggernaut of development. They immediately moved to redistribute land and attend to the complaints of urban workers. Revolutionary presidents rebalanced society while throwing the inclusionary mantle of nationalism over all Mexicans.

NOTES

Introduction

1. Colin M. MacLachlan and Jaime E. Rodríguez O., *The Forging of the Cosmic Race: A Reinterpretation of Colonial Mexico* (Berkeley and Los Angeles: University of California Press, 1980), 144–95, and Rodríguez O., *Down from Colonialism*. A 2007 study by two economists supports the conclusions of the two earlier works. See Rafael Dobado and Gustavo A. Marrero, *Mining-Led Growth in Bourbon Mexico: The Role of the State and the Economic Cost of Independence*, Working Paper no. 06/07-1, David Rockefeller Center for Latin American Studies, Harvard University.

2. Manuel Miño Grijalva, *El mundo novohispano: Pobalción, ciudades y economía, siglos XVII y XVIII* (Mexico City: Fondo de Cultura Económica, 2001), demonstrates the complex and prosperous commercial network that included all of New Spain.

3. While the influence of pre-European societies and the New World frontier experience also separated them, they shared an overarching culture.

4. "Ideology" is used here to mean a system of ideas as well as socially patterned rationalizations that form group values and ideals.

5. The notion of Greater Mexico follows the thesis developed in MacLachlan and Beezley, *El Gran Pueblo*, with its focus on the movement of people rather than geography.

1. Spain and Its Empire in Crisis

1. Unfortunately, Aldama, an eyewitness, described the contents only, not the exact words. The heroic myth supplied words that do not match Aldama's report. See MacLachlan and Rodríguez O., *The Forging of the Cosmic Race*, 311–12.

2. Indian tribute had been imposed on the defeated indigenous

population as a result of the conquest. It followed European custom pertaining to the treatment of conquered peoples.

3. Carlos María de Bustamante (1774–1848) founded the *Diario de México* in 1805 and subsequently made full use of the Constitution of 1812's freedom of the press. With the end of the Morelos insurgency he would be imprisoned in the fortress of San Juan de Ulúa but lived to play a role in the politics of the early republic.

4. See Jaime E. Rodríguez O., "*Nosotros somos ahora los verdaderos españoles": La transición de Nueva España de un reino de la monarquía española a la República federal mexicana, 1808–1824* (Mexico City: El Colegio de Michocán, in press). In a similar vein, American colonists saw themselves as true Englishmen wronged by the mother country.

5. Provincial deputations theoretically represented the Cortes, with the authority to make interim decisions subject to legislative approval by the larger body.

6. Jaime E. Rodríguez O., "The Transition from Colony to Nation: New Spain, 1820–1821," in Rodríguez O., *Mexico in the Age of Democratic Revolutions, 97–132.*

7. See table 5 in Romero Flores Caballero, *Counter Revolution: The Role of the Spaniards in Independence of Mexico, 1804–38,* trans. Jaime E. Rodríguez O. (Lincoln: University of Nebraska Press, 1974), 109.

8. Anna, *Forging Mexico,* 204–8. It ended the notion that the executive branch could remain above partisan politics.

9. Similar tensions characterized the 1800 elections in the United States that led to the suspected Burr conspiracy in 1805 to merge Mexico and the Louisiana Purchase into a competing republic.

10. Quoted in Julia Tuñón Pablos, *Women in Mexico: A Past Unveiled* (Austin: University of Texas Press, 1999), 58.

2. Santa Anna's Era

1. The tithe, in theory one-tenth of material goods that Christians owed the Church for its support, became an important source of revenue for the colonial state, with some of the proceeds transferred to support the Church.

By making it voluntary, the government reduced the Church to a supplicant and greatly reduced its income.

2. How many Tejanos supported the restoration of federalism and how many supported independence is difficult to determine. Confusion over goals led many to withdraw into the countryside without taking sides. Ramos, *Forging Mexican Ethnicity*, 151–53.

3. Foos, *A Short Offhand Killing Affair*, 61–79.

4. McCaffrey noted that arsenals had a plentiful supply of the new muskets, but they would not be distributed. The rush to battle left no time to train solders. McCaffrey, *Army of Manifest Destiny*, 38–41.

5. General Winfield Scott, who studied tactics in Europe, wrote a three-volume study of infantry tactics and believed in a well-trained and disciplined army. While also an Indian fighter against various indigenous groups, he became a modern professional soldier.

6. Leticia Reina, "The Sierra Gorda Peasant Rebellion, 1847–50," in *Riot, Rebellion, and Revolution: Social Conflict in Mexico*, ed. Friedrich Katz, 276–83 (Princeton: Princeton University Press, 1988).

7. Yellow fever, popularly called yellow jack, after the yellow flag flown by ships under quarantine, killed 20 percent of its victims. Complications from liver failure led to "black vomit," actually congealed blood, soon followed by death.

8. McCaffrey, *Army of Manifest Destiny*, 172–85.

9. The details are not clear, or the extent to which the patriotic myth has embellished a heroic last stand.

10. McCaffrey, *Army of Manifest Destiny*, 52–53.

11. Mariano Otero, "Consideraciones sobre la situacion política y social de la República Mexicana en el año 1847," in *Obras*, vol. 1, ed. Jesus Reyes Heroles, 95–137 (Mexico City: Editorial Porrua, 1967).

12. Gastón García Cantú, *La intervención francesa en México* (Mexico City: Clío, 1998).

3. Liberalism, Reform, and Napoleon III

1. Nineteenth-century protectorates required the protected party to surrender control over foreign affairs while retaining a negotiated degree of

internal control. The territory of the protected party remained distinct from the other party, and its citizenship remained unchanged. The subordinate entity became in essence an apprentice state. A protectorate could easily end up as a colony. Mexican Liberals had in mind an economic arrangement only.

2. That plan became a reality in 1883.

3. Santa Anna, ignored and impoverished, died in 1876.

4. Berry, *The Reform in Oaxaca*, 176–78.

5. Michael T. Ducey, "Liberal Theory and Peasant Practice: Land and Power in Northern Veracruz, Mexico, 1826–1900," in *Liberals, the Church, and Indian Peasants: Corporate Lands and the Challenge of Reform in Nineteenth-Century Spanish America*, ed. Robert H. Jackson (Albuquerque: University of New Mexico Press, 1997), 80–82.

6. Hamnett, *Juárez*, 53–56.

7. Pope Pius IX, faced with anticlericalism in Colombia, denounced that government in 1852 and 1861. In 1853 he established the Latin American Pontifical College in Rome to train priests for what he viewed as a prolonged struggle. In the Mexican case the Pope issued his condemnation of the constitution on September 30, 1861. An embattled pontiff unsuccessfully clung to temporal rule over the papal state under pressure from the Young Italy movement, which brought about Italian unification.

8. Marshal Forey, speaking on the floor of the French legislature in February 1866, declared that it would require 150,000 French soldiers to pacify Mexico.

9. Erika Pani, *Para mexicanizar el Segundo Imperio: El imaginario político de los imperialistas* (Mexico City: Colegio de México / Instituto Mora, 2001), 189–99. See appendix 2 for the careers of important Mexican imperialists before, during, and after the empire.

10. Pani, *Para mexicanizar el Segundo Imperio*, 273, 277.

11. Hamnett, *Juárez*, 194. "Anáhuac" referred to pre-Hispanic Mexico. As used by Juárez, it suggested historical unity across time, including the colonial period revered by Conservatives.

4. The Restored Republic

1. As Enrique Krauze observed, it made the point that before the creation of the states, Mexico existed as the overarching concept; therefore, states had to accept a subordinate position. Presidents became the dominant force in politics at that moment. Enríque Krauze, *Siglo de caudillos: Biografía política de México (1810–1910)* (Mexico City: Tusquets Editores, 1994), 283–84. The U.S. Civil War had a similar political impact.

2. Top military commanders received better treatment, perhaps a political office or continuation in the army. Porfirio Díaz, in addition to his army command, received the La Noria hacienda, close to the city of Oaxaca.

3. Luis Gonzáles y Gonzáles, Emma Cosío Villegas, and Guadalupe Mouroy, eds., *Historia moderna de México*, 8 vols. (Mexico City: Editorial Hermes, 1955), 3:332.

4. John M. Hart, "Agrarian Precursors of the Mexican Revolution: The Development of an Ideology," *The Americas* 29, no. 2 (1972): 131–50.

5. The number of schools reported by state authorities in some instances may have been inflated. Voss, *On the Periphery of Nineteenth-Century Mexico*, 197–203.

6. Gonzáles y Gonzáles, *Historia moderna de México*, 3:650–51. Eighteenth-century reformers suggested similar changes, although with economics in mind. The Constitution of 1812 subsequently recognized the importance of indigenous political participation.

7. Daniel Cosío Villegas, *The United States versus Porfirio Díaz* (Lincoln: University of Nebraska Press, 1963), 29–31.

8. In Mexico, those who drew up the Constitution of 1824 debated the relationship of the north with the republic. In Mexican California the *Californios* discussed the notion of an independent arrangement, and prominent New Mexicans toyed with the creation of a República Mexicana del Norte. In similar manner, many in the United States questioned the wisdom of a republic cut off from the West by mountains attempting to govern territory beyond the Appalachians. Only after the opening of the Erie Canal did it appear feasible to govern beyond the East Coast. Peter L. Bernstein, *Wedding of the Waters: The Erie Canal and the Making of a Great Nation* (New York: W. W. Norton, 2006), 62–63.

9. Gonzáles y Gonzáles et al., *Historia moderna de México*, 3:190–94.

10. Lawrence D. Taylor, "The Mining Boom in Baja California from 1850 to 1890 and the Emergence of Tijuana as a Border Community," in *On the Border: Society and Culture Between the United States and Mexico*, ed. Andrew Grant Wood, 1–30 (Wilmington DE: Scholarly Resources, 2004).

11. Charles H. Harris and Louis R. Sadler, *Bastion on the Border: Fort Bliss, 1854–1943* (El Paso: United States Army, 1993), provides an overview of the economic importance of the U.S. Army to the region.

12. Estimates of demand for local products are from Thompson, *Warm Weather and Bad Whiskey*, 6.

13. Timmons, *El Paso*, 138–41.

14. Mora-Torres, *The Making of the Mexican Border*, 48–50.

15. Cortina, appointed by President Juárez to be general of the Mexican Army of the North, fought against the French. He died in 1894. Jerry Thompson, "Juan Nepomuceno Cortina," in *The Handbook of Texas Online* (accessed December 6, 2007).

16. Thomas E. Sheridan, *Los Tucsonenses: The Mexican Community in Tucson, 1854–1941* (Tucson: University of Arizona Press, 1986), 132.

17. Until 1917 no restrictions on immigration from Mexico interfered with the circulation. Demand for labor remained high until the sharp economic downturn in the early 1920s.

18. Hoyt, *The Guggenheims and the American Dream*, 91. Mora-Torres, *The Making of the Mexican Border*, 130–33.

19. Camarillas are political groups, often centered on one individual or an extended family, that exercise political power, either directly in elective office or through their agents.

20. Early tracks made of wood with an iron strap on the running surface required constant inspection and replacement, in some cases in less than a year. Iron strap tracks fractured easily and could twist into snakeheads, derailing the locomotive. They continued to be used into the 1860s because of cost considerations, although rolled-steel tracks became available in the 1830 in the still standard T-bar that cut down on derailments. In the 1890s the Bessemer open-hearth process produced much stronger and longer steel tracks that could carry more tonnage, thereby cutting shipping costs.

21. Van Hoy, *A Social History of Mexico's Railroads*, 15–20.

22. The laws of 1883 and 1894 as they impacted northern Mexico must be viewed as part of the explanation of why the Mexican Revolution of 1920 started in the north and swept the country. After Álvaro Obregón initiated land reform in the 1920s, the revolution became controllable.

5. Constructing the Porfiriato

1. Sebastian Lerdo de Tejeda died in New York in 1889. His remains, perhaps fittingly, are in the Rotunda de los Hombres Ilustres in the capital's Dolores cemetery. President Lerdo established the Rotunda in 1872 for those who brought honor to their country. Significantly, Porfirio Díaz is not so honored.

2. The success of Mariachi de Justo Villa prompted them to move to the capital. They recorded (1907–8) for Edison, Columbia, and Victor under the name the Cuarteto Coculense. Hermes Rafael, *Cuarteto Coculense*, pamphlet accompanying *Cuarteto Conculense: The Very First Mariachi Recording, 1908–1909* (Arhoolie Records, album no. 7037, 1998), 3–7.

3. The Eighth Cavalry Band, directed by Encarnación Payen, inspired wild enthusiasm for Mexican music. Local myth maintains that the band's musicians influenced the development of early jazz and the formation of brass bands in New Orleans. Fragmentary information appears in "The Mexican Band Legend: Myth, Reality, and Musical Impact. A Preliminary Investigation," *The Jazz Archivist: A News Letter of the William Ransom Hogan Jazz Archive* 6, no. 2 (1991), and 9, no. 1 (1994).

4. Emiliano Zapata's village of Anenecuilco, Morelos, lost land despite a judicial appeal. Zapata's revolt broke out as a direct consequence of land appropriation.

5. Fernando Rosenzweig, "El desarrollo económico de Mexico de 1877 a 1911," *El Trimestre Económico* 32 (July–September 1965): 405–54. Roger D. Hanson, *The Politics of Mexican Development* (Baltimore: Johns Hopkins University Press, 1974), 19–27 and 18–20. Saragoza, *The Monterrey Elite*, 52–63. Barbara Hibino, "Cervecería Cuauhtémoc: A Case Study of Technological and Industrial Development in Mexico," *Mexican Studies / Estudios Mexicanos*, Winter 1992, 27.

6. A competition of sorts swept Latin America as various capitals revamped colonial cities into versions of the city beautiful. In the 1880s Argentina spent lavishly on public grandeur. Rio de Janeiro reoriented the city toward the sea in the early 1900s and demolished its old center. Many republican regimes also built grand opera houses, and many cities claimed to be the Paris of Latin America.

7. Johns, *The City of Mexico*, 50.

8. Piccato, *City of Suspects*, 165–67, 176.

9. Pulque, or *octli* in Nahautl, is of ancient origins. Made from the fermented sap of the agave, it has a milky and slightly sour taste and a distinctive smell. Its alcohol content ranges from 2 to 8 percent, depending on fermentation and various additives.

10. Philadelphia's Walnut Street Jail, established in 1790, became an expensive showcase with complete separation of inmates according to their offenses and workshops for inmates. Norman Johnson, "Prison Reform in Pennsylvania," Pennsylvania Prison Society, prisonsociety.org/history.shtml.

11. Moisés González Navarro, "El Porfiriato: La Vida Social," in *Historia moderna de México*, 4:438–52. Buffington noted the contradictions between Enlightenment rationalism and popular notions of criminality that defined the issue as a lower-class problem. Robert M. Buffington, *Criminal and Citizens in Modern Mexico* (Lincoln: University of Nebraska Press, 2000), 35–37, 114–17.

6. The Socioeconomic Pyramid

1. James W. Wilkie and Paul D. Wilkens, "Quantifying the Class Structure of Mexico, 1895–1970," in *Statistical Abstract of Latin America*, ed. James W. Wilkie and Stephen Haber (Los Angeles: UCLA Latin American Center Publications, 1981), 21:577–90. José Iturriaga, *La estructura social y cultural de México* (Mexico City: Fondo de Cultura Económica, 1951), chap. 3. Based on the 1895 census, Iturriaga estimated that in urban Mexico the class breakdown indicated 2 percent upper, 30 percent middle, and 68 percent lower class.

2. Mora-Torres, *The Making of the Mexican Border*, 70–74.

3. The Army and Navy establishment served the British Empire. It required customers to deposit money into an account and order from a catalog that listed every conceivable item needed to stay up to date.

4. See the discussion in Victor Bulmer-Thomas, *The Economic History of Latin America since Independence* (Cambridge: Cambridge University Press, 2003), 151.

5. The Council of Notables appointed Labastida as regent pending the arrival of Emperor Maximilian. Juárez permitted him to return from exile in 1871.

6. González Navarro, "El Porfiriato: La Vida Social," 389.

7. James Creelman, "President Díaz: Hero of the Americas," *Pearson's Magazine* 19, no. 3 (1908): 231–77, 240.

8. Hiro de Gortari, "Los años difíciles: Una economia urbana. El caso de la ciudad de México (1890–1910)," *Iztapalapa* 3, no. 6 (1982): 101–14.

9. Patricia Arias, ed., *Guadalajara, la gran cuidad de pequeña industria* (Zamora: El Colegio de Michoacán, 1985). Carlos Alba Vega, introduction, "La industrialización en Jalisco: Evolución y perspectivas," in *Cambio Regional, mercado de trabajo y vida obrera en Jalisco*, ed. Guillermo de la Peña and Augustín Escobar Latapí, 102–6 (Guadalajara: El Colego de Jalisco, 1986).

10. The proposed constitution rejected foreign control of railroads and telegraph lines and other infrastructure projects, suggesting the army and workers could construct them. Taxes levied on the general population based on income would amass the capital necessary. Gaston Garcia Cantu, "De la Republica de Trabajadores (Una utopia mexicana del siglo XIX)," *Revista Mexicana de Sociología* 29, no. 2 (1967): 347–60.

11. Arturo Obregón, ed., *El congreso obrero de 1876: Antologia* (Mexico City: Centro de Estudios Históricos del Movimiento Obrero Mexicano, 1980), 7–13, 158–160, 193.

12. González Navarro, "El Porfiriato: La Vida Social," 401–2.

13. Harry E. Cross, "Debt Peonage Reconsidered: A Case Study in Nineteenth Century Zacatecas, Mexico," *Business History Review* 53, no. 4 (Winter 1979): 473–95.

14. John Mason Hart, *The Silver of the Sierra Madre: John Robertson, Boss*

Shepherd, and the People of the Canyons (Tucson: University of Arizona Press, 2008), 155.

15. Lanny Thompson, "Artisans, Marginals, and Proletarians: The Household of the Popular Classes in Mexico City, 1876–1950," in *Five Centuries of Mexican History / Cinco siglos de historia de México*, ed. Virginia Guedea and Jaime E. Rodríguez O. (Mexico City: Instituto Mora; Irvine: University of California, 1990), 2:309. In secondary cities and towns with fewer factories the percentage would be much higher.

16. Beatriz Ruiz Gaytán F., "Un grupo trabajadoras importante no incluido en la historia laboral Mexicana (trabajadoras domesticas)," in *El trabajo y los trabajadores en la historia de México*, ed. Elsa Cecilia Frost, Michael C. Meyer, and Josefina Zoraida Vázquez, 419–49 (Mexico City: El Colegio de México; Tucson: University of Arizona Press, 1979).

17. Garza, *The Imagined Underworld*, 30.

18. While women could not vote until 1947 or run for elective office until 1953, nineteenth-century women established that they represented a constituency entitled to consideration.

19. Susie S. Porter, *Working Women in Mexico City: Public Discourses and Material Conditions, 1879–1931* (Tucson: University of Arizona Press, 2003), 161.

20. See François, *A Culture of Everyday Credit*, appendix 3, table M, 330–31.

21. Kroeber, *Man, Land and Water*, 182. González Navarro, "El Porfiriato: La Vida Social," 389.

22. François, *A Culture of Everyday Credit*, 161.

23. Pilcher, *The Sausage Rebellion*, 167. The objection of public heath officials that corn cobs had no food value led to permission being rescinded.

24. Pilcher, *The Sausage Rebellion*, 22–23.

25. Lanny Thompson, "Households and the Reproduction of Labor in Mexico, 1876–1970," PhD diss., State University of New York, Binghamton, 1989, esp. 69–76. Lanny Thompson, "Artisans, Marginals, and Proletarians," 2:307–19.

26. These are estimates. It cannot be assumed that the authorities

received notification of all deaths or that the cause of death was correctly determined. Alfredo J. Pani, *Hygiene in Mexico: A Study of Sanitary and Educational Problems* (New York: G. P. Putnam's Sons, 1917), 33,179. Comparable living conditions for those at the bottom existed in the United States in the nineteenth century.

27. Quoted in Carl J. Mora, *Mexican Cinema: Reflection of a Society, 1896–1980* (Berkeley and Los Angeles: University of California Press, 1982), 6–12.

7. Soft Diplomacy

1. Daniel Cosío Villegas has observed that Zamacona's command of English, while adequate, did not allow him to bring his "rhetorical temperament" fully into play. Cosío Villegas, *The United States versus Porfirio Díaz*, 143.

2. Brigham Young officially accepted polygamy in 1852, complicating Utah's efforts to achieve statehood. The Morrill Act of 1862 made polygamy illegal in American territories, and the Edmunds-Tucker Act in 1882 dissolved the Mormon Church Corporation. Under threat of destruction, the leadership banned polygamy in 1890.

3. Thomas Cottam Romney, *Mormon Colonies in Mexico* (Salt Lake City: University of Utah Press, 2005), 148.

4. The family left Mexico with the fall of the regime of General Victoriano Huerta, settled in Oklahoma, and in 1927 established Brantiff Airlines.

5. Hart, *Empire and Revolution*, 201–34.

6. Pletcher, *Rails, Mines, and Progress*, 57. See also Schell, *Integral Outsiders*. Schell offers an insightful view of the role of the American community.

7. N. O. Winters, *Mexico and Her People Today* (Boston: L. C. Page, 1907), 390.

8. Díaz on several occasions rescued his foreign friends from financial disasters with timely contracts and loans. A. K. Coney, the ship's purser who saved Díaz from Lerdo's soldiers at the beginning of the Tuxtepec Revolt, would not be forgotten. In 1887 Díaz appointed him the Mexican consul in San Francisco. When he subsequently fell on hard times, Díaz lent him money to start a business. Weetman Pearson, the English engineering magnate, repaid Díaz's generosity when the ex-president struggled in exile in Paris.

9. The free zone initially emerged because of less expensive goods on the American side, which resulted in depopulation of the Mexican settlements. Juárez, alarmed at the northward migration, confirmed earlier efforts to create a duty-free area with a decree in 1861. The tide reversed during the American Civil War as northern Mexico became a conduit for Confederate cotton, depopulating South Texas and flooding the state with European goods, causing Washington to protest. Francisco R. Calderón, "La Republic restaurada: La vida economica," in *Historia moderna de México*, 2:283.

10. General Treviño played a weak hand in his dealing with General Ord, but eventually they became close friends, and Treviño married Ord's daughter. Tragedy marred the union. Cosío Villegas, *The United States versus Porfirio Díaz*, 210–11.

11. Rio Grande City was founded in 1847 on the U.S. side of the river, a hundred miles upstream from Brownsville. It had a population of 1,800 in 1896 and was a busy riverboat port with connections to New Orleans.

12. Francisco Madero overthrew the government in 1911, becoming president. Venustiano Carranza led the forces that restored the constitutional government in 1914, serving as president until his death in 1920. Jesus Flores Magón, the eldest of the three Flores Magón brothers, played an early role in opposing Díaz.

13. The United States viewed the Central American republics as proto-states. As Elihu Root observed in a private letter in 1907, failing a long period of intervention, which he opposed, these "half-civilized people will have to work out their own salvation." Quoted in Buchenau, *In the Shadow of the Giant*, 74.

14. Roosevelt followed the same geopolitical plan that Napoleon III had envisioned earlier.

15. An abortive attempt by Washington to justify its actions in Panama suggested that had Colombia nationalized the assets of the French company, France might have swept aside the Monroe Doctrine and intervened. Thomas D. Schoonover, *The French in Central America: Culture and Commerce, 1820–1930* (Wilmington DE: Scholarly Resources, 2000), 119.

16. Creelman, "President Díaz," 230.

8. Fatal Vulnerabilities

1. The presidential term changed to six years in 1904. Díaz accepted reelection in 1910 and would have been eighty-six at the end of the term in 1916. He died in 1915.

2. Ramón Corral, a former governor of Sonora, had a reputation for harshness in dealing with Indians. In 1900 he became governor of the Federal District (Mexico City), with mixed success. In 1903 he served as minister of the interior. After Díaz experienced a brief illness, he accepted the reestablished vice presidency in 1904. Ramón Corral died in exile in Paris in 1912. His reputedly unsavory private life made him unacceptable to the oligarchy.

3. Ross blamed Reyes's inept politics for his failure to seize the moment. Had he played the game with more skill, the outcome might well have been an updated version of the Porfiriato. Ross, *Francisco I. Madero*, 73.

4. González, *San José de Gracia*, 99.

5. Subsoil problems, followed by the revolution, delayed completion until 1934, when it was considerably changed from the original design, including the use of art deco interiors and rearrangement of space. Completion of the exterior areas as designed by Boari concluded in 1994.

6. Charles Harris and Louis R. Sadler, *El Paso during the Mexican Revolution* (Albuquerque: University of New Mexico Press, forthcoming).

7. Porfirio Díaz died in Paris in 1915 and is buried in the Montparnasse cemetery. Carmen lived on in Paris supported by rents on her property sent during the violent years of the revolution. She returned to Mexico in 1931 and died in 1944.

Conclusion

1. Mansel G. Blackford, *The Rise of Modern Business in Great Britain, the United States, and Japan*, 2nd ed. (Chapel Hill: University of North Carolina Press, 1998), 52–53.

2. The importance of organization is demonstrated in Edward N. Muller and Mitchell A. Seligson, "Inequality and Insurgency," *American Political Science Review* 81, no. 2 (1987): 425–50.

SUGGESTED READINGS IN ENGLISH

The following works have provided details and information reflected in this book. All of them have extensive bibliographies of works in Spanish, English, and French for those interested in further study. The two-volume *Encyclopedia of Mexican History*, edited by Michael Werner (Routledge, 1997), provides mini-essays on important events, people, and institutions. More broadly focused, but with excellent articles on Mexican topics, is the multivolume *Encyclopedia of Latin American History*, edited by Barbara A. Tanenbaum. *The Handbook of Latin American Studies*, edited by the Hispanic Foundation, Library of Congress, provides an on-line review of the latest books and articles.

Alexius, Robert Martin. "The Army and Politics in Porfirian Mexico." PhD diss., University of Texas, 1975.

Anderson, Rodney D. *Outcasts in Their Own Land: Mexican Industrial Workers, 1906–1911*. DeKalb: Northern Illinois University Press, 1976.

Andrews, Gregg. *Shoulder to Shoulder? The American Federation of Labor, the United States and the Mexican Revolution, 1910–1924*. Berkeley and Los Angeles: University of California Press, 1991.

Anna, Timothy E. *Forging Mexico: 1821–1835*. Lincoln: University of Nebraska Press, 2002.

———. *The Mexican Empire of Iturbide*. Lincoln: University of Nebraska Press, 1990.

Archer, Christon I. "La Causa Buena: The Counterinsurgency Army of New Spain and the Ten Years War." In *The Independence of Mexico and the Creation of the New Nation*, edited by Jaime E. Rodríguez O., 254–72. Los Angles: UCLA Latin American Center Publications, 1989.

Arrom, Silva Marina, *The Women of Mexico City, 1790–1857*. Stanford: Stanford University Press, 1985.

Baldwin, Deborah J. *Protestants and the Mexican Revolution: Missionaries, Ministers, and Social Change.* Urbana: University of Illinois Press, 1990.

Bazant, Jan. *Alienation of Church Wealth in Mexico: Social and Economic Aspects of Liberal Revolution, 1856–1875.* Cambridge: Cambridge University Press, 1971.

Beezley, William H. *Judas at the Jockey Club and Other Episodes of Porfirian Mexico.* Lincoln: University of Nebraska Press, 1987.

Benson, Nettie Lee. *Mexico and the Spanish Cortes, 1810–1822.* Austin: University of Texas Press, 1968.

———." Territorial Integrity in Mexican Politics, 1821–1833." In *The Independence of Mexico and the Creation of the New Nation,* edited by Jaime E. Rodríguez Jaime O., 275–307. Los Angeles: UCLA Latin American Center Publications, 1989.

Berry, Charles R. *The Reform in Oaxaca, 1856–76: A Microhistory of the Liberal Revolution.* Lincoln: University of Nebraska Press, 1981.

Brunk, Samuel. *Emiliano Zapata: Revolution and Betrayal in Mexico.* Albuquerque: University of New Mexico Press, 1995.

Buchenau, Jurgen. *Tools of Progress: A German Merchant Family in Mexico City, 1865-Present.* Albuquerque: University of New Mexico Press, 2004.

———. *In the Shadow of the Giant: The Making of Mexico's Central American Policy, 1876–1930.* Tuscaloosa: University of Alabama Press, 1996.

Coatsworth, John. *Growth Against Development: The Economic Impact of Railroads in Porfirian Mexico.* DeKalb: Northern Illinois University Press, 1981.

Coerver, Donald M. *The Porfirian Interregnum: The Presidency of Manuel González of Mexico.* Fort Worth: Texas Christian University Press, 1979.

Dabbs, Jack A. *The French Army in Mexico, 1861–1867.* The Hague: Mouton, 1962.

Eisenhower, John S. D. *So Far from God: The U.S. War with Mexico, 1846–1848.* New York: Random House, 1989.

Foos, Paul. *A Short Offhand Killing Affair: Soldiers and Social Conflict During the Mexican-American War.* Chapel Hill: University of North Carolina Press, 2002.

François, Marie Eileen. *A Culture of Everyday Credit: Housekeeping, Pawnbroking, and Governance in Mexico, 1750–1920*. Lincoln: University of Nebraska Press, 2006.

Garner, Paul. *Porfirio Díaz*. New York: Longman, 2001.

Garza, James Alex. *The Imagined Underworld: Sex, Crime, and Vice in Porfirian Mexico City*. Lincoln: University of Nebraska Press, 2008.

González, Luis. *San José de Gracia: Mexican Village in Transition*. Austin: University of Texas Press, 1974.

Guardino, Peter F. *Peasants, Politics, and the Formation of Mexico's National State: Guerrero, 1800–1857*. Stanford: Stanford University Press, 1996.

Gutiérrez, Ramón A. *When Jesus Came, the Corn Mothers Went Away: Marriage, Sexuality, and Power in New Mexico, 1500–1846*. Stanford: Stanford University Press, 1991.

Haber Stephen H. *Industry and Underdevelopment: The Industrialization of Mexico, 1890–1940*. Stanford: Stanford University Press, 1989.

Hale, Charles A. *Mexican Liberalism in the age of Mora, 1821–1853*. New Haven: Yale University Press, 1968.

———. *The Transformation of Liberalism in Late Nineteenth-Century Mexico*. Princeton: Princeton University Press, 1989.

Hamnett, Brian. *Juárez*. New York: Longman. 1994.

Harris, Charles H. III. *A Mexican Family Empire: The Latifundo of the Sánchez Navarro Family, 1765–1867*. Austin: University of Texas Press, 1975.

Hart, John Mason. *Anarchism and the Mexican Working Class, 1860–1931*. Austin: University of Texas Press, 1987.

———. *Empire and Revolution: The Americans in Mexico Since the Civil War*. Berkeley and Los Angeles: University of California Press, 2002.

———. *Revolutionary Mexico: The Coming and Process of the Mexican Revolution*. Berkeley and Los Angeles: University of California Press, 1997.

———. *The Silver of the Sierra Madre: John Robinson, Boss Shepherd, and the People of the Canyons*. Tucson: University of Arizona Press, 2008.

Hoyt, Edwin P. *The Guggenheims and the American Dream*. New York: Funk and Wagnalls, 1967.

Jackson, Robert H. ed. *Liberals, the Church, and Indian Peasants: Corporate Lands and the Challenge of Reform in Nineteenth-Century Spanish America*. Albuquerque: University of New Mexico Press, 1997.

Johns, Michael. *The City of Mexico in the Age of Díaz*. Austin: University of Texas Press, 1997.

Jones, Oakah L. *Santa Anna*. New York: Twayne, 1968.

Katz, Friedrich. *Riot, Rebellion, and Revolution: Rural Social Conflict in Mexico*. Princeton: Princeton University Press, 1988.

———. *The Life and Times of Pancho Villa*. Stanford: Stanford University Press, 1998.

Knapp, Frank A. *The Life of Sebastián Lerdo de Tejada, 1823–1889: A Study in Influence and Obscurity*. Austin: University of Texas Press, 1951.

Knight, Alan. *The Mexican Revolution*. 2 vols. Cambridge: Cambridge University Press, 1984.

Krauze, Enrique. *Mexico: Biography of Power*. New York: Harper Perennial, 1998

Kroeber, Clifton B. *Man, Land and Water: Mexico's Farmlands Irrigation Policies, 1885–1911*. Berkeley and Los Angeles: University of California Press, 1983.

LaFrance, David G. *The Mexican Revolution in Puebla, 1908–1913*. Wilmington DE: Scholarly Resources, 1989.

Lewis, Daniel. *Iron Horse Imperialism: Southern Pacific of Mexico, 1880–1951*. Tucson: University of Arizona Press, 2007.

Lomnitz, Larissa A., and Marisol Pérez-Lizaur. *A Mexican Elite Family, 1820–1980*. Princeton: Princeton University Press.

MacLachlan, Colin M. *Anarchism and the Mexican Revolution: The Federal Trials of Ricardo Flores Magón in the United States*. Berkeley and Los Angeles: University of California Press, 1991.

MacLachlan, Colin M., and William H. Beezley. *El Gran Pueblo: A History of Greater Mexico*. 3rd ed. Upper Saddle River NJ: Prentice Hall, 1996.

McCaffrey, James M. *Army of Manifest Destiny: The American Soldier in the Mexican-American War, 1846–1848*. New York: New York University Press, 1992.

Meyer, Michael C. *Mexican Rebel: Pascual Orozco and the Mexican Revolution*. Lincoln: University of Nebraska Press, 1967.

Meyers, William K. *Forge of Progress, Crucible of Revolt: The Origins of the*

Mexican Revolution in La Comarca Lagunera, 1880–1910. Albuquerque: University of New Mexico Press, 1994.

Mora-Torres, Juan. *The Making of the Mexican Border: The State, Capitalism, and Society in Nuevo León, 1848–1910.* Austin: University of Texas Press, 2001.

Olivera, Ruth R., and Liliane Crété. *Life in Mexico under Santa Anna, 1822–1855.* Norman: University of Oklahoma Press, 1991.

Olliff, Donathan C. *Reforma Mexico and the United States: A Search for Alternatives to Annexation, 1854–1861.* Tuscaloosa: University of Alabama Press. 1981.

Piccato, Pablo. *City of Suspects: Crime in Mexico City, 1900–1931.* Durham NC: Duke University Press, 2001.

Pilcher, Jeffrey M. *The Sausage Rebellion: Public Health, Private Enterprise, and Meat in Mexico City, 1890–1917.* Albuquerque: University of New Mexico Press, 2006.

Pletcher, David M. *Rails, Mines and Progress: Seven American Promoters in Mexico, 1867–1911.* Ithaca NY: Cornell University Press, 1958.

Ramos, Raúl A. *Forging Mexican Ethnicity in San Antonio, 1821–1861.* Chapel Hill: University of North Carolina Press, 2008.

Rice, Jacqueline. "The Porfirian Political Elite: Life Pattern of Delegates to the 1892 Union Liberal Convention." PhD diss., University of California, Los Angeles, 1979.

Richmond, Douglas W., ed. *Essays on the Mexican War.* College Station: Texas A&M University Press, 1986.

Rodríguez O., Jaime E. *The Divine Charter: Constitutionalism and Liberalism in Nineteenth-Century Mexico.* Lanham MD: Rowman and Littlefield, 2005.

———. *Down from Colonialism.* Los Angeles: The Chicano Studies Research Center, 1983.

———. *The Emergence of Spanish America: Vicente Rocafuerte and Spanish Americanism, 1808–1832.* Berkeley and Los Angeles: University of California Press, 1975.

———. "The Struggle for the Nation: The First Centralist-Federalist Conflict in Mexico." *The Americas* 49, no. 1 (July 1992): 1–22.

————, ed. *Mexico in the Age of Democratic Revolutions, 1750–1850*. Boulder CO: Lynne Rienner Publishers, 1994.

————, ed. *Patterns of Contention in Mexican History*. Wilmington DE: Scholarly Resources, 1992.

Rohlfes, Lawrence J. "Police and Penal Correction in Mexico City, 1876–1911: A Study of Order and Progress in Porfirian Mexico." PhD diss., Tulane University, 1983.

Ross, Stanley R. *Francisco I. Madero: Apostle of Mexican Democracy*. New York: Columbia University Press, 1955.

Salvucci Richard J. *Textiles and Capitalism in Mexico: An Economic History of Obrajes, 1539–1840*. Princeton: Princeton University Press, 1887.

Santoni, Pedro. *Mexicans at Arms: Puros, Federalists, and the Politics of War, 1845–1848*. Fort Worth: Texas Christian University Press.1996.

Saragoza, Alex M. *The Monterrey Elite and the Mexican State, 1880–1940*. Austin: University of Texas Press, 1988.

Schell, William Jr. *Integral Outsiders: The American Colony in Mexico City, 1876–1911*. Wilmington DE: Scholarly Resources, 2001.

Schoonover, Thomas D. *Dollars Over Dominion: The Triumph of Liberalism in Mexican-United States Relations, 1861–1867*. Baton Rouge: Louisiana State University Press, 1978.

Stevens, Donald F. *Origins of Instability in Early Republican Mexico*. Durham NC: Duke University Press, 1991.

Stewart, Kenneth L., and Arnoldo de León. *Not Room Enough: Mexicans, Anglos, and Socioeconomic Change in Texas, 1850–1900*. Albuquerque: University of New Mexico Press, 1993.

Tenenbaum, Barbara. *The Politics of Penury: Debts and Taxes in Mexico, 1821–1856*. Albuquerque: University of New Mexico Press, 1992.

Thompson, Jerry D. *Warm Weather and Bad Whiskey: The 1886 Laredo Election Riot*. El Paso: Texas Western Press, 1991.

Timmons, W. H. *El Paso: A Borderlands History*. El Paso: Texas Western Press, 1990.

Tuñón Pablos, Julia. *Women in Mexico: A Past Unveiled*. Austin: University of Texas Press, 1999.

Van Hoy, Teresa. *A Social History of Mexico's Railroads: Peons, Prisoners, and Priests*. Lanham MD: Rowman and Littlefield, 2008.

Vanderwood, Paul J. *Disorder and Progress: Bandits, Police and Mexican Development*. Wilmington DE: Scholarly Resources, 1992.

Voss, Stuart F. *On the Periphery of Nineteenth Century Mexico: Sinaloa and Sonora 1810–1877*. Tucson: University of Arizona Press, 1982.

Warren, Richard A. *Vagrants and Citizens: Politics and the Masses in Mexico City from Colony to Republic*. Lanham MD: Rowman and Littlefield, 2007.

Wasserman, Mark. *Everyday Life and Politics in Nineteenth Century Mexico: Men, Women, and War*. Albuquerque: University of New Mexico Press, 2002.

Weber, David J. *The Mexican Frontier, 1821–1846: The American Southwest under Mexico*. Albuquerque: University of New Mexico Press, 1982.

Weeks, Charles A. *The Juárez Myth in Mexico*. Tuscaloosa: University of Alabama Press, 1987.

Womack, John. *Zapata and the Mexican Revolution*. New York: Vintage, 1970.

Zea, Leopold. *Positivism in Mexico*. Austin: University of Texas Press, 1975.

INDEX

transportation, 245; road network, 49, 51–52.
See also railroads
Travis, Ben, 59
Treaty of Ciudad Juárez, 237
Treaty of Guadalupe Hidalgo, 1, 4, 73, 74, 242;
provisions of, 71, 120, 207
Treviño, Gerónimo, 115, 208, 260n10
Tucson AZ, 126
Tuxtepec, Plan of (1876), 116, 117, 131, 183

United States: Americans living in Mexico,
202–7; annexation of Texas, 4, 62; and anti-
Díaz revolutionaries, 211, 224; Civil War in,
91, 99, 124–25, 260n9; Constitution of, 34,
86; and discussions on Mexican protectorate, 79, 83, 87; economic development of,
244–45; economic ties with, 124–25, 131,
136, 139, 221, 242; education system in, 112;
and French intervention in Mexico, 99,
100; and Gadsden Purchase, 80–81, 121,
242; investments in Mexico, 131, 157, 204–7;
labor unions in, 184–85; naval bases of,
213; North-South divide before Civil War,
63, 79–80; and Panama, 210, 212, 213–14,
260n15; Porfirio Díaz and, 117–19, 146–47,
201–2; railroad ties with, 4, 80–81, 116, 124,
136, 137, 242; regional diplomacy by, 210–13;
restrictions on immigration to, 254n17; as
threat to Mexico, 4, 56–57, 241–42, 250n9;
treaty of 1857 with, 87–88; Treaty of Guadalupe Hidalgo, 1, 4, 71–72, 74, 120, 207, 242;
treaty with Britain, 62–63; and War of the
Reform, 89–90; Western expansion of, 2, 56,
241–42, 253n8. *See also* U.S.-Mexican border;
U.S.-Mexican War
Urbina, Luis, 199, 200
U.S.-Mexican border, 120–27, 207–9; Cortina Wars, 125–26; cultural hybridization
along, 4, 120, 121, 126, 242, 249n5; as free
zone, 207–8, 260n9; and Mexican labor,
126–27; military incursions across, 208–9;
revolutionaries' use of, 209; Salt War, 125;
smugglers and bandits along, 119, 207–8;
during U.S. Civil War, 124–25, 260n9; and
U.S.-Mexican War, 73, 120–21
U.S.-Mexican War (1846–48), 4, 63–74;

battle for Mexico City, 68–70; disease toll
in, 70–71; impact of in Mexico, 71, 73–74,
96; political/military moves during, 65, 67;
seizure of Veracruz, 67–68; U.S. Army in,
63–64, 251n4; U.S. pretext for, 63. *See also*
Treaty of Guadalupe Hidalgo

Valladolid, 14–15
Valladolid conspiracy (1809), 13
Vallarta, Ignacio, 133, 134
Valle Nacional, 189
vendors, street, 161–62, 192–93
Venegas, Francisco Javier, 13, 18
Veracruz (city), 62, 67–68, 75, 88, 89
Veracruz (state), 40, 225
Vicario, Doña Leona, 17–18
Victoria, Guadalupe, 35–36, 37
Vidaurri, Santiago, 97, 98
Villa, Pancho, 235, 236
Virgin Islands, 213

War of the Reform (1858–61), 88–90
wealth distribution, 175, 220; gap between rich
and poor, 170, 244, 256n1
Wellington, Duke of, 21
Western Federation of Miners (WFM), 185
Whig Party, 63
Wines, Enoch C., 166
women: as domestic servants, 190, 258n15; and
education, 45–46, 47–48, 113–14; in factories,
193; and Mexico City department store,
177–78; middle-class, 194; modernization of
role of, 45, 190, 192; mutual aid societies of,
193–94; notion of vulnerability about, 164,
177, 191; of oligarchy, 176–77; and prostitution, 164, 191; right to vote of, 258n18; as
street vendors, 192–93; traditional gender
roles of, 45, 47–48, 189–90, 192
Women's Club, 177
Wordsworth, William, 50
working class: in agriculture, 186–87, 233–34;
Catholic Church and, 219; in countryside,
186–89, 219; dependency on credit and debt,
170, 187–88, 197; diet of, 195, 197; industrial,
181–85, 222; low wages of, 160, 186–87, 197,
219, 221, 243–44; and Mexico's class structure, 170, 256n1; and Porfiriato, 220,

working class (*cont.*)
225, 245; in railroads, 139–40; socialism and
anarchism among, 182–83; strikes by, 182,
183, 211, 221, 225; and unions, 183, 184, 185;
and U.S.-Mexican border, 126–27; wages of,
160, 186–87, 197, 219, 221, 243–44; women
in, 193
Worth, William J., 69, 70

yellow fever, 67, 68, 166, 251n7
Yorkinos. *See* Masonic order, York Rite lodge
Young, Brigham, 259n2

Yucatán, 32, 58, 186, 188; henequen plantations
in, 156, 188–89

Zacatecas, 33, 43, 56, 186
Zalacosta, Francisco, 130
Zamacona, Manuel María de, 201–2, 259n1
Zapata, Emiliano, 82, 235, 247, 255n4
Zaragoza, Ignacio, 93
Zavala, Lorenzo, 40
Zelaya López, José Santos, 214
Zuloaga, Félix, 88–89
Zuloaga family, 171